AF352566

Impoliteness in Corpora

Pragmatic Interfaces

Series Editors:
Németh T. Enikő, University of Szeged
Dániel Z. Kádár, Hungarian Academy of Sciences
Károly Bibok, University of Szeged

In the last two decades it has become increasingly clear that language and language use cannot be studied separately and independently of each other. This new approach assumes an interaction between grammar (phonology, morphology, lexicon, syntax and semantics) and pragmatics. An analysis of the interfaces between each component of grammar and pragmatics (the 'interface view') can also be applied to hard-pragmatics and soft-pragmatics research. Hard-pragmatics studies the field of language use from philosophical, linguistic and logical points of view, while soft-pragmatics explores phenomena of language use from a social and socio-cultural perspective.

The definitions hard- and soft-pragmatics, adopted around the 1980s, have become somewhat dated since pragmatics has become a field of its own, and so these two trends have merged to some extent. Also, various pragmaticians made important attempts to blend these approaches. Nevertheless, a border between these areas continues to exist: hard-pragmaticians rarely venture into socio-pragmatic issues, and, vice versa, soft-pragmatic studies rarely make use of formal tools of hard-pragmatics.

Pragmatic Interfaces fills an important knowledge gap in the field of pragmatics as the first major publication project devoted to studying grammar-pragmatics interfaces and merging of soft-pragmatics with hard-pragmatics. Through this merging many pragmatic phenomena could be essentially revisited. *Pragmatic Interfaces* follows an interdisciplinary approach, allowing scholars from different areas of grammar and pragmatics to collaborate.

Forthcoming:

Face and Face Practices in Chinese Talk and Interaction
Wei-Lin Melody Chang

Politeness Phenomena across Chinese Genres
Xinren Chen

Impoliteness in Corpora
A Comparative Analysis of British English and Spoken Turkish

Hatice Çelebi

SHEFFIELD UK　BRISTOL CT

Published by Equinox Publishing Ltd.

UK: Office 415, The Workstation, 15 Paternoster Row, Sheffield, South Yorkshire S1 2BX
USA: ISD, 70 Enterprise Drive, Bristol, CT 06010

http://www.equinoxpub.com/home/

First published 2015

British Library Cataloguing-in-Publication Data

A catalogue record for this book is available from the British Library.

ISBN 978 1 78179 070 0 (hardback)

Library of Congress Cataloging-in-Publication Data
Çelebi, Hatice.
   Impoliteness in corpora: a comparative analysis of British English and spoken Turkish / Hatice Çelebi.
      pages cm. – (Pragmatic interfaces)
   Originally published as the author's PhD under the title "Extracting and analyzing impoliteness in corpora a study based on the British National Corpus and the spoken Turkish corpus"; Middle East Technological University
   Includes bibliographical references and index.
   ISBN 978-1-78179-070-0 (hb)
1. Politeness (Linguistics) 2. Politeness (Linguistics)–Great Britain.
3. Politeness (Linguistics)–Turkey. 4. Corpora (Linguistics) 5. Power (Social sciences) 6. Grammar, Comparative and general. 7. Interpersonal relations. I. Title.
   P299.H66C45 2014
   401'.41–dc23
                        2014011971

Typeset by S.J.I. Services, New Delhi
Printed and bound by Lightning Source Inc. (La Vergne, TN), Lightning Source UK Ltd. (Milton Keynes), Lightning Source AU Pty. (Scoresby, Victoria).

Contents

List of Figures

List of Tables

List of Abbreviations

ASA	Advertising Standards Authority
BBC	British Broadcasting Corporation
BNC	British National Corpus
BSC	Broadcasting Standards Commission
CA	Conversation Analysis
CBL	Corpus Based Linguistics
CDL	Corpus Driven Approach
COLT	Bergen Corpus of London Teenage Language
CP	Cooperative Principle
FTA	Face Threatening Act
IR	Interpersonal Rhetoric
MCD	Membership Categorization Device
METU	Middle East Technical University
PP	Politeness Principle
RTF	Rich Text Formatting
SIP	Socio-Interactional Principles
STC	Spoken Turkish corpus
STR	Speaker Rights Theory
TEI	Text Encoding Initiative
XML	Extensible Markup Language

Acknowledgements

The research from the STC, reported in this study, has been supported by TÜBİTAK 108K283 and METU BAP-05-03-2011-001.

Next I would also like to acknowledge and thank the series editors Enikő Nemeth T., Daniel Z. Kadar, and Karoly Bibok for their helpful comments and feedback on the manuscript and Janet Joyce, Val Hall and George Moore of Equinox for facilitating efficient publishing process. This book has received critiques from three external Equinox reviewers. I wish to express my deepest thanks for their thorough and extensive comments.

Preface

The book you are holding is a result of my PhD thesis that I diligently worked on with my advisor Şükriye Ruhi from 2009 to 2012. I would like to acknowledge her support and input which made it possible to complete this project and turn it into a book. I owe her a great debt and give her my deepest heartfelt thanks. I would also like to acknowledge Yeşim Aksan whose feedback immensely helped and thank her.

Next I would also like to acknowledge and thank the series editors Enikő Németh T., Dániel Z. Kádár, and Károly Bibok for their helpful comments and feedback on the manuscript and Janet Joyce and Val Hall of Equinox for facilitating efficient publishing process. This book has received critiques from three external Equinox reviewers. I wish to express my deepest thanks for their thorough and extensive comments.

Many friends and colleagues viewed and commented on the chapters and I am very grateful for all their support. I would like to acknowledge them (in alphabetical order): Serpil Demir-Vegter, Mathew Howell, Hale Işık-Güler, Gaele Macfarlane, Jennifer Mcready, Sarah Metzker, Blake Shedd, and friends including Yıldız Altuntaş, Ahmet Çolak, Nihal Gökgöz Gördeslioğlu and Hatice Karaaslan were very supportive throughout the process.

Last, but by no means least, I would like to thank my family and my husband Abdullah Çelebi whose presence and love have always lifted up my spirit. I dedicate this book to my Mother Ayse, the woman who represents every little good thing in life and my two daughters Ayşegül and Yasemin, who are the future.

CHAPTER 1

Introduction: Impoliteness in Spoken Corpora

1.1 Why impoliteness?

'Hear no evil, speak no evil – and you will never be invited to cocktail parties.'

Oscar Wilde

It is said that the below is an actual letter (http://www.dslreports.com/forum/ r26944193-Letter-from-Newfoundlander-about-renewing-a-passport) received by the UK Passport Office.

Dear Sirs,

I'm in the process of renewing my passport, and still cannot believe this. How is it that Sky Television has my address and telephone number and knows that I bought a bleeding satellite dish from them back in 1977, and yet, the Government is still asking me where I was bloody born and on what date.

For Christ sakes, do you guys do this by hand? My birth date you have on my pension book, and it is on all the income tax forms I've filed for the past 30 years. It is on my National Health card, my driving license, my car insurance, on the last eight damn passports I've had, on all those stupid customs declaration forms I've had to fill out before being allowed off the plane over the last 30 years, and all those insufferable census forms.

Would somebody please take note, once and for all, that my mother's name is Mary Anne, my father's name is Robert and I'd be abso-fucking-lutely astounded if that ever changed between now and when I die!!!!!!

I apologise, I'm really pissed off this morning. Between you an' me, I've had enough of this bullshit! You send the application to my house, then you ask me for my fucking address!!!!

What is going on? Do you have a gang of Neanderthal arseholes workin' there? Look at my damn picture. Do I look like Bin Laden? I don't want to dig up Yasser Arafat, for shit sakes. I just want to go and park my arse on some sandy beach somewhere. And would someone please tell me, why would you give a shit whether I plan on visiting a farm in the next 15 days? If I ever got the urge to do something weird to a chicken or a goat, believe you me, you'd be the last fucking people I'd want to tell!

Well, I have to go now, 'cause I have to go to the other end of the poxy city to get another fucking copy of my birth certificate, to the tune of £30. Would it be so complicated to have all the services in the same spot to assist in the issuance of a new passport the same day?? Nooooooooooooooo, that'd be too damn easy and maybe make sense. You'd rather have us running all over the fuckin' place like chickens with our heads cut off, then have to find some arsehole to confirm that it's really me on the damn picture – you know, the one where we're not allowed to smile?! (bureaucratic fuckin' morons) Hey, do you know why we couldn't smile if we wanted to? Because we're totally pissed off!

Signed,

An Irate Citizen

I would say there is no possibility of knowing whether this was actually written by a citizen and sent to the passport office or written by some person to spice up the Internet world. Regardless, this letter has found a great applause from the audience on various blogs it has been read by: 'hilarious,' 'very funny,' 'absolutely beautiful,' 'loved it,' claps,' 'tears … I'll keep this forever' are some of the comments it received. Part of the reason why it was 'hilarious' to the audience is that the language is creative, impolite and humorous in its own way.

Creativity and humour have been associated with each other for a long time (see Barsoux, 1993; Murdock and Ganim, 1993) and it has been suggested that there is always an element of creativity in humour: 'During the creative process people go through a series of stages and steps that involve humour in some way. The experience/manifestation of humour becomes part of this overall creative process' (Murdock and Ganim, 1993:58). In discussing whether impoliteness is creative or not Culpeper (2011b:240) refers to the two types Carter (2004) argued for:

> There are clearly two levels of 'creative' interactions: first, more overt, presentational uses of language, open displays of metaphoric invention, punning, uses of idioms and departures from expected idiomatic formula-tions (*pattern-reforming*); second, less overt, may be even subconscious and

> subliminal parallelisms, echoes and related matchings which regularly result
> in expressions of affective convergence, in signals of intimacy and in explicit
> symmetries of feeling (*pattern forming*). (Carter, 2004:109)

Culpeper (2011b:241) further expands on the other two types Leech (1969:182; Coupland, 2007:84) and Carter mentioned (Carter, 2004:134): situational deviation and unusual implicitness. He then takes the task of evaluating whether impoliteness is creative. He concludes that in his data there is good evidence to 'counter the everyday view that impoliteness, rather like views of slang, is a debased form of language – simplistic without finesse' (p. 239). It is this observation that I have had in my everyday encounters with impoliteness that motivated this book. I have found it intriguing how people managed to be impolite yet could get by with a true or false 'I did not mean to ...' explanation. This point has brought up the long debated issue of what impoliteness is. How is it possible to decide whether an utterance is impolite or not given that it will be perceived differently depending on various factors such as previous encounters, culture, prosody, semantic schema and so on?

This book aims at taking steps towards understanding: (a) what does impoliteness, which makes up of some portion of our daily life because it serves different purposes, consist of? and (b) how can we extract impoliteness from corpora, given that it is such a complex notion to define? The first question is closely related to our daily lives and encompasses a broad focus. The second question aims at bringing an academic dimension to it.

1.2 An overview of the book

As the world becomes more closely knit, owing to rapid progress in transportation and communication systems, we are now confronted by situations in which we have to engage with people from different backgrounds and with different communicative styles. We use language to transmit information and manage relationships. Language is more often used in a manner intended to avoid friction between the participants, which is the reason why there is a growing interest in linguistic politeness research. The language use associated with smooth communication or appropriate speech is what is referred to as linguistic politeness (Lakoff, 1973; Brown and Levinson [1978] 1987). However, appropriateness differs between cultures as well as subcultures due to competing differences. Therefore, studies regarding language provide valuable insights into locating the cultural ideologies underlying discourses as they reflect speakers' choices and understanding of the situation and the interaction. Through this kind of relationship we also project the identity that we wish to construct in the culture of the community to which we belong. It is for this reason that the diversity of languages should be acknowledged and studies carrying languages into an arena where such diversity will be acknowledged deserve special interest.

The topic of this book, however, is not linguistic politeness but its twin: impoliteness. The concept of impoliteness has been largely neglected in linguistic studies until only very recently since pragmatic and sociolinguistic studies mainly focused on politeness and its strategies. A further reason why impoliteness has not received much attention is the assumption that impoliteness is 'rather marginal to human linguistic behaviour in normal circumstances' (Leech, 1983). However, such a 'conceptual bias' (Eelen, 2001) has been criticized by several researchers. It was argued that an adequate discussion of the dynamics of interpersonal communication should include hostile as well as harmonious communication. If politeness is related to 'face', an image of self formed in terms of approved social attributes (Brown and Levinson, 1987), and involves the idea that we like other people to have positive thoughts about us, it is essential to understand the motivations behind impoliteness. If self-esteem is dependent on how others feel about you and when you lose face you feel bad about how you are seen in other people's eyes, an investigation of the contexts of impoliteness is important as such situations threaten the positive value we have of ourselves. Although Brown and Levinson's (1987) treatment of facework has been applied most widely among different theories of politeness, approaches emphasizing that impoliteness is not only related to 'face' and that other factors should be taken into account have been developed (Culpeper, 1996; Spencer-Oatey, 2000, Watts, 2003; Arundale 2006a; Ruhi and Işık-Güler, 2007). This book presents an approach that takes the concept of face and discusses its role in impoliteness in relation to the context and the co-text in spoken interaction.

What lies in the centre of Brown and Levinson's (1987) politeness theory is face as the public self-image that individuals want to claim for themselves and that it consists of two aspects; negative and positive face. Arundale (2006a) points out that Brown and Levinson critiqued their own theory by stating that their models were not well equipped for the emergent character of social interaction and that interaction is the field where new conceptualizations of politeness are likely to emerge (p. 195). He claims that Brown and Levinson's theory is based on Grice's pragmatics and Searle's speech act, to which one can add Goffman's account of the interaction order (p. 195). Bargiela-Chiappini (2003) makes a re-examination of face related to politeness and proposes a study of 'cultural conceptualizations, the social self and its relationship to others as an alternative and possibly more fruitful way of studying relevance, and dynamics of "face" and "facework" in interpersonal contacts' (p. 1463). This approach emphasizes that 'face' is not an individual phenomenon; rather it is relational and interactional. Arundale (2006a) argues that the models based on Brown and Levinson's face theory frame language use or communication as encoding and decoding meanings. In this model, a speaker has a meaning that he or she intends the hearer to get, encodes it with the knowledge of language, transmits that meaning through an utterance and in turn the hearer decodes the utterance by using his or her knowledge of language. Sperber and Wilson (1995) are also two scholars who previously added to this model the planning and reconstruction of the hearer's inferences and the speaker's intentions.

Culpeper (1996) proposes a complementary model of face related to politeness by his emphasis on discourse type and activity type. By doing so, Culpeper adopts a more contextually and culturally sensitive model of face. He suggests that conclusions arising from a model of impoliteness based on the hearer's perception would be unreliable. Işık-Güler (2008) takes a similar approach for her study investigating the metapragmatics of (im)politeness in Turkish. By bringing an emic dimension to her study, she aims at laying out the conceptualizations of 15 (im)politeness lexemes in Turkish by getting the native speakers to narrate anecdotes that they found to be(im)polite and why they evaluated events in these anecdotes as (im)polite. Other scholars further expanded on understanding of context and culture. For instance, Garcés-Conejos Blitvich, Lorenzo-Dus and Bou-Franch (2010) narrowed their study by taking a genre approach. They focused on Spanish TV talk shows and collected data from a variety of sources such as corpus, questionnaires and focus groups. In addition, the role conversational patterns and phenomena related to impoliteness and interaction played in the context were explored and previous arguments were revisited. Angouri and Locher (2012) discussed the tendency to theorize disagreement as an instrument generating impoliteness since it is perceived as an attack to positive face. They pointed out that in different cultural contexts, disagreement could as well be used to address positive face.

Given the complexity of factors such as face, context and culture that generate impoliteness in interaction, a contrastive study of impoliteness demands a depth of theorizing both at the level of extracting and at the level of analysing impoliteness. The present book aims to indicate the necessity of such theorizing both for extraction and analysis and to demonstrate how corpus linguistics could be made use of for a contrastive study of two languages in terms of how impoliteness is generated. It illustrates how impoliteness can be extracted and analysed in a contrastive manner between diverse languages, namely British English and Turkish in a genre approach (Garcés-Conejos Blitvich, Lorenzo-Dus and Bou-Franch,

2010; Garcés-Conejos Blitvich, 2010). It focuses on conversation as a genre or discourse type in spoken interaction and discusses issues related to impoliteness as in a corpus driven approach (Römer, 2005). Since the study illustrated is a contrastive analysis of two languages (English and Turkish) looking into spoken conversations extracted from two different corpora – the British National Corpus and the Spoken Turkish Corpus – it has strong implications for how corpus studies can be expanded to study factors such as context and co-text.

1.3 The scope of the book

Modern politeness theory was initially shaped by Robin Lakoff (1973, 1989), who related politeness to Grice's Cooperative Principle (CP), which is based on the maxims of quantity, quality, relation and manner. In the CP framework, the inter-actants follow these maxims and reach an interpretation of utterances. However, since these maxims are almost never followed strictly in informal conversations, Lakoff (1973) complemented the clarity maxims of Grice with a politeness rule. She argued that when the hearers realize that the speakers are not following Gricean maxims, they search for a logical explanation in the politeness rules which are as follows: (1) do not impose; (2) give options; (3) make A [addressee] feel good – be friendly. She further developed her theory and explained that, since different cultures have different understandings of politeness, cultures tend to abide by the rules of distance, deference and camaraderie in different ways. Distance refers to the strategy of impersonality, deference is related to hesitancy, and camaraderie is about informality.

Similar to Lakoff, Brown and Levinson ([1978] 1987) define politeness in a conflict avoidance frame but what lies in the centre of their theory are the concepts of face and rationality. According to these scholars, face consists of two opposing wants, which can be threatened by face threatening acts (FTAs hereafter). To address politeness, they use superstrategies. The superstrategies that they propose are:

1. Bald on-record politeness: The FTA is performed in the most clear and concise way possible and is maximally in line with Grice's maxims.
2. Positive politeness: The FTA is performed towards redressing the positive face threat to the hearer by claiming common ground (e.g. noticing, attending to hearer's needs, exaggerating approval, sympathy with the hearer, seeking agreement), conveying that speaker and hearer are cooperators (e.g. being optimistic, offering, promising, assuming

reciprocity), fulfilling the hearer's want for something (e.g. giving gifts to hearer).

3. Negative Politeness: The FTA is performed towards redressing the negative face threat to the hearer by being indirect, not presuming (e.g. question, hedge), not coercing hearer, communicating speaker's want to not impinge on hearer, and redressing other wants of hearer.

4. Off-record: the FTA is performed through an indirect illocutionary act. It allows the deniability of the utterance if the recipient takes offence. Output strategies are inviting conversational implicatures (e.g. giving hints, giving association rules, presupposing) and being vague or ambiguous by violating Manner maxim.

5. Do not perform the FTA.

Brown and Levinson (1987) point out that, since their theory is based on social harmony, the lower the face threat to the hearer the FTA utterance is, the lower the superstrategy used by the speaker. In other words, for the lowest threat in the FTA performed to the hearer, the first, or bald on record superstrategy would be used. Negative face is the want that others do not impede one's actions, and positive face is the wants of the member to be at least desirable to the others. They claim that when speech acts threaten face wants, speakers apply politeness strategies to redress their face wants, which are positive, negative and off-record politeness, and do-not-do the FTA. Moreover, these three politeness strategies can be regarded as rational deviations from CP, which supposedly underlies all human interactions. With the introduction of FTA, they propose that depending on the calculation of the weightiness of the speech act, which is determined by certain social values, speakers tend to choose a strategy. Although there is the concept of a Model Person, a universal speaker/hearer, 'who is a wilful fluent speaker of a natural language, further endowed with two special properties – rationality and face' (Brown and Levinson, 1987:58), their theory explains the management of social relationships as attendance to face. It is only as a result of this that certain politeness strategies are preferred or disregarded. Therefore, despite the criticisms the theory receives, context is assumed to play a major role and as such this is noteworthy.

Leech's theory of politeness is expanded along with an emphasis on interpersonal rhetoric and bridges semantics and pragmatics by arguing that messages are conveyed through a form of sound mapping; 'message transmission,' a text, 'textual transaction,' and a discourse, 'interpersonal transaction' (Leech, 1980). While the interpersonal transaction provides clues to shape the judgments about the text in terms of language-internal factors such as clarity, interpersonal rhetoric ensures that the utterance adheres to the situational demands of the conversation, one of which is politeness (Leech, 1980). He develops his theory further by adding another principle to the Gricean cooperative principle, the Politeness Principle (PP), the maxims of which are tact, generosity, approbation, modesty, agreement and sympathy. The PP model was to receive criticisms later for the arbitrary number of the maxims arguing that, for the PP model to be reliable, the unrestricted number of PP maxims had to be restricted (Jucker 1988, Thomas, 1995).

Over time, as discussed in detail in Section 2.1, the validity of the models proposed by Brown and Levinson, Lakoff and Leech was questioned and the need for new approaches was emphasized. This book proposes a new methodological approach to impoliteness studies consisting of two levels: extraction and analysis. The two levels require methods and tools that facilitate the retrieval of impoliteness in different corpora in English and Turkish. It presents a corpus driven approach to conversation analysis (CA hereafter).

The main purpose of the study presented in this book is to devise a methodological framework for extracting and analysing impoliteness from corpora. Within this methodological framework, the discussion on the epistemological issues which have governed the politeness and impoliteness models and theories are detailed and conferred further to bring out new implications. Some major concerns are touched upon briefly in this section in order to explain why it is important to devise such a methodological framework and how two approaches, namely discursive and cue-based, can be combined for that purpose.

Bousfield and Locher (2008) were first to present a collected volume with a thorough discussion of impoliteness and power. Their aim was to demonstrate a massive imbalance in terms of academic interest between the studies of politeness and impoliteness. The notions of conflict and aggression came into the discussion of impoliteness theory and inspired further studies on impoliteness. Bousfield (2008) focused on an analysis of impoliteness in face-to-face spoken interaction, in which politeness – perceived to be the governing principle – allows for exploration of how impoliteness comes into play. His study was followed by Culpeper's (2011b) publication which also used naturally-occurring language data and combined both a discussion of layperson's views and a theoretical discussion of what shapes their views. In addition, he brings linguistic pragmatics and social psychology into the discussion of impoliteness, and by doing so, expands the boundaries to a level where researchers of impoliteness should consider the use of naturally occurring data and how a layperson's views of impoliteness are shaped by linguistic impoliteness and vice versa.

As mentioned in Section 2.1, during the 1990s, as a result of the move from theoretical to societal norms that informs the theory of politeness, a distinction between how sociolinguists defined politeness and how laypeople (the individuals in a society) defined politeness was made. In other words, scholars found it essential to discuss how theoretical stances about whether or not ordinary speakers' views and evaluations of politeness, termed *first order politeness*, and thus the social norms, informed and affected the researchers' theoretical views of politeness, termed *second order politeness*. Watts, Ide and Ehlich (1992) argued that a distinction between first order and second order politeness requires different interpretations, the first referring to a commonsense notion that we use and understand in our daily lives and thus it is a layman's concept, and the latter referring to a linguistic and scientific concept that is used as a theoretical construct to explain social behaviour and language use (Watts, 1992). The acknowledgment of this distinction generated attention and turned a critical eye on the theoretical underpinning of politeness theory.

Eelen (2001), for example, pointed out that the unquestioning incorporation of the first order (or politeness1) concepts into scientific theory, second order politeness (or politeness2) confounds politeness1 with politeness2. He added that the opposite move is also possible with the danger of transferring politeness2 concepts into everyday life and as such, methodological and epistemological issues in politeness studies occur (p. 31). On the other hand, he emphasized that these concepts are inseparably interconnected and salient in all politeness studies for the reason that the basic characteristics of politeness1 inevitably will provide a researcher with the aspects of a social phenomenon to lay out a scientific description. The features of politeness1 – evaluativity (the judgment that a social behaviour is polite or impolite), argumentativity (the immediate action that other's behaviour is approved or condemned), normativity (the association of politeness with appropriateness evaluated against a standard), modality and reflexivity (despite the social norms the optionality that speakers have to choose to be evaluated as polite or impolite) – gives an *emic* analysis for an *etic* analysis for politeness2.

By incorporating the terms *emic* and *etic* into the discussion of politeness1 and politeness2, Eelen (2001) aims to bridge the informants' conscious statements about their notion of politeness and spontaneous evaluations made during the course of interaction, that is, an *emic* approach, which is related to politeness1, and the outsiders' (researchers') accounts of insiders' behaviour, involving distinctions not relevant to those insiders – an *etic* approach, which is related to politeness2 (p. 78). It seems that studies of politeness have to include an emic analysis and incorporate politeness1 to reach politeness2, although the main aim of politeness2 is to arrive at a theoretical analysis. In other words, it is a must that studies seeking an understanding of politeness2 include an emic analysis since:

> [s]cientific accounts always intend to have some kind of surplus value over
> lay accounts. At the very least, a description of human behaviour involves
> making explicit the actor's unconscious distinctive practices, which in itself
> already entails a description in analytical as opposed to folk categories
> (Eelen 2001:78).

However, Eelen (2001) cautions researchers against creating a theoretical
ambiguity for using politeness1 and politeness2 without a conscious discussion of
the position of their study regarding how these two concepts are related in their
particular study:

> At each point in the analysis one must remain thoroughly aware of the position
> of one's concepts in relation to the distinction, or the possible conclusions or
> next steps this position warrants. If this is not properly done, one runs the risk
> of arbitrarily jumping from one side to the other without taking the necessary
> precautions, which ultimately results in confusion regarding the status of the
> concepts. *In practice, such awareness thus takes on the form of making explicit
> what in most current approaches is left implicit.* (p. 76, emphasis mine)

Along the same line, Mills (2009) cautions us against mixing politeness1 and
politeness2 and argues that the folk linguistic beliefs, '... should be examined in
their own right; these beliefs may have an effect on interactants' performance, but
we need to keep these beliefs separate from our analysis at the level of politeness2'
(p. 1058). This study, for the very reason of 'making explicit what in most current
approaches is left implicit,' acknowledges that the theory of (im)politeness has
to integrate first order and second order politeness into the discussion without
mixing the two. Mills (2009) suggests a Foucauldian move to integrate the two
without mixing them:

> [w]hat needs to be developed in a more Foucauldian move, is an analysis of
> the means by which these supposed norms are held in place, or are asserted
> to be norms in the first place; that is, we analyse the discursive mechanisms
> by which cultural stereotypes about language are developed and circulated.
> (Foucault. [1969] 1972 cited in Mills, 2009:1048)

The features of politeness1, evaluativity, argumentativity, normativity, modality
and reflexivity, are taken into account both at the extraction and at the analysis
level of naturally occurring data, and are interpreted to the extent the cues in the
conversation allow. These features are taken to be the discursive mechanisms Mills
(2009) is referring to and attended to by taking metapragmatic comments (e.g. 'You
are rude!'), reactive responses, language or paralanguage indicating interpersonal

conflict in verbal and non-verbal forms (e.g. change in structural patterns such as turn taking, topic change, repetition, seeking of disagreement) into account for the interpretation. In addition, both the implications of the co-text, by examining conventionalized impoliteness formulae (Culpeper 2010; 2011b) and the context, by attending to non-conventionalized implicational impoliteness (2011b), are taken into consideration. In this sense, the study illustrated in the book presents a Foucauldian move: how the discussion of what the discursive mechanisms offer can be combined with a cue-based approach to reach the underlying theory and in this way explain how second order politeness is developed.

1.4 The aims of the book

There are a number of studies which have been conducted investigating politeness in Turkish, focusing on various dimensions such as speech acts, power relations, gender issues and identity which were explored within the Turkish language or with contrastive studies of Turkish with other languages. For instance, Martı (2006) focused on the realization of politeness through requests and compared Turkish monolingual speakers and Turkish-German bilingual returnees. She tested the possibility that these two groups differed since Turkish-German returnees might be affected by pragmatic transfer from German. Doğançay-Aktuna and Kamışlı (in Bayraktaroğlu and Sifianou, 2001:75–104) investigated the norms and behaviour of native speakers of Turkish expressing disagreement in an environment where these speakers were of unequal status. In the situations they examined, they found that professors' sociolinguistic behaviour differed from the workplace managements', which can be related to the pedagogic roles they assumed. Zeyrek (in Bayraktaroğlu and Sifianou, 2001:43–74) examined the influence of socio-cultural phenomena on language. She explored the key concepts such as family organization and cordiality to provide a background about how appropriate and polite behaviour can be understood. She then discussed the issues of power and gender and how these issues influenced deference terms and forms of address. In another study, Bayraktaroğlu (in Bayraktaroğlu and Sifianou, 2001:177–208) demonstrated the differences existing between American/British English and Turkish through case studies in regard to the speech act of advice-giving. Hatipoğlu (2007) focused on nationality identity composed in calls for papers for international conferences and discussed how different politeness strategies were applied.

There are also studies bridging theoretical underpinnings of politeness to speech acts. For example, Ruhi (2006) analysed a corpus of compliment responses in

Turkish with the aim of reanalyzing of the Maxim approach (Leech, 1983) and the face-management approach by Brown and Levinson (1987). Other studies bring a socio-pragmatic dimension to the concept of politeness and, in doing so, discuss how impoliteness is perceived in relation to politeness. For instance, Ruhi and Işık-Güler (2007), explored the conceptualization of face, how it is related to the social person and self-presentation in Turkish, and the implications of their findings for relational work in (im)politeness in Turkish. They did a discourse-analytic investigation on two key concepts: *yüz* (face) and *gönül,* roughly 'heart/mind/desire' and examined metonymic and metaphorical expressions in the METU Turkish Corpus (Say, Zeyrek, Oflazer, and Özge, 2004). Based on their analysis, they maintain that relational work in the Turkish setting is not only conceptualized around the perceived social image and communicative goals but it is also conceptualized around the inner self. One of the implications their study suggested was that the concept of impoliteness is strongly motivated by self-concerns.

In a later study, Işık-Güler (2008) further investigated the metapragmatics of (im)politeness in Turkish as mentioned above. She found that the lexical items most frequently associated with the concept, IMPOLITE (*KABA* in Turkish) are: inconsiderate (*düşüncesiz*); disrespectful (*saygısız*); tactless (*nezaketsiz*); arrogance (*küstahlık*); indiscretion (*patavatsızlık*); offensive (*kırıcı*); selfish (*bencil*); ugly (*çirkin*); ignorant (*cahil*); and inability to empathize (*empati kuramayan*). These lexemes were given special attention at the extraction level as explained in Chapter Three.

As the literature presented above suggests, the line of study carried out focusing on politeness has moved towards a more inclusive dimension, as sociopragmatic and metapragmatic aspects of politeness were discussed in depth. Along with this, impoliteness has started to get attention among scholars. In the meantime, studies of politeness have started to take all aspects into consideration, and just as it was in the beginning for politeness studies, studies on impoliteness have attempted to lay out a theoretical framework. Two of the most recognized frameworks of politeness are Leech's (1983) and Brown and Levinson's (1987) approaches. Leech (1983) proposed a Politeness Principle Theory consisting of six maxims which are tact, generosity, approbation, modesty, agreement and sympathy. Brown and Levinson (1987) continued along the same line proposing a framework of Face Threatening Acts (FTAs) and four superstrategies: bald-on record, positive, negative politeness and off-record.

A similar approach was followed for impoliteness: Culpeper (1996), taking Brown and Levinson's (1987) model for politeness as the underlying departure point for his framework for impoliteness, proposed that impoliteness can be theorized under four superstrategies in relation to FTAs, which he then developed into a five point model: bald, on record impoliteness, positive impoliteness, negative impoliteness, off-record impoliteness, withhold politeness (Culpeper 2005). The modification Culpeper (2005) made to the model with the addition of *bald, on record impoliteness*, came as a result of the discussions about the degree to which face is at stake when the speaker's intention is to attack the face of the hearer and / or where the speaker does not have the power to reply with an impolite utterance and not suffer from the consequences. Therefore, as it has been for politeness, the concept of face and sociological aspects such as power relations and culture have been at the centre of impoliteness frameworks.

In addition to face and culture, the issue of intention emerged together with the question of whether it is possible to determine a speaker's intention given the fact the hearer's interpretation could well be different from what the speaker intended to say. For example, Culpeper (2005) claimed that impoliteness came about when '(1) the speaker communicates face-attack intentionally, or (2) the hearer perceives and/or constructs behaviour as intentionally face-attacking, or a combination of (1) and (2)' (p. 38) although later he revised his definition of impoliteness and claimed that impoliteness may occur when '[s]ituated behaviours are viewed negatively – considered impolite – when they conflict with how one expects them to be, how one wants them to be and/or how one thinks they ought to be' (2011b:23). For Bousfield (2008), impoliteness constituted the communication of intentionally gratuitous and conflictive verbal FTAs, which were purposefully delivered:

i.   unmitigated in contexts where mitigation is required, and/or
ii.   with deliberate aggression that is with the face threat exacerbated, 'boosted' or maximized in some way to heighten the face damage inflicted. (p. 72)

Terkourafi (2007) made a distinction between rudeness and impoliteness:

> [m]arked rudeness or rudeness proper occurs when the expression used is not conventionalised relative to the context of occurrence; following recognition of the speaker's face-threatening intention by the hearer, marked rudeness threatens the addressee's face ... impoliteness occurs when the expression used is not conventionalised relative to the context of occurrence; it threatens the addressee's face ... but no face-threatening intention is attributed to the speaker by the hearer. (p. 70)

Such subtleties brought out methodological concerns and the theoretical validity and applicability of such models were questioned as broader theories such as Spencer-Oatey's (2002) approach, which consists of two components, face (quality face and social identity face) and sociality rights (equity rights and association rights) emerged. Still, some scholars have continued to propose models aiming to account for the discussion on the issues mentioned above. Bousfield (2008) summarized Culpeper's (1996, 2005) emergent model of impoliteness under two over-arching 'tactics:' (1) on-record impoliteness; and (2) off-record impoliteness which consists of (a) sarcasm and (b) withhold politeness.

Impoliteness studies applying models of impoliteness proposed by Culpeper (1996, 2005) and Bousfield (2008) in fact demonstrate and confirm the need for separating the extraction level from the analysis level to overcome a circular way of developing a theory of impoliteness. What comes about in these studies is that the extraction of impoliteness is incorporated into analysis level and results in the following fallacy: utterances that function to *ignore, snub, fail to attend to hearer's interests, wants, needs and goods, etc.* which is a substrategy listed under the superstrategy positive impoliteness (Culpeper 1996), are impolite because '*ignore, snub, fail to attend to hearer's interests, wants, needs and goods, etc.*' is a substrategy of the superstrategy positive impoliteness. In fact, this issue was later taken up, perhaps with the same line of logic, by Culpeper (2010) himself. He carried out an intensive study on 'conventionalized formulaic expressions' which signalled potential for impoliteness since these formulaic expressions accompanied with matching context and co-text could be interpreted as insults, personalized negative assertions, challenging or unpalatable questions and/or presuppositions, condescension, message enforcers, dismissals, silencers, threats, negative expressives (e.g. curses, ill-wishes). Culpeper (2011b) further developed a theoretical approach to go beyond the conventionalized formulaic expressions to be able to define impoliteness when it is implied without necessarily making use of conventionalized formulaic expressions, which he refers to as 'non-conventionalized implicational impoliteness.' Culpeper (2010, 2011b) hints at the methodological shift of impoliteness studies from the analysis to extraction: from frameworks of super and substrategies to expressions and co-text and the context that make an utterance impolite.

Overall, the study at hand does not constitute the first study about impoliteness in the field of linguistics in Turkish or in English but it is significant in that it aims to investigate impoliteness in two layers, both in extraction and analysis. In addition, the interaction type for this study is spoken interaction through a contrastive analysis for British English by using a fairly well-acknowledged corpus, BNC, for its representativeness for its spoken component, and STC. Throughout the study the theoretical approach to data supplied by the corpora is corpus driven as opposed to many studies in corpus linguistics and it will be argued that the corpus driven approach changes the nature of research and that it should be the preferred choice over a corpus-based approach (Römer, 2005). Natural data findings do not always fit into existing theories; therefore, the researcher theorizes from scratch to generate new ideas and to move a step further, which is the main aim of scientific research.

1.5 The data and challenges

The data used for the study illustrated in this book have been retrieved from two different corpora, the British National Corpus (BNC) XML edition and the Spoken Turkish Corpus, STC hereafter (Ruhi, Eyrılmaz, and Acar, 2012) which is currently under construction as a project sponsored by TÜBİTAK (Scientific and Technological Research Council of Turkey) 108K283; and ODTÜ (Middle East Technical University) BAP-05-03-2011-001.

There are some limitations regarding the data extraction and analysis, and the methodological approach developed in the study. In Chapter Three, it is explained that in extracting and at times simultaneously analysing impoliteness events in conversation, metapragmatic comments, conventionalized impoliteness formulae (Culpeper, 2010; 2011b) and cues for non-conventionalized implicational impoliteness (Culpeper, 2011b) present in the co-text and context are taken into consideration. Non-verbal forms such as structural patterns and a change in the pattern in conversation (e.g. turn taking, overlaps, topic retention, repetition signalling a potential for impoliteness, continuous disagreements), metadata features such as the relationship of speakers, paralinguistic forms such as prosodic aspects (e.g. pauses and rise in intonation or pitch) or annotations describing the utterance (e.g. speaker laughing, yawning) played a major role in interpreting the data as far as the corpora BNC and STC allowed. However, not all the data the corpora offered were used due to some limitations.

First, since data encoding and transcription schemes are different for BNC and STC, non-verbal and paralinguistic forms existing in the data retrieved differed depending on the corpus. The interpretation of certain forms was not attempted at the levels of extraction or analysis. For BNC paralinguistic phenomena such as pauses, speech management phenomena (e.g. truncation, false starts, correction), and overlaps in the data were disregarded due to the complexity of the data retrieval and instead the conventional script was used. The BNC offers two different formats to retrieve data; Extensible Markup Language (XML henceforth) and the 'fancy' format which is closer to a conventional script. XML is the format through which alignment in speech is given in the BNC with the 'align with' mark followed up with the speaker whose utterance is overlapping, followed by the utterance it is overlapping with (see Figure 3.6, in Section 3.5).

If a researcher wants to include alignment of speech into his/her discussion of overlaps as potential for impoliteness, he or she must find a systematic way of putting together all the 'align with' marks on the XML format in a conversation as well as a way of presenting both the data about the speakers and the utterances overlapping to the readers of the study. However, the focus of that intent would be then transcribing corpus data. Therefore, although XML format supplies information about alignment of speech (which may give important clues about overlaps and interruptions signalling a potential for impoliteness, due to the complex process) 'fancy' format was preferred. This limited the study, especially at the analysis level, as paralinguistic data such as speech alignment was lost and the discussion, which would have been broader, was relatively restricted.

Similarly, STC supplies different formats (e.g. [TEI], [Praat], [Folker], RTF), which provide different nuances for different purposes. For this study, the data in the Rich Text Formatting (RTF hereafter) file were used. For all the excerpts that are discussed from STC, musical score written files in RTF were used since it allowed a detailed discussion of conversational conventions, co-text and context by providing details of overlaps, turn-taking, and clues provided by the annotations in the script. Additional analyses were included through the use of the software [Praat] for acoustic descriptions and a discussion of prosodic nuances such as pitch and intonation, change in voice and speed of speech. Referring to Crystal and Davy (1969) and Arndt and Janne (1987), Culpeper (2011a) points out that all prosodic cues are gradient and relative. He continues to argue that '[i]t is precisely the gradience and relativity of prosody that makes it crucial to account for the pragmatic inferencing that underpins its role in communication' (p. 63). The key point for acoustic descriptions is then to decide 'what counts as fast or slow, high pitch or low pitch' since:

> [i]t could be relative to the local context, for example, the rest of speaker's utterance or the immediately preceding speaker's utterance. It could be relative to the general context, for example, what is usual for that type of speaker (e.g. a man or woman, young or old person). It could also be relative to an aspect of the context somewhere between global and local, such as what is usual for that speech activity or event, e.g. increased loudness addressing a public meeting. (Culpeper 2011a:62)

All the acoustic descriptions of prosodic nuances that are analysed with the extracts from the STC in [Praat] are checked against the local context. Although such analysis offers a limited view of the complex ways prosody may play a role in communication in interaction, it gives important indications about how it may aggravate impoliteness combined with other contextual and co-textual clues.

Second, the study presented in the book focused mostly on linguistic and certain paralinguistic nuances, especially at the extraction level, and did not have an equal discussion of sociolinguistic factors such as power, age, social relations, gender or culture and subcultures despite their important roles in how impoliteness occurs. The role sociolinguistic factors play is acknowledged but, to increase the explanatory power of the study, greater attention was given to determinants such as conventionalized and non-conventional implicational impoliteness, which generated a method to search for and extract data from different corpora.

Third, there is a time gap of 12 years between today and the year BNC spoken corpus was collected and completed. Although written texts were selected from roughly the same period, some texts date back to 1964. The intention was not to include texts further back than 1975 but that criterion was not followed very strictly with especially imaginative works which continued to be popular among readers and influential on language over time. However, the spoken corpus used in this study does not go as far back. The building of the corpus started in 1991 and was completed in 1994. The British Market Research Bureau hired 124 volunteers who recorded all their conversations over two or three days. Revisions were made and new editions were released without adding new texts. In terms of sampling and its scale, the BNC offers a good degree of representativeness as the data source; however, the time difference can be can be viewed as a limitation because language changes over time.

Fourth, only naturally occurring data from the corpora was used. Other triangulation instruments such as diary or field notes, where information about how informants perceive or report incidents of impoliteness were not referred to. Since data were extracted from corpora already recorded from anonymous interactants in the past, the researcher was not a participant in collecting the data. In other words, it was not possible to ask interactants to provide, for instance, a report explaining whether they perceived the incidence extracted as impolite. Spencer-Oatey (2007) calls these documents post-interview reports and highlights their importance. Ruhi (2010) suggests that alternative documents should be used to bring a different dimension to the analysis of face as discussed in Section 5.4. Although the need for such alternative methods are acknowledged, the study in general looked at interaction in the 'ordinary sense' (Haugh and Bargiela-Chiappini, 2010) but confirmed that additional documents would have brought a depth to the issues such as membership organization and related background assumptions and brought out valuable findings. However, considering the nature of the corpora used for the study and the purpose of proposing a methodological perspective for extraction and analysis for corpus studies on naturally occurring data about impoliteness, such analytical documents had to be discounted.

Fifth, although the data were collected from rich databanks, the BNC and the STC, which allowed a large set of impoliteness incidences at the extraction level, the number of examples discussed in the analysis level were limited to seven and five. Conversation analysis combined with a focus on impoliteness requires a tremendous effort. With various purposes set for the study, the number of the discussion-level examples could not be extended despite the desire to reach conclusive generalizations on impoliteness by looking at large-scale co-occurrences of impoliteness data. Therefore, the contrastive aspect of the analysis between British English and Turkish did not go far beyond suggestions for further studies although it offered originality to the study.

1.6 The contributions of the book

There are a number of studies which have been conducted investigating politeness. They have focused on various dimensions such as speech acts, power relations, gender issues and identity which have been explored within the Turkish language or with contrastive studies of Turkish with other languages (Doğançay-Aktuna and Kamışlı, 2001; Zeyrek, 2001; Bayraktaroğlu and Sifianou, 2001; Martı, 2006; Ruhi, 2006; Hatipoğlu, 2007). However, impoliteness has been specifically and systematically discussed in reference to Turkish with more recent studies in relation to the face and relational work and its metapragmatic manifestation (Ruhi and Işık-Güler, 2007; Işık-Güler, 2008).

This book is about impoliteness studied in the Turkish language and it is the first volume that tackles impoliteness in Turkish with natural/corpus data. Moreover, since the data selection has been based on semi-comparable corpora, namely the BNC and the STC, extracted from naturally occurring spoken interaction, it is a good resource to exemplify how different corpora can be used for contrastive studies in pragmatics. At the extraction level, it lays out a well-defined methodology to the extraction of impoliteness from everyday spoken interaction, which is to minimize the degree of subjectivity in extracting the impoliteness and prevent the epistemological fallacies in the analysis. The discursive and the cue-based approaches combined together required a close look at metapragmatic comments, lexical and non-lexical reactive responses and conventionalized impoliteness formulae (Culpeper, 2010), cues for non-conventionalized implicational impoliteness (Culpeper, 2011b), verbal and non-verbal forms signalling interpersonal conflict, and nuances emerging through semantic prosody (Sinclair 1998, 2004; Stubbs

2002; Morley and Partington, 2009; Bednarek, 2008). Such detailed extraction allowed impoliteness phenomena which would go unnoticed to be noticeable to the researcher. This as a result broadened the perspective impoliteness phenomena have been discussed so far. In addition, since the STC is still under construction, the book will provide a reference for future studies which will be carried out on the STC and naturally occurring Turkish conversation at large.

Throughout the study, the theoretical approach to data supplied by the corpora is corpus driven as opposed to many studies in corpus linguistics which are not. It has been argued that the corpus driven approach changes the nature of research and that it should be the preferred choice over a corpus-based approach (Römer, 2005). Natural data findings do not always fit into the existing theories; therefore, the researcher theorizes from scratch to generate new ideas and to move a step further, which is the main aim of scientific research. To illustrate with the book, during the course of the study it presents, certain issues emerged and various insights were gathered on these issues. The issues, which were formed as new research questions that evolved as the study proceeded, did not replace the earlier ones. Therefore, they are considered as part of the cyclic approach: the progression of the study has brought out new questions and perspectives. For instance, two such questions were related to corpus linguistics and contrastive studies with corpora: (1) to what extent is the extraction of impoliteness possible when the corpora used for a study, the BNC and the STC in the case of this study, are not fully comparable? and (2) to what extent can such semi-comparable corpora be used for contrastive studies, which in this case is the present study? A discussion of such emerging issues and perspectives is provided in the concluding chapter.

1.7 Outline of the book

This book consists of six chapters. Following the overview in Chapter One, Chapter Two reviews studies on politeness and impoliteness phenomena and the concept of face. Since the study presented focuses on conversation as the discourse type and the data collected from corpora, these chapters are followed by a discussion of conversation and conversation analysis. Similarities of the methodological concerns between conversation analysis and corpus driven linguistics, and the implications of these for the impoliteness studies focusing on conversation extracted from corpora will also be discussed. Chapter Three will delve into the methodological framework proposed by the book. It will provide a detailed exploration of the methodological issues related to extracting and analysing impoliteness from semi-comparable corpora within the corpus driven linguistics (CDL) approach. Further investigation of how encoding the data and the annotations in the corpora influence the analysis of impoliteness are provided in the relevant sections. Chapter Four illustrates how the extracted conversations including impoliteness from the BNC and the STC have been analysed. The role that semantic prosody and acoustic prosody play in impoliteness are demonstrated and their implications for impoliteness phenomena are further investigated. Chapter Five, gives an evaluation of the methodological approach proposed by the book, the emerging issues, and a contrastive analysis of the impoliteness in British English and Turkish. It also touches briefly on the suggested areas for future research. The final chapter, Chapter Six, gives an overview of how the book has implicitly addressed some recent discussions formed around corpora related studies and impoliteness.

CHAPTER 2

Impoliteness Phenomena, Conversation and Corpus Linguistics

2.1 Perspectives on Politeness

In the area of politeness theory, Brown and Levinson's (1987) view has been the most influential and widely investigated, and has therefore attracted a great deal of attention from commentators and critics. One of the criticisms is that the bald on-record superstrategy functions as a threat to negative face since it impedes the actions of the hearer and, as such, 'bald, on record (im)politeness does not and cannot exist when we take into account (a) context, and more importantly here, (b) the fact that there is no communication without face' (Bousfield, 2008:64). Another criticism against Brown and Levinson's view is that it deals with single acts of politeness within single utterances rather than on the level of discoursal exchange and this creates a single, universal Model Person.

Leech's theory of politeness is expanded through an emphasis on interpersonal rhetoric and bridges semantics and pragmatics by arguing that messages are conveyed through a version of sound mapping; 'message transmission,' a text, 'textual transaction,' and a discourse, or 'interpersonal transaction' (Leech, 1980). While the interpersonal transaction provides clues to shape judgments about the text in terms of language-internal factors such as clarity, interpersonal rhetoric ensures that the utterance adheres to the situational demands of the conversation, one of which is politeness (Leech, 1980). He develops his theory further by adding another principle, Politeness Principle (PP) to the Gricean CP; the maxims of which are tact, generosity, approbation, modesty, agreement and sympathy. The PP model was later to receive criticisms for the arbitrary number of maxims arguing that, for the PP model to be reliable, the unrestricted number of PP maxims should be restricted (Jucker, 1988; Thomas, 1995).

Following the abovementioned approaches, in the 1990s, more emphasis started to be placed on how societal aspects shaped the theory of politeness. For instance,

Watts (1992) aimed at making a distinction between polite and politic behaviour. He explained that politeness is 'marked forms of elaborated speech codes in open groups' (p. 134), whereas politic behaviour is unmarked in the sense that it is intended to establish and/or maintain social equilibrium. Therefore, his theory also attempted to cover both the politeness and societal norms that informed the theoretical aspect. Some other scholars based their theory of politeness on societal norms. For instance, Gu's (1990) concept of politeness is derived from Chinese, while Ide (1993) discussed the concept of politeness in the Japanese context, and Blum-Kulka (1992) based the discussion on the Israeli-Jewish context. During the 1990s, a huge amount of empirical research was carried out within the existing models of linguistic politeness and the data were mostly collected through the use and analysis of Discourse Completion Tests, including formal and informal situations. However, Watts (2003) broke away from the current trend by including data of real-life speech situations, and argued that the object of the study of politeness theory must be commonsense notions of what politeness and impoliteness are, and that they should be investigated through the discursive approach. He further argued that a more appropriate model would be based on Bourdieu's (1991) social practice, in which the struggle for power dimension is central.

In line with the new focus of politeness theory that societal norms, cultural issues, the subtleties of power struggle and common sense (or lay persons' views) should inform the theory of politeness, Lakoff and Ide (2005) presented a collection of studies mostly conducted in non-Western languages, such as Japanese, Thai, and Chinese as well as Greek, Swedish and Spanish, which offered new insights. These studies went beyond semantics and incorporated non-language insights to the linguistic work and covered various theoretical topics such as social levels, gender-related differences in language use, and directness and indirectness. Watts, Ide and Ehlich (1992, 2005) published another collection of papers containing a theoretical discussion of the existing politeness models. They presented the problems by developing a theory of linguistic politeness which must deal with the crucial differences between lay notions in different cultures and the term 'politeness' as a concept within a theory of linguistic politeness. The validity of the models proposed by Brown and Levinson, Lakoff and Leech was questioned and the need for new approaches was emphasized.

Bousfield and Locher (2008) were the first to present a collected volume containing a thorough discussion of impoliteness and power. Their aim was to demonstrate a massive imbalance in terms of the academic interest between the studies of politeness and impoliteness. The notions of conflict and aggression came into the discussion of impoliteness theory and inspired further studies on impoliteness. Bousfield (2008) focused on an analysis of impoliteness in face-to-face spoken interaction, in which politeness was perceived to be the governing principle, and explored how impoliteness comes into play. His study was followed by Culpeper's (2011b) publication, which also used naturally-occurring language data and combined both a discussion of the lay person's views with a theoretical discussion of what shapes these took. He brought linguistic pragmatics and social psychology into the discussion of impoliteness and, by doing so, expanded the boundaries to a level where researchers of impoliteness should consider the use of naturally-occurring data and how a lay person's views of impoliteness are shaped by linguistic impoliteness and vice versa.

2.2 Perspectives on Impoliteness

Eelen (2001) discusses how impoliteness theory has been defined by politeness theories and thus, due to this conceptual bias, failed to account for a comprehensive view of impoliteness. Bousfield (2008) summarizes politeness theories under three main headings and extensively critiques how each one deals with the concept of impoliteness.

The first view is the social norm, or lay person's view of impoliteness. With the acknowledgment that politeness studies have to deal with social norms to varying degrees and that both first order and second order politeness are essential, Bousfield (2008) suggests that the distinction should be taken into consideration for further understanding of impoliteness. The second view is the conversational maxim approach to politeness. As mentioned above, Leech's research (1983, 2005) comes under this heading. Leech (1983, 2005) complements Grice's CP with the term Interpersonal Rhetoric (IR) and proposes that IR consists of PP and CP. His theory has been criticized for not attempting to explain how IR, which is based on a social goal-sharing principle, could explain the impoliteness that occurs in conflictive and aggressive communication (Bousfield, 2008; Eelen, 2001). Leech (2005) argues that his position is that '... a theory of politeness is inevitably a theory of impoliteness, since impoliteness is a non-observance or violation of the constraints of politeness' (p. 18). This approach creates a tendency to give priority to politeness and see impoliteness 'as always socially aberrant,' while impoliteness is 'not "normal" in a lay sense,' this approach overlooks the fact that it is 'ubiquitous across and within virtually all modes of human communication' (Bousfield, 2008:50).

The third view is the face management view, which was typified by Brown and Levinson (1987). As mentioned above, Brown and Levinson (1987) subdivide face into two parts – positive and negative face – and claim that members of a society subscribe to the needs of the two faces and, as such, adhere to politeness for social harmony. This idea of face management was adapted to impoliteness models. For example, in line with Brown and Levinson's (1987) superstrategies, Culpeper (1996) proposed a model that views impoliteness as an attack on the addressee's positive or negative face wants (pp. 349–350), and defined the following five superstrategies:

1. Bald on-record impoliteness
2. Positive impoliteness
3. Negative impoliteness
4. Sarcasm or mock politeness
5. Withheld politeness

Under positive impoliteness, which is defined as the use of strategies designed to damage the addressee's positive face wants, he lists the following output strategies:

1. Ignore, snub, fail to attend H's interests, wants, needs, goods, etc.
2. Exclude the other from the activity.
3. Disassociate from the other. Deny common ground or association.
4. Be disinterested, unconcerned, unsympathetic.
5. Use inappropriate identity markers.
6. Use obscure or secretive language.
7. Seek disagreement-sensitive topics or just disagree outright (act as 'Devil's advocate').
8. Avoid agreement. Avoid agreeing with H's position (whether S actually does or not).
9. Make the other feel uncomfortable.
10. Use taboo language – swear, be abusive, express strong views opposed to H's.
11. Call H names – use derogatory nominations.
12. Etc.

The following output strategies are listed under negative impoliteness, which is defined as the use of strategies designed to damage the addressee's negative face wants:

1. Frighten. Instil a belief that action detrimental to other will occur.

2. Condescend, scorn or ridicule. Emphasize own power, use diminutives to other (or other's position), be contemptuous, belittle, do not take H seriously.
3. Invade the other's space, literally (positioning closer than relationship permits) or metaphorically (ask for intimate information given the relationship).
4. Explicitly associate H with negative aspect. Personalize, use pronouns '*I*' and '*you*.'
5. Put H's indebtedness on record.
6. Hinder – physically (block passage), conversationally deny turn, interrupt.
7. Etc.

Culpeper (1996) claimed that this model of impoliteness takes Brown and Levinson (1987) into account but also departs from their model. Although he used similar superstrategies, he explained that impoliteness causes disharmony and social disruption since it is defined as the use of utterances that are designed to attack the interlocutor's face. Later, Culpeper et al. (2003), following Eelen (2001), point out that all theories of politeness mention impoliteness but they all fall short in explaining the intricacies of impoliteness since they cannot be 'straightforwardly applied to impoliteness … to fully account for the confrontational interaction in impolite discourses' (Bousfield, 2008:71). Therefore, later, Culpeper (2005) revised the five superstrategies and replaced his 'sarcasm or mock politeness' with 'off-record impoliteness.' Culpeper's (1996) modification of his model into Culpeper (2005), the replacement of sarcasm or mock politeness by the off-record impoliteness superstrategy, is a result of the shift in his focus of an intentional, impolite face attack to a more contextually and culturally sensitive model (Culpeper, 2005:40).

The model Culpeper (2005) revised suggests that Spencer-Oatey's (2002) approach, Rapport Management, which consists of two distinct features, Face and Sociality Rights, should be integrated into impoliteness theory. Face consists of quality face and social identity face and sociality rights are divided into equity rights and association rights. Still, Bousfield (2008:92) criticizes Culpeper's new model (2005):

> In doing so his approach remains sympathetic and complementary to the work done previously on this model. However, simply relating Brown and Levinson's Positive/Negative approach to face Spencer-Oatey's (2002) approach to Rapport Management (including 'Face' and 'Sociality Rights'); by, in short, linking the two together, simply does not solve the issue of the,

> more often than not multi-face directedness of the linguistic impoliteness
> strategies. Indeed, when we consider that Spencer-Oatey (2007:16) argues
> that face is a multi-faceted phenomenon, then it is obvious that the linguistic
> impoliteness strategies identified by Culpeper (1996), Culpeper et al. (2003)
> and Cashman (2006) don't purely indict one type of face, or one type of
> sociality right over another. I would therefore suggest, though, that the
> evolutionary steps that Culpeper (2005:41–42) makes have not *yet* gone far
> enough to solve such issues facing the model.

Despite Bousfield's (2008) criticism, Culpeper's (1996, 2005) face management view and models of impoliteness have been applied to various discourses and real data. It was claimed that Culpeper's (1996, 2005) model provides adequate analysis power as it works both at the application and analysis level, with some modifications. For example, Lauer (1996) analysed complaint letters, and Cashman (2006) applied the model to impolite interactions taking place between Spanish and English bilingual children. However, his model proposes an open-ended list of superstrategies, and the open-endedness of the list of positive and negative face damage strategies could be argued as the weakness of the model, similar to Thomas's (1995) criticisms of Leech's (1983) PP model in that it 'makes the theory at best inelegant, at worst virtually unfalsifiable' (p. 167). Bousfield (2008) also acknowledges this claim and postulates, 'if we are to simply invent a new strategy for every new regularity in language than the model could soon become impervious to counterexamples' (p. 91).

Bousfield (2008) also applies Culpeper's (1996, 2005) model with some modifications, as he believes:

> [r]esearch into impoliteness should not unduly concern itself with the
> discovery of additional linguistic output strategies but should now be concen-
> trated upon how the discourse 'builds up', how context affects the generation
> of impoliteness and how dynamism of impolite illocutions is dealt with. (p. 91)

In his analysis, Bousfield (2008) takes a more inclusive approach to these superstrategies and summarizes the superstrategies under two titles as the following:

1.   On-record impoliteness
2.   Off-record impoliteness
     (a) Sarcasm
     (b) Withheld politeness

He explains on-record impoliteness as being 'the use of strategies designed to *explicitly* a) attack the face of an interactant, b) construct the face of an interactant in a non-harmonious or outright conflictive way, c) deny the expected face wants, needs, or rights of the interactant, or some combination thereof' (p. 95, emphasis in the original). Off-record impoliteness, on the other hand, is the use of strategies 'where the threat or damage to the interactant's face is conveyed indirectly by way of implicature following Grice (1989) and can be cancelled (e.g. denied, or an account/post-modification/elaboration offered, etc.)' (p. 95).

This study proposes a model that breaks away from the summarized criticisms which are that: (1) the superstrategies are open-ended and thus the theory is impervious to counterexamples and (2) the theory of face does not constitute the main defining tool for the theory of impoliteness. In order to address these issues, this study adds a new layer to the model, namely extraction, which is based on the notions of the conventionalized impoliteness formulae (Culpeper, 2010; 2011b), and non-conventionalized implicational impoliteness (Culpeper, 2011b), instead of the superstrategies existing in the current model. This additional layer is then followed by an analysis level. The discussion at this level originates from existing theories but is developed more in the light of the findings the natural data at the extraction level supply.

Two further core issues of impoliteness research so far have centred around the following two questions: (1) Where does the meaning lie? In other words, what speech acts or linguistic expressions define what is impolite? and (2) How is the notion of face related to the concept of impoliteness?

In terms of the first question, the literature vacillates between two opposing views – whether meaning is inherent in the speech act and whether meaning is inherent in forms (Culpeper, 2010). Brown and Levinson (1987:65–68) imply that FTAs can be intrinsic to speech acts, as they define FTAs as 'what is intended to be done by a verbal or non-verbal communication, just as one or more "speech acts" can be assigned to an utterance.' Their view has been criticized for being deterministic for the reason that some speech acts, such as orders which are beneficial to the hearer, can be interpreted differently in different cultures. Thus, generalizations about FTAs being inherent in speech acts could only be specific to cultures. It has also been pointed out that speech acts do not have a degree of determinacy and stability (Leech, 1983:23–24). Therefore, the view that meanings are inherent in speech acts has been claimed as a 'theoretical non-starter' (Culpeper, 2010:3234). The other view – that meaning is inherent in linguistic expressions – has received different responses, which can be examined under three positions. The first one takes a positive stance and makes the line between semantic and pragmatic meaning more visible: meaning is 'more a matter of truth conditions than felicity conditions, more conventional than non-conventional and more non-contextual (and thus non-relative) than contextual' (Culpeper, 2010:3234).

Although scholars have not argued explicitly whether politeness or impoliteness is inherent in linguistic expressions, the focus on linguistic expressions implied that context was less important. The other view takes a relatively negative stance. Fraser and Nolen (1981) claim that, '... no sentence is inherently polite or impolite. We often take certain expressions to be impolite, but it is not the expressions themselves but the conditions under which they are used that determine the judgment of politeness' (p. 96). Locher and Watts (2008) argue that 'there is ... no linguistic behaviour that is inherently polite or impolite' (p. 78). Nevertheless, even within the 'no' camp, there is a recognition that in determining the interpretation of politeness, expressions play a role that 'lend themselves to individual interpretation' (Watts, 2003:168) and that they constrain the interpretation. The third stance is the 'discursive' approach. Culpeper (2010) explains that 'the focus of the discursive approach is on the micro level, that is, on participants' situated and dynamic evaluations of politeness, not shared conventionalized politeness forms or strategies.' He adds that discursive studies emphasize that the meanings are unstable, negotiable, and fuzzy, and that shared conventions of meaning enforce stability and certainty to communication. In this respect, discursive studies on politeness received critical reactions in that if everything is relative, descriptions of individual encounters cannot account for an explanatory theory of politeness, and thus they do not have predictive power (Watts, 2003; Terkourafi, 2005a). Culpeper (2010) defines his own approach as the dual view to argue that impoliteness is partly inherent in linguistic expressions:

> My own position is dual in the sense that I see semantic (im)politeness and pragmatic (im)politeness as inter-dependent opposites on a scale. (Im)politeness can be more inherent in a linguistic expression or can be more determined by context, but neither the expression nor the context guarantee an interpretation of (im)politeness. What is different about semantic (im)politeness from, say the semantics of the noun 'table' is that it is the relationship between the expression and its interpersonal contextual effects that must be the central semanticized component for it to exist. (p. 3237)

He relates 'the dual view' to conventionalization. Terkourafi (2005b) defines conventionalization as 'a relationship between utterances and context, which is a correlate of the (statistical) frequency with which an expression is used in one's experience of a particular context' (p. 213). Similar to Terkourafi (2005b),

Culpeper (2010) argues that there is a big difference between conventional and conventionalized inferences: for example, although *cunt* was viewed as the most offensive word in British English in the year 2000, an undergraduate student reported in a diary that a friend used this word to mean 'guy' or 'dude' (Culpeper, 2010:3237). Culpeper (2011b:22) touches upon the level of subjectivity and evaluative aspects of the notion of impoliteness by stating that impoliteness 'is very much in the eye of the beholder, that is, the mind's eye. It depends on how you perceive what is said and done and how that relates to the situation.' Eelen (2001), Watts (2003) Spencer-Oatey (2005), Ruhi (2008), Terkourafi (2001), Haugh (2007) and Fraser and Nolen (1981) are among the scholars who discussed the same idea in relation to different emphases. For instance, Ruhi (2008) argues that the reason why utterances that are perceived to be polite can as well be perceived impolitely, depending on their meta-representation of verbal and/or non-verbal acts, and on 'conceptualizing interpretation of acts relative to actions and relative to the perceptions that interlocutors have of each other' (p. 305). She proposes that 'politeness is an (optional) metarepresentation of (non)verbal acts, which concerns people's representations of others' words, attitudes, beliefs, actions and relational and/or transactional goals' (p. 305). In further discussing how metarepresentations are formed, Ruhi (2008) states:

> [t]he belief that it is polite to say 'thank you' when one receives a gift would be generated through a causal chain of repeated public productions of the act and would stabilize both as a public and a mental representation. The act would thus gain the status of a socially institutionalized category and become part of one's encyclopaedic knowledge of expectations in social interaction. The act could then be triggered in production and comprehension in the context of its associated action schema. (p. 305)

In this respect, not all conventional utterances are conventionalized formulae, and the conventionalized impoliteness formulae are closely linked to the idea of co-occurrence regularities, a casual chain of productions of an act referred to in the quotation above, between language forms and specific contexts. Following this line of thought, Culpeper (2010, 2011b) carried out an inclusive study to identify conventionalized impoliteness formulae and studied specific contexts and metadiscourse to reveal the linguistic behaviour governing impoliteness. To arrive at the conventionalized impoliteness formulae, he used video recordings and written texts, 100 informant reports containing a description of impoliteness events, corpus data in particular from the Oxford English Corpus, and an impoliteness perception questionnaire. The table below displays his findings.

Table 2.1. Conventionalized Impoliteness Formulae (Culpeper, 2010)

1. Insults	1. Personalized negative vocatives – [you][fucking/rotten/dirty/fat/little/etc.] [moron/fuck/ plonker/dickhead/berk/pig/shit/bastard/loser/liar/minx/ brat/slut/squirt/sod/bugger, etc.] [you] 2. Personalized negative assertions - [you][are][so/such a] [shit/stink/thick/stupid/bitchy/ bitch/hypocrite/disappointment/gay/nuts/nuttier than a fruitcake/hopeless/pathetic/fussy/terrible/fat/ugly/etc.] - [you] [can't do] [anything right/basic arithmetic/etc.] - [you] [disgust me/make me] [sick/etc.] 3. Personalized negative references - [your] [stinking/little] [mouth/act/arse/body/corpse/ hands/guts/trap/breath/etc.] 4. Personalized third-person negative references (in the hearing of the target) - [the] [daft] [bimbo] - [she] ['s] [nutzo]
2. Pointed criticisms/ complaints	- [that/this /it] [is/was][absolutely/ extraordinarily/ unspeakably/etc.][bad/rubbish/crap/terrible/horrible/etc.]
3. Challenging or unpalatable questions and/or presuppositions	- why do you make my life impossible? - which lie are you telling me? - what's gone wrong now? - you want to argue with me or you want to go to jail?
4. Condescensions	- [that] ['s/is being] [babyish/childish/etc.]
5. Message enforcers	- listen here (preface) - you got [it/that]? (tag) - do you understand [me]? (tag)
6. Dismissals	- [go] [away] - [get] [lost/out] - [fuck/piss/shove] [off]
7. Silencers	- [shut] [it]/[your] [stinking/fucking/etc.] [mouth/face/trap/ etc.] - shut [the fuck] up
8. Threats	- [I'll/I'm/we're] [gonna] [smash your face in/beat the shit out of you/box your ears/bust your fucking head off/straighten - you out/etc.] [if you don't] [X] - [X] [before I] [hit you/strangle you]
9. Negative expressives (e.g. curses, ill-wishes)	- [go] [to hell/hang yourself/fuck yourself] - [damn/fuck] [you]

The dual view Culpeper (2010) describes has various implications for this study. The conventionalized impoliteness formulae together with the non-conventionalized implicational impoliteness, as opposed to speech acts associated with impoliteness, will be the driving forces at the extraction level in regard to the debates as to whether what is impolite can be defined through speech acts or linguistic expressions. Still, not at the extraction but at the analysis level, some speech acts will inevitably be touched upon through the discussion of co-text and context again for the reason that no linguistic expression is inherently polite or impolite; context is the determining factor.

Disagreement, for instance, is one of the speech acts referred to in the analysis level. It is a speech act which has been theorized traditionally in relation to identity construction and impoliteness research (Angouri and Locher, 2012:1); 'it is typically related to confrontation and conflict' and 'evaluated as having negative effects' (p. 2) 'in CA terms' (Sifianou, 2012:1). Levinson (1983) argued that agreement is generally the preferred act; that is, why seeking disagreement and avoiding agreements have been associated with damaging speakers' positive face wants. Likewise, Leech's (1983) Politeness Principle included the Maxim of Agreement: to minimize disagreement between *self* and *other* and maximize agreement between *self* and *other*. Pomerantz (1984) and Heritage (1984) characterized disagreement as creating a conflict and a threat to social solidarity. However, research ensued indicating opposing findings: disagreement can be chosen to ensure sociability and intimacy (Tannen, 1984; Kakavá, 1993, 2002; Locher, 2004). Angouri and Locher (2012), along similar lines with Gumperz (1992), argue that any view on disagreeing would be incomplete unless there is an analysis of 'how it is embedded in speech activity and how this speech activity is part of wider discourses' (p. 2). Sifianou (2012) states that disagreements are both multidirectional and multifunctional. They can affect both positive and negative faces of both interlocutors and serve a variety of functions such as hostility or affiliation (p. 6). If disagreement is studied in context through the lens of relational work (Locher and Watts, 2005), it would be more useful for studies on interpersonal interaction:

> [a]s linguists we are not only interested in the presence or absence of disagreement but in observing how disagreement is enacted and achieved and what the effects of different renditions might be. Ultimately we study whether the linguistic form we observe (for example direct or mitigated disagreement) will contribute to face-aggravating, face-maintaining or face-enhancing *effects*.
> (Angouri and Locher, 2012: emphasis in the original)

The direction Angouri and Locher (2012) are suggesting towards studies of disagreements in relation to face can be observed in various studies, for example, studies which focus on how the presence of other participants influences the interpretations of disagreement in interaction, and which take the effects of different renditions into account. Watanabe (2011:316–317) points out that our actions and thoughts are influenced by the presence of others even if they do not actively participate in interaction. These bystanders or third parties can be the determining factor in the escalation or solution of a dispute: 'The presence of third parties may influence the construction, interpretation and outcome of a disagreement' (Sifianou, 2012:5). Sifianou (2012) gives Kangasharju's (2002) study as an example to support her point. Kangasharju (2002) compared multiparty and dyadic interactions in Finnish committee meetings and the impact they had on arguments and forming alliances. Kangasharju's (2002) study bears in mind the complexities mentioned in that disagreements among participants in conversations are analysed in this study. If the disagreement as a speech act is used as a tool to extract impoliteness, it would be a major methodological drawback. However, since disagreement is both multidirectional and multifunctional, discussing it in relation to how it contributes to 'face-aggravating, face-maintaining or face-enhancing *effects*' (Angouri and Locher, 2012:2, emphasis in the original) strengthens the study. In this sense it brings a new depth to how it has been presented in CA studies; 'a "dispreferred" second' (Sacks, 1973/1987; Pomerantz, 1984 quoted in Sifianou, 2012:1).

Discussion of disagreements as speech acts in relation to the impoliteness studies brought out another issue, which is the notion of adjacency pairs. Kakavá (1993, p. 36) states that:

> Since disagreement can lead to a form of confrontation that may develop into an argument or dispute, disagreement can be seen as a potential generator of conflict. Not only can disagreement create conflict but it can also constitute conflict, since an argument is composed of a series of disputable opinions or disagreements. (p. 36)

That is why Locher (2004:95) explains that disagreements naturally require a first part and a second part, or an adjacency pair. Based on Schegloff (1972) and Schegloff and Sacks (1973), Schriffin (1994:236) elucidates adjacency pairs as 'a sequence of two utterances, which are adjacent, produced by different speakers, ordered as a first part and a second part, and typed so that the first part requires a particular second part or range of second parts' (quoted in Locher, 2004:95). Going back to the idea of the different renditions disagreement may be present in and their various effects (Angouri and Locher, 2012:2); what becomes very important for impoliteness studies is whether the sequence of adjacency pair for disagreement was followed, whether there were pauses in between the first part and the second part, how many times the pair was repeated, and whether these issues triggered face-aggravation. That is one of the reasons why CA offers valuable tools for impoliteness studies, if the CA approach is wide enough to take the complexities context and co-text put forward.

Culpeper (2011b) states that impoliteness is 'very much about signalling behaviours that are attitudinally extreme or understanding them to be so' (p. 139). He maintains that impoliteness formulae do not necessarily signal impoliteness unless they are intensified; that is, used in ways that make them less ambiguous and equivocal. Modifiers, taboo words, certain prosodies, and some non-verbal features are among examples of ways in which they are intensified. Quoting from McEwen and Greenberg (1970:340), Culpeper (2011b) explains message intensity as 'the strength or degree of emphasis with which a source states his attitudinal position towards a topic' (p. 140). He draws attention to the fact that all conventionalized impoliteness formulae naturally have a degree of intensity but certain features are added which increase their level of offensiveness. Message intensity can be increased through use of lexis, grammar, prosody, and non-verbal signals. For instance, 'you're so stupid' and 'you're stupid' have different effects as the former is intensified through a modifier. Lexical choices may also function as intensifiers. Culpeper (2011b) uses Leech's ([1974] 1981:15) 'affective meaning' to explain why a variation of lexical items (e.g. 'bad/rubbish/ horrendous/crap/shit') in a frame 'that's X' would give different degrees of negative attitude to what is referred to in X. Affective meaning is about 'how language reflects the personal feelings of the speaker, including his [sic] attitude to the listener, or his attitude to something he is talking about' (Leech, 1981:15). Adjectives of taboo words in conventionalized impoliteness formulae act towards giving an affective meaning since they 'intensify descriptions' (Jay, 1992:63 quoted in Culpeper, 2011b:141).

Culpeper's (2010) findings of taboo words acting as intensifiers in conventionalized impoliteness formulae are strongly confirmed by another study, Millwood-Hargrave (2000), carried out jointly by the Advertising Standards Authority (ASA), The British Broadcasting Corporation (BBC), the Broadcasting Standards Commission (BSC) and the Independent Television Commission. The project was designed to test people's attitudes towards swearing and offensive language and to examine the role of context. First, qualitative study using group discussions together with interviews were carried out with the prompts from television programs and advertisement clips followed by a quantitative study through the analysis of an in-home questionnaire given to 1,033 adults. Figure 2.1 summarizes the findings of a questionnaire about the most offensive words in Britain in 2000.

	Position	*(1997)*
Cunt	1	(1)
Motherfucker	2	(2)
Fuck	3	(3)
Wanker	4	(4)
Nigger	5	(11)
Bastard	6	(5)
Prick	7	(7)
Bollocks	8	(6)
Arsehole	9	(9)
Paki	10	(17)
Shag	11	(8)
Whore	12	(13)
Twat	13	(10)
Piss off	14	(12)
Spastic	15	(14)
Slag	16	(18)
Shit	17	(15)
Dickhead	18	(19)
Pissed off	19	(16)
Arse	20	(20)
Bugger	21	(21)
Balls	22	(22)
Jew	23	(24)
Sodding	24	(23)
Jesus Christ	25	(26)
Crap	26	(25)
Bloody	27	(27)
God	28	(28)

Base: Total sample

Figure 2.1. Ranking of 'very severe' words
Source: Millwood-Hargrave (2000:9)

The taboo words above, which signal a negative affective meaning and act as intensifiers, were used for word queries in the BNC as explained in detail in Chapter Three.

Prosody and kinesic features have been neglected, despite the major role they might play in impoliteness incidences (Culpeper, 2011b:146). Arndt and Janne (1987:275 quoted in Culpeper, 2011b:147) argue that prosody and kinesic features interact with words and structures, and create meaning. According to Arndt and Janney, attitudinally-marked prosody, which is not clearly motivated by syntactic considerations, triggers further interpretations in different ways:

1. *rising pitch* together with declarative, imperative or wh-interrogative utterance types would be considered attitudinally marked.
2. *falling pitch* together with all other interrogative utterance types would be considered attitudinally marked.
3. *falling-rising pitch*, as a mixed contour, would be considered attitudinally relevant regardless of the utterance type with which it is combined.
4. *all remaining combinations* of pitch direction and utterance type – i.e., the so-called normal ones, grammatically speaking, would be considered attitudinally relevant only in conjunction with other types of cues or cue combinations. (Arndt and Janne 1987:275 quoted in Culpeper, 2011b:147)

In this study, discussion of prosody was limited to the annotations present in the BNC and the STC. Further analysis such as what Praat – a software used to analyse prosodic speech events (e.g. pitch, intonation, etc.) – would offer were followed only to a limited extent with the STC. This is acknowledged in Section 1.5.

Conventionalized impoliteness formulae offer a frame for impoliteness co-occurrences in British English, which has been applied to extract data from Turkish in this study. Conventionalized impoliteness is only one aspect of impoliteness and is noticed in more obvious ways compared to non-conventionalized implicational impoliteness. Culpeper (2011b) classifies implicational impoliteness in three categories: form-driven, convention-driven; internal, external, and context-driven; unmarked behaviour and absence of behaviour. By form-driven, Culpeper (2011b) is referring to the 'implicit messages which are triggered by formal surface or semantic aspects of a behaviour and which have negative consequences for certain individuals' (p. 157). He explains that form-driven implicational impoliteness may look similar to off-record politeness superstrategy; however, there are two major differences. One, this notion is not linked to politeness, and two, with the incidences of impoliteness, an alternative interpretation of politeness is impossible to make (p. 157). Intensifying techniques, as well as prosody, provide an evaluation of impoliteness in context. With the form-driven category, Culpeper (2011b) proposes the Gricean cooperative principles and the echoic mention view (e.g. Sperber and Wilson 1981, 1995 [1986]). Culpeper (2011b) explains that mimicry and echoic mention is another type of implicational impoliteness. He defines mimicry as 'a caricatured re-presentation' (p. 161). Referring to Goffman (1974:539), he points out that quoting is part of mimicry. When someone quotes 'too much,' for instance all the prosodic features of the speaker, the quoter becomes 'suspect' (p. 161). He further discusses inferential steps taken when quoting is inferred as too much. For Sperber and Wilson (1995 [1986]), echo, in their term 'echoic irony,' is more than verbal utterances or thoughts. It is of someone's behaviour, which is usually a characteristic behaviour pattern and depends on the following condition to be inferred as echoic irony: 'first, on a recognition of the utterance as an echo; second, on an identification of the source of the opinion echoed; and third, on a recognition that the speaker's attitude to the opinion echoed is one of rejection or disapproval' (p. 240). Culpeper (2011b) proposes an adjustment to broaden this condition:

> [f]irst, on a recognition of the behaviour as an echo; second, on an identification of the source of the behaviour echoed, third, the recognition that the source behaviour is a characteristic of the identity of the speaker who gave rise to it, and fourthly, on a recognition that the speaker's attitude to the behaviour echoed is one of rejection or disapproval. (p. 161)

He summarizes impolite mimicry and caricatured (re)presentation in five points:

1. An echoed behaviour. A behaviour referenced by an echo.
2. An echo. A behaviour which is recognized as an earlier behaviour.
3. A marked echo and the implied echoed behaviour. The echo is marked (usually involving distortion or exaggeration), thus signalling the need for further inferencing. Moreover, the marked echo implies that the behaviour it echoes is also marked, that is, abnormal in some way. This is the implied echoed behaviour.
4. An implied echoed behaviour and the echoer. The implied echoed behaviour is attributed to the person who gave rise to it; more specifically, it is typically attributed to an identity characteristic of that person.
5. The echoer and the echoed. The recognition that the discrepancy between the echoed behaviour and the implied echoed behaviour reflects the negative attitude of the echoer towards the echoed person. (p. 165)

The following excerpt is extracted from the BNC (Text ID: KCP, conversations recorded by PSOGM). It is a part of an extended family conversation and the speakers are exchanging opinions on TV programs. The extract, which is discussed in section 4.2 in more detail, is an example of impoliteness since how the conversation unfolds exemplifies both conventionalized impoliteness formulae and implicational impoliteness:

> (GU) She knew a lot of telly.
> (GU) Neighbours
> (GM) Oh!
> (GU) and bloody Coronation Street and all that crap!
> (GM) Ooh!
> (GT) Ooh!
> (GU) You'd hear all that!
> (GV) And don't say crap, that's a very good programme!
> (GM) What is? I
> (GV) Coronation
> (GU) Coronation
> (GV) Str
> (GM) Oh what a load of dip!
> (GV) I lo, I've recorded whatever's on tonight, is it Eastenders?
> (GV) K Y T V I've got on tonight recorded that.
> (GU) S H I T more like!
> GT laughs
> (GM) Yeah.
> (GV) K Y T V is very good, K Y T V.
> (GT) Hang on! *(laughing)*
> (GT) K Y T V, what's that?
> (GM) I didn't think you'd be a Coronation Street addict.
> (GT) No, I wouldn't!
> (GV) The best people are.
> (GV) Princess Anne.

The reason why Culpeper (2011b) applies Grice's cooperative principle to the discussion of impoliteness when cooperative principles are associated with politeness is that when Grice's maxims are flouted, the utterance can be interpreted differently from what it literally means, since it acts as indirect speech and so is implicational. Indirect speech acts are closely related to those principles proposed by Grice:

1. Indirect speech acts violate at least one maxim of the cooperative principle.
2. The literal meaning of the locution of an indirect speech act differs from its intended meaning.
3. Hearers and readers identify indirect speech acts by noticing that an utterance has characteristic 1 and by assuming that the interlocutor is following the cooperative principle.
4. As soon as they have identified an indirect speech act, hearers and readers identify its intended meaning with the help of knowledge of the context and of the world around them. (Finnegan, 1999:305)

People need to cooperate in communicating with each other since they need to 'honour the conventions' (Finnegan, 1999:301) of speech. Hearers assume that the speakers take the 'conventions of interpretation' into account while constructing their utterances; speakers on the other hand, assume that the hearers trust the speakers and that they value the conventions of speech. In short, speakers rely on this cooperation to make their speech meaningful. The maxims are: maxim of quantity, which requires the speaker to be appropriately informative; maxim of quality, which requires being orderly and clear; maxim of manner, which requires being truthful; and maxim of relevance, which requires being relevant. An example Culpeper (2011b) gives for non-conventionalized form-driven implicational impoliteness that occurs through violation of Gricean maxims is as follows:

> Sitting with housemates in the lounge and one comes in after finishing making her tea. She sits close to me and my other housemate i.e. within close earshot and says, 'See I made a curry that doesn't come out of a jar' knowing full well that I eat food like that which she clearly looks down upon. (p. 159)

In this incidence of implicational impoliteness, Culpeper (2011b) suggests that the offender supplies more information about the curry than seems to be necessary, thus flouting the maxim of quantity. The context that ensures this interpretation is the context that the informant eats 'food like that.' It is this kind of contextual clue which will be sought in this study for the purposes of extraction and analysis of impoliteness. In this example, and with Culpeper's (2011b) data collection approach, giving questionnaires and asking informants to describe impoliteness events gives more clues about the violation of maxims. Here, the informant points out, 'knowing full well that I eat food like that.' However, since the data in the present study consist of spoken interaction only, unless one of the speakers makes an explicit confrontational comment, contextual clues have to be searched for explicitly.

The essential feature of convention-driven impoliteness, which can be internal or external, is that it occurs when 'there is a mismatch in the context projected by or associated with the conventionalized formulae and either some other aspect of behaviour performed or the wider context' (Culpeper, 2011b:166). For instance, 'Could you just fuck off?' is an example of convention-driven implicational impoliteness since it mixes conventionalized politeness formulae with conventionalized impoliteness formulae through uses of *could you* and *fuck off*. Such a mixed use of formulae assures interpretation of the utterance as impolite since it provides 'a measure of extreme distance' between conventionalized politeness formulae and conventionalized impoliteness formulae (p. 168).

With context-driven implicational impoliteness Culpeper (2011b) refers to cases where there is no mismatch between the conventionalized politeness formulae since the 'trigger is not marked' (p. 180). Instead, impoliteness interpretation comes out with the strong expectations in a context. For instance he proposes the example of impoliteness below occurs because it is driven by what is triggered with the context even when there is no marked behaviour of impoliteness:

> TO SHOP ASSISTANT: You've not given me the pound.
> SHOP ASISTANT: I think I did [Abruptly]
> TO SHOP ASISTANT: Well it's not there. Look. (opened wallet to show him)
> SHOP ASISTANT: Go like that. [Implied I was trying to con him](he pointed to his sleeves, gesturing to loosen them)
> TO SHOP ASISTANT: See. [Raised volume] (opened sleeve to him) (He handed me a pound)
> TO SHOP ASISTANT: Thank you.

In this example the utterance 'go like that' seems to be a cooperative utterance by Gricean maxims but Culpeper (2011b) explains that it triggers impolite implications since 'our knowledge about hiding things in sleeves, or magicians or pickpockets is triggered.' It is the context that brings out the implication and so is impolite, especially when it was clear the person did not put the pound up their sleeve and that the shop assistant did not apologize afterwards.

Further discussion of conventionalized and non-conventionalized implicational impoliteness will be provided with examples at the extraction level of this study in Chapter 3. The next section summarizes the history of how the concept of face has changed in politeness studies over time and how the notion of face is linked to the concept of impoliteness.

2.3 Perspectives on the Concept of Face

Bargiela-Chiappini (2003) gives a very detailed historical analysis of how the concept of face and facework came to be used and how it has taken on new meanings over time. China is commonly acknowledged to be the place where the concept of 'face' originated, and Goffman, who first used the concept *face* or *facework* in his collected volume of essays *Interactional Ritual, Essays on Face-to face Behaviour* (1967), acknowledges this (Bargiela-Chiappini; 2003:1454). In her article, Bargiela-Chiappini (2003:1456) explains that, in footnote 1, Goffman (1967) mentions the sources which most influenced his thinking. For him, Emile Durkheim is one of the most influential scholars as his references to Durkheim's *The Early Forms of Religious Life* (1924) indicate. This, as Bargiela-Chiappini (2003:1456) points out, also explains why Goffman's (1967:45) notion of facework has some religious resonances (e.g. moral rules, ritual equilibrium). In fact, many other aspects of Durkheim's model of society are echoed in Goffman's discussion of how individuals behave in relation to others. For instance, rights and duties arise from collective thinking; ritual is maintained by the fulfilment of these duties in Durkheim's society and the idea of interdependence of individuals in society is emphasized. Similarly, Goffman's discussion of the interactant's maintenance of face focuses on the idea of interdependence with its emphasis on other interactants' reactions and feelings:

> an awareness of other interactants' reactions and feelings is famously expressed in Goffman's face as 'the positive social value a person effectively claims for himself by the line others assume he has taken during a particular contact' where a 'line' is the interactants' own evaluation of the interaction and all of its participants, which includes self-evaluation. (Goffman 1967:5 quoted in Bargiela-Chiappini 2003:1458)

This is significant to note since Goffman's notion of face has been frequently referred to and claimed to be adopted by scholars, but the nuance has been missed that the concept is very much related to the interdependence of the individual on the society and to self-evaluation of the interaction. This, in turn, brought out a criticism that the notion of face is ethnocentric, which will be discussed shortly.

Twenty years after Goffman's work, Brown and Levinson published their revised essay *Politeness: Some Universals In Language Use* (1987), which begins with a remark that their notion of face is 'highly abstracted' and requires 'cultural elaboration' (quoted in Bargiela-Chiappini, 2003:1460). Their use of negative politeness is significantly different from Goffman's face and facework and Durkheim's positive and negative rituals. First, for Goffman, facework concerned 'not the individual and his psychology, but rather syntactical relations among the acts of *different persons mutually present to one another*' (1967:2, quoted in and emphasis added by Bargiela-Chiappini 2003:1460), which certainly does not ground face in culture-relativistic terms. Second, as Bargiela-Chiappini 2003:1460) points out, Brown and Levinson's concept of negative face and negative politeness, inspired from 'avoidance rituals' corresponding to Durkheim's work and Goffman's discussion of 'avoidance,' is radically different since there is a clear-cut distinction between 'freedom of action and freedom from imposition' characterizing the negative face which does not exist in the notion of 'avoidance.'

Brown and Levinson (1987), therefore, seem only to define face through a Durkheimian line (Bargiela-Chiappini, 2003; Bousfield, 2008) by subdividing face into positive and negative face. They treat face as the basic wants every member of society has, and knows the other members also desire on some level. In addition, they argued that where urgent cooperation is necessary, face can be ignored for efficiency at the cost of social breakdown. Their definition of face is different from the face defined as norms or values that the members of society subscribed to as echoed in Goffman's (1967) definition. For Goffman (1967) face '... is an image of self, delineated in terms of approved social attributes – albeit an image that others may share, as when a person makes a good showing for his profession or religion by making a good showing for himself' (Goffman 1967:5).

Brown and Levinson's (1987) concept of face has received criticisms for the reasons touched upon. It is assumed that face is universally applicable to all cultures, and that it is discussed in a highly individualistic sense with an emphasis on how face acts as a public self-image. Locher (2004), for instance, argued that there are layers of face and that face can be internal or external; these layers get lost in Brown and Levinson's discussion (Locher, 2004:55). Bousfield (2008:34–35) agreed on the argument quoting from O'Driscoll (1996) who explains the confusion as follows:

> Goffman (1967:5) refers to the origin of face in 'the line others assume [a person] has taken.' It is 'an image.' Thus it is bestowed from the outside and post-factum (note the perfective aspect here). B[rown] and L[evinson], on the other hand, stress that face consists of 'wants' (1987:62). Thus it is bestowed from the inside, and pre-facto. B[rown] and L[evinson], however, confuse the issue somewhat by also referring to face as 'something that ... can be lost, maintained or enhanced' (1987:61), thus also using the term in Goffman's sense. (O'Driscoll, 1996:6)

Although Bousfield (2008) acknowledges O'Driscoll's (1996) criticism of Brown and Levinson's (1987) face, he argues that there is still confusion: face is treated as consisting of semantic opposites, positive-negative or internal-external, and that there is 'dualism' rather than dichotomy, and therefore face is scalar (p. 35). In his attempt to re-conceptualize face, Bousfield (2008) mentions some problematic areas in literature. His first argument is that there is confusion as to what negative face actually is, especially in the research discussing the concept of negative face outside the so-called 'western' setting, as pointed out in Matsumoto (1988) and Gu (1990). For instance, in opposition to Gu's argument that ill-fame and reputation is part of negative face, Bousfield (2008) claims 'with positive face being the want to be approved of by others in one's society, then in my view, ill-fame and reputation must be considered aspects of positive face, not aspects of negative face as Gu seems to claim. This "confusion" may actually be the result of the fact that there appears to be no sharply defined line between positive and negative face' (p. 37).

However, Bousfield (2008) further clarifies a second issue; that his view regarding the confusion of positive and negative face in research on non-western cultures does not imply that negative face, or the aspects of the desire to be free from restriction, do not exist in other cultures. In fact, he argues that 'the type, quantity, strength, and salience of different aspects of face will vary from culture to culture, discourse to discourse, and, of course, context to context' (p. 37). He concludes that the remarks coming from researchers who argue for a different notion of negative and positive face for non-western cultures are, in fact, neglecting the heart of the issue, which is that the notion of face is not and cannot be dichotomous; rather it is and can only be 'dual.'

In this sense, Bousfield (2008) suggests a return to Goffman (1967) since Goffman's idea of face is that it is a public property and as such it can only be realized in social interaction (p. 38). Therefore, he agrees with de Kadt (1998) in that face is mutually constructed and with Terkourafi (2007) in that there is no faceless communication. However, he further argues that Terkourafi's notion of face (2007) is always constituted or damaged and therefore is always external (Bousfield, 2008:39), whereas Bousfield's notion of face is also internal as suggested by the *duality* of face. Bousfield (2008) claims that when individuals interact with each other, they expect the interlocutors to recognize how they want their faces to be constituted, and act accordingly. This expectation is internal, since how individuals want the interlocutors to act in constituting their face is closely related to one's feeling of self-worth and understanding of previous, similar encounters (p. 39).

Bousfield (2008:110–11) attempts to illustrate the argument that the boundaries of positive and negative face become superfluous, using an example from the excerpt taken from The Clampers, Extract 12 below:

[14] *Context:* It is 7.30 in the morning. Bailiff S1 is making his first call of the day to a female driver (S2) who has repeatedly ignored parking ticket payment requests. Her husband (S3) is also present. S1 has just knocked on S2's door and S3 has answered it.

1. S1: Court bailiffs is she in
S2:
S3: yeah yeah at the moment why what's the
2. S1: we've got a court order been issued sir for non payment of
S2:
S3: problem
3. S1: fines on this vehicle ... Harrow council have authorized removal of
S2:
S3:
4. S1: the vehicle for non-payment of fines if you can manage to get that sir
S2:
S3:
5. S1: she's now got a sum payable of three hundred and twenty one pounds
S2:
S3:
6. S1: twenty five and the vehicle will be going into court storage once
S2:
S3:
7. S1: she's paid the fine she can go and collect her vehicle from the court
S2:
S3:

<S2 pushes then hits S1>

8. S1: storage fali facility alright
S2: what the fuck you doing excuse me.
S3:
9. S1: the car is going he has a court order
S2: what are you *fucking* doing
S3:

<S2 hits S1 in mouth- S1 starts dialling on the phone>

10. S1: police please yeah

S2: really you want some *fucking* money right
S3:
11. S1: <indistinct >
S2: all you have to do is ask for the money you don't
S3: all you have to do is ask for the *fucking* money right
12. S1: you can't get in the car madam
S2: have to *fucking* take the car
S3:
13. S1:
S2: *piss off* <indistinct >
S3: Jackie come here come here
[...]

With this example, Bousfield (2008:111–12) explains that with the use of *piss off*, unlike other taboo words she used, S2 aims directly at S1 and comments that it was to offend, on record, the face of S1, *purposefully* and *gratuitously* (emphasis in the original).

> Note as with the vast majority of impoliteness strategies, the overall *effect* is that the utterances of S2 are both in Culpeper's original (1996) terms, positively and negatively impolite. She is negatively impolite because the overall command she is making throughout her utterances is for S1 to 'go away' – an impingement on his freedom of action (including his power, his right, and indeed his obligation to remove the vehicle). In the context in which such a command is delivered, note, the lexical choices she makes (not to mention the physical violence she inflicts on S1) adds a clear dimension positive face attack in that she is showing extreme disapproval. As such this 'combined positive and negative face 'strategy of impoliteness (a) creates the overall evaluation of the fact of command to 'go away' as being one of impoliteness and (b) further strengthens the argument that a division between the two types is superfluous.

Although Bousfield (2008) relates his discussion of duality of face to O'Driscoll's (1996) criticism of Brown and Levinson's (1987) face as quoted above, his formulation of face which is phrased as 'duality of face' is different from O'Driscoll's (2007). O'Driscoll (2007) argues that Brown and Levinson's (1987) positive and negative face strongly suggest an opposition and that there is asymmetry between positive and negative politeness; 'positive is too large and negative is apparently too small' (p. 474). Moreover, he points out that positive face(work) includes both the desire to belong and desire to be approved of, but that dividing face into subcategories will overlook the connection between the positive and the negative. Therefore, he proposes a new look at face(work), which he claims is similar to Lim and Bowers's (1991) fellowship face:

> Just as negative face(work) pertains to separation and individuation, so positive face(work) should pertain solely to connection and belonging (something akin to Lim and Bowers's fellowship face). In terms of interaction, it should describe only those moves which can be interpreted as 'moves toward,' as predications or implications of togetherness, as opposed to negative's 'moves away.' (O'Driscoll, 2007:474)

In other words, O'Driscoll embraces the polarity of positive and negative in face(work) with the caution that they lie on a 'a uni-dimensional spectrum, which necessitates that the meanings of the two faces, especially positive, be constrained' (p. 465) and that not all aspects of face are at play at any one time during interaction. It is also noteworthy that O'Driscoll uses the phrase *face(work)* to refer to affective aspects of moves in interaction, as opposed to 'face' within the frame of politeness as Brown and Levinson (1987) framed it. Brown and Levinson's (1987) theory is built around 'scientific predictability,' which is more in line with second-order politeness, or politeness2, and ignores first-order politeness, or politeness1. To put it differently, if the scientific findings, constructed in this way, confirm the data on how interactants conceptualize what is (im)polite, it is only coincidental. This is one of the reasons why Locher and Watts (2005) argue that Brown and Levinson's (1987) theory is a one of facework, not politeness, and O'Driscoll (2007) puts forth a similar theorization.

Both O'Driscoll (2007) and Bousfield (2008) have expanded on the traditionally accepted 'dichotomy' of face and argued for different perspectives more recently, but earlier scholars also theorized on the notions of positive and negative face. For instance, Haugh (2005:44) argued that positive and negative face could be considered as one undifferentiated notion that can be 'lost' or 'saved,' which is more in line with Bousfield's (2008) expansion. Spencer-Oatey (2007:645) also exemplified this with an authentic example that the distinction between Brown and Levinson's ([1978] 1987) positive and negative face is 'no help in unpacking the complex face claims that people make in real-life situations, and which others need to be sensitive to if they are to address people's concerns in suitable ways' (p. 646):

> A group of Chinese businessmen, at the end of a visit to a British company with which they had been doing business, got embroiled in a protracted argument with their British hosts over money. One of the Chinese became

> concerned about the impression they were conveying, and said privately
> to the others: one thing is that we should not let people say we are stingy;
> secondly, we should not give the impression of being too weak; thirdly, we
> should not negotiate in a friendly manner. (Spencer-Oatey, 2005:115)

Through this example, Spencer-Oatey discusses the complexity of the face issue and explains that what is potentially face-threatening in this example is the mismatch between what the speaker values as positive attributes and negative attributes: not stingy, not weak, and friendly versus stingy, weak and unfriendly. In other words, the discussion of face cannot be carried out with a limited understanding of face consisting of positive and negative face.

Yet other scholars discussed some other aspects of face. In her re-examination of face, Bargiela-Chiappini (2003) proposes an alternative to its conceptualization as 'social self,' which focuses more on the dynamics of facework in interpersonal communication (p. 1463). Arundale (2006a) argues further along the same lines, and proposes that face or facework is relational and interactional. He starts his argument with a critical look at decoding/encoding models of communication, which explain 'communication as an output of one system that serves as an input to a separate, independent system' (p. 196) as opposed to the interactional way in which he views the communication. Quoting from Heritage (1984), he points out that 'communicative action is both relationship-shaped and relationship-renewing (1984:242), and like context, relationship is endogenously generated within talk, rather than exogenous to it (1984: 280)' (quoted in Arundale, 2006a:201). This has strong implications for how face or facework is conceptualized:

> In the alternative ontology, face is not a matter of the individual actor's
> public self-image. Instead, because social selves emerge in relationships
> with other social selves, face is an emergent property of relationships, and
> therefore a relational phenomenon, as opposed to a social psychological one.
> Importantly, framing face as relational rests directly on framing it as interac-
> tional (Arundale, 2006a:201)

Some implications of such a conceptualization are as follows. Face is both an interactional and a relational phenomenon and, as such, is not bound to individualistic framings of wants. Since it does not only reflect individualistic characteristics of wants and desires, it is not the equivalent of identity (Arundale, 2006a:202). Moreover, since it is 'interactional,' face is 'conjointly co-constituted' (Arundale, 2004; 2006a) and the analysis of face requires a change in methodological approaches for researchers. This change 'foregrounds interpretative methods that examine resources and practices for facework in specific instances of verbal and visible contact' (Arundale, 2006a:209) or in interaction. The present study examines interaction while taking this conceptual change into consideration.

Later, Spencer-Oatey (2007) draws attention to the relationship between face and identity, face in interaction and the cognitive side of the face concept. She starts off by pointing out that it is necessary to discuss the relationship between face and identity. There have been debates on whether face is an individual or social, private or public, situation-specific or context independent notion. Identity has always been a strand of discussion but has not been explicitly discussed so far (p. 640). Referring to Hecht et al. (2005), Arundale (2005), for instance, treats identity situated within an individual and face as a relational or social phenomenon: 'Both relationships and identity arise and are sustained in communication, but a relationship, and hence face, is a dyadic phenomenon, whereas identity is an individual (and much broader) phenomenon' (p. 202). However, Spencer-Oatey (2007) proposes that identity and face are similar in the sense that they are both about self-aspects and attributes and consist of individual, relational, and collective constructions of self. She then goes on to discuss the role of attributes, analytic frames and the dynamic unfolding of face in interaction. She claims that different attributes, depending on their connotations, gain different meanings and become face-sensitive during interactions. In terms of the role of the analytic frames (individual, relational, or collective) through which face is situated, she discusses an example from Spencer-Oatey and Xing, (2004:207). In this example, a group of Chinese businessmen are guests to British businessmen, and during the initial meeting the British chairman gives a welcome speech to the Chinese, but does not invite them to give a return speech. The comment below is what the Chinese delegate, Sun, said in a follow-up interview translated from original Chinese to English (Spencer-Oatey, 2007:646):

> Sun: According to our home customs and protocol, speech is delivered on the basis of reciprocity. He has made his speech and I am expected to say something ... In fact, I was reluctant to speak, and I had nothing to say. But I had to, to say a few words. Right for the occasion, right? But he had finished his speech, and he didn't give me the opportunity, and they each introduced themselves, wasn't this clearly implied that they do look down upon us Chinese?

This example illustrates that both relational and collective frames are required for the analysis since relational attributes, 'the relative status of business partners and rights and obligations associated with their relationship' and collective face emerging through the speaker's phrase 'us Chinese' are at stake (Spencer-Oatey 2007:646).

Although both Arundale (2005, 2006a) and Spencer-Oatey (2007) describe face as relational, their approach is different. For Arundale (2006a), face is relational because it is 'an emergent property of relationship' (see quotation above). For Spencer-Oatey, face is relational because relational 'refers to the relationships between participants (e.g. distance-closeness, equality-inequality, perceptions of role rights and obligations) and the ways in which this relationship is managed or negotiated' (p. 647). This is highly significant since it sets out how rapport, which has become quite an important concept with Spencer-Oatey's Rapport Management model for (im)politeness, is different from 'relational':

> I thus take it [relational] to be narrower in scope than rapport, which I define as (dis)harmony or smoothness-turbulence in relationships. Of course, rapport is partly dependent on relational (mis)management, but the latter is not the only factor that can influence it; for example, people's transactional 'wants' and the ways they are handled can also affect the rapport between the interlocutors (Spencer-Oatey 2005). My interpretation of rapport is thus close to Holmes and Schnurr's [2005] concept of 'relational practice,' but since this meaning is significantly different from that of 'relational,' as used by Locher and Watts (2005) and Arundale (2005), I use the term 'rapport' for the former and relational for the latter. (Spencer-Oatey, 2007:647)

The third aspect of face in interaction Spencer-Oatey (2007) elaborates upon is the 'dynamic unfolding.' In addition to the range of strategies participants use to manage a relationship, in ongoing relationships, attributes existing at individual, relational, or collective levels and other participants' attributions and anticipations of face at each level play a big role. Yet, since an interactional analysis looking into how interpretations on face-sensitive issues will not suffice, 'cognitive underpinnings' of face should also be considered to achieve a better analysis of face in interaction. Under the heading of cognitive underpinnings, Spencer-Oatey (2007) discusses values and obligations and how they are related to the concept of face referring to the social psychologist Shalom Schwartz and his value constructs (Schwartz, 1992; Schwartz et al., 2001). She refers to the figure below to point out the complexity of the value constructs that play a role in face sensitive issues.

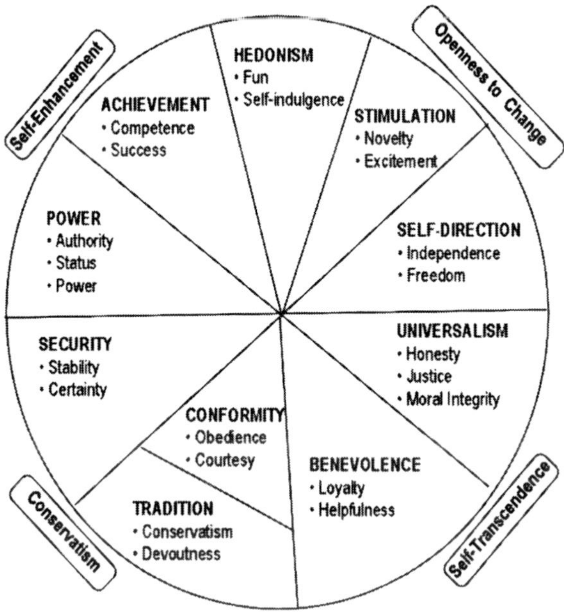

Figure 2.2. Schwartz's value constructs and their structured relationship
Source: quoted in Spencer-Oatey (2007:650) from Schwartz (1992:44).

She further argues that the negative and positive face described by Brown and Levinson ([1978] 1987) fall short in taking into account all these constructs, which may change from culture to culture. Spencer-Oatey (2007:650–651) explains that the figure illustrates the only values that can be considered 'negative face,' according to Brown and Levinson's model, would be self-direction, stimulation and hedonism in that they represent self-seeking. All the other values would be 'positive face.' However, that is not the case. Brown and Levinson ([1978] 1987) limit the positive face and exclude, for instance, the 'conformity' and 'tradition' through which Sun, the Chinese delegate in the example above, defines his positive face.

Through these discussions, Spencer-Oatey (2007) aims to raise two crucial questions: 1) to what extent is face always an interactional phenomenon? and 2) what kind of data is needed for research into face? In discussing the first question, she gives an example; in some cultures, if a journalist publishes a story describing a certain person in negative terms, that certain person may argue that they have lost face, although the readers of the story are unknown to that person. Spencer-Oatey suggests that interaction should therefore be defined very broadly if it is to be argued that face is always interactionally constituted. For the second question, she argues that post-event comments offer valuable information on people's evaluative reactions or attributions which may vary from person to person and culture to culture. Post-event comments were not used for data collection for this study since it is assumed that they would create a different type of interaction.

2.4 Conversation as Discourse Type

Garcés-Conejos Blitvich *et al.* (Garcés-Conejos Blitvich, Lorenzo-Dus and Bou-Franch, 2010) carried out a study focusing on Spanish television talk shows. They explain that their aim was to 'examine the bases underlying Peninsular Spanish speakers' *situated* (emphasis mine) assessments of im-politeness1,' and their analysis was 'grounded in a genre approach' (p. 690). Mills (2009) cautions us against mixing the analysis of politeness1 and politeness2, and creating cultural stereotypes:

> There is a tendency to draw on beliefs more recognisable as politeness1 than those from politeness2. What is needed is to analyse the linguistic behaviours of cultures in their own terms and not to elide stereotypical beliefs which may well derive from politeness1 beliefs with those of politeness2. The folklinguistic beliefs about a particular culture's usage of politeness are very interesting and should be examined in their own right; these beliefs may have an effect on interactants' performance, but we need to keep these beliefs separate from our analysis at the level of politeness2. (p. 1058)

Garcés-Conejos Blitvich *et al.* (2010) argue that a genre approach is a way of maintaining the fine balance between politeness1 and politeness2 and avoiding the pitfalls Mills (2009) draws attention to: '[Genre approach] provides a contextualized frame of analysis fit for inter/intra-cultural studies. However, because of their hybridity and fluidity, genre conventions will be permeated by societal norms. Genres thus bridge the individual and the societal' (p. 694). Elsewhere, to support her argument, Garcés-Conejos Blitvich (2010) summarizes the reasons in favour of this argument in seven items, and includes a detailed discussion of the role of the issues such as face, dyadic communication, predictive power of top-down and bottom-up approaches. For similar reasons to those outlined and discussed by Garcés-Conejos Blitvich (2010) and Garcés-Conejos Blitvich *et al.* (2010), a genre approach is adopted for this study.

Fairclough (2003) distinguishes between pre-genres, using Swales' (1990) suggestion for the term, *disembedded genres* and *situated genres*. He defines conversation as pre-genre, since it is on a high level of abstraction. There are categories which transcend particular networks or social practices and hence the term pre-genre is preferred (Fairclough 2003:68). The mentioned level of abstraction makes conversation particularly interesting for impoliteness studies. Other reasons, which will be discussed in this section, have also played a role in the selection of conversation as the discourse type in this study.

One of the reasons why conversation is selected for this study is related to frequency correlations and impoliteness formulae present in daily interactions. As a response to Terkourafi (2005b), Culpeper (2010) states that, where politeness is concerned, the frequency correlations between impoliteness formulae may not be as strong as the correlations between forms and particular contexts. He points out that impolite formulae are less frequent than politeness formulae, and one cannot find many examples during 'everyday' interactions. For this reason, he explains that he collected his data from particular discourses to study impoliteness formulae and that 'impoliteness plays a central role in army recruit training, interactions between car owners and traffic wardens, exploitative TV' (p. 32–38). His argument is that for impoliteness formulae these 'abnormal circumstances are indeed such specific contexts.' In fact, although Culpeper (2010) puts forward the reason for his selection of army training, interactions between car owners and traffic wardens as specific contexts that impoliteness formulae *can and do develop* (emphasis mine), and that 'in "everyday" interactions (e.g. interacting with my family, buying a ticket for the bus, talking to colleagues at work), examples of impoliteness are relatively rare' (p. 3238), a selection of what Warren (2006) names as specialized discourse reinforces the assumption that impoliteness is 'rather marginal to human linguistic behaviour in normal circumstances' (Leech, 1983), which has been argued to be 'conceptual bias' (Eelen, 2001) in impoliteness studies. Nevertheless, most recent studies on (im)politeness (Bousfield, 2008; Culpeper, 1996) focus on data collected from the interactions which would likely contain conflictive, impolite illocutions. For instance, Bousfield (2008) uses 101 example extracts from the video-taped television series representing the discourse types of driver-clamper encounters, military training discourse, police-public encounters, employer-to-employee discourse and person-to-person encounters.

While explaining the nature of the data set he used, Bousfield (2008) selects the following discourse types, since confrontational and impolite linguistic behaviour is more likely to occur: driver-clamper encounters (BBC's *The Clampers,* ITV's *Parking Wars*), person-to-person-encounters (*The Clampers, Soldiers To Be, Parking Wars*), military discourse (*Soldiers To Be, Red Caps*) police-public encounters (stop and enquiry, arrest) as well as employer-employee discourse. For instance, *Soldiers To Be* and *Redcaps,* serial television programmes dealing with military training discourse, illustrate the 'extreme inequality of power which is rigidly enforced.' Moreover, with 'the particular training philosophy,' which, Culpeper (1996) postulates, 'aims to depersonalize recruits in order that they may be remoulded as model soldiers' (p. 11), this discourse type offers up a lot of potential for impolite linguistic behaviour to occur. However, this discourse type does not represent the kind of interaction which this study aims to analyse.

Extract 28, from *Soldiers to Be,* will be discussed below to further explain why the types of discourse which Bousfield (2008) and Culpeper (1996) studied would not suffice for this study, and why they would result in shortcomings.

Soldiers To Be, Extract 28:

(9) *Context*: Recruit rifleman Parry has, for the second time, been fighting with his fellow recruits while under the influence of alcohol. This second time, he beat a recruit so badly that the other recruit was sent for medical treatment. The attack was relatively unprovoked and is primarily due to Parry's inability to conduct himself in an appropriate manner while under the influence of alcohol. As it is the second offence of this nature, Parry's punishment cannot be dealt with by either his platoon commander or his company commander. He is to be referred to the OC-Officer commanding the training regiment. In the meantime, (S1) the CSM-Company sergeant major – a very senior and experienced NCO – has called Parry (S2) into his office. The reasons for this are unclear. It may be because the CSM is angry with Parry and wishes him to be aware of this, or it may be in order for the CSM to be able to make a recommendation to the Commanding Officer when Parry's case comes up, based on how he reacts to the line of questioning (Bousfield 2008, p. 104):

> 1. S1: right come in ... *right my young fellow* explain your fucking actions
> S2:
> 2. S1: to me because I am not a happy ted.
> S2: [...]
> 6. S1: you know something *my young feller* It's a good job you was not in
> S2:
> 7. S1: the army ten years ago when I was at a rank where I could actually
> S2:
> 8. S1: beat the living daylights out of you
> S2: [...]
> 12. S1: me Parry you have got a drink problem *my friend* do you
> S2: yes sir
> 13. S1: understand that
> S2. yes sir

Bousfield carries out his analysis by applying Culpeper's (1996) impoliteness strategies discussed in Section 2.2, and explains that the interaction presents an example of impoliteness since the CSM is using one of Culpeper's strategies (1996): 'Use inappropriate identity markers – for example, use title and surname when a close relationship pertains, or a nickname when a distant relationship pertains.'

Bousfield's (2008) discussion of Extract 28 above is as follows:

> In no less than three instances does S1 appear to use insincere and inappropriate identity markers. The use of the first two – *my young fellow* (stave 1) and *my young feller* (stave 6) appear to be overtly patronizing and insincere. The third instance of an inappropriate identity marker is perhaps the clearer example with the use of the phrase *my friend* (stave 12). Clearly the relationship pertaining between these two; the CSM and the sometimes-violent when drunk recruit; is not so close as to permit either to consider themselves friends of the other and so the use is somewhat sarcastically inappropriate.

Another example he analyzes occurs through staves 10, 11, and 12 during the same interaction between the CSM and Parry:

[...]
10. S1: I'm hoping the OC recommends you to be discharged from the army
S2:
11. S1:. I don't want you. Because you are a pathetic individual do you
S2:
12. S1: understand
S2:
[...]

The strategy Bousfield (2008) analyzes this example with is Culpeper's (1996) [c]*all h names – use derogatory nominations:*

> Here we see S1 disassociate himself on a personal level from S2 by saying *I don't want you* and indirectly disassociating S2 from the army in general when he says *I'm hoping the OC recommends you to be discharged from the army*. Of course discharge need not, necessarily be a matter of impolite disassociation. The clause *you are a pathetic individual* is crucial to our understating here as, through the traditional use of the insulting *pathetic individual* (captured in Culpeper's (1996) Call h names – use derogatory nominations, S1, in the role of sergeant major, is disassociating recruit Parry from himself.

Both of these examples would be considered impolite because they follow the conventionalized impoliteness formulae (Culpeper, 2010, 2011b). For instance, *it's a good job you was not in the army 10 years ago when I was at a rank where I could actually beat the living daylights out of you* is a threat, *do you understand that* is a silencer and in between, there is a dismissal *I don't want you*, an insult in the form of personalized negative assertion *you are a pathetic individual* and another message enforcer *do you understand*. However, the data in the interaction are not rich enough for a discussion of how impoliteness unfolds or how impoliteness is encountered in interaction since these examples illustrate that the hearer in this case does not have equal power to the speaker. If the hearer decides to reply to the impoliteness with anything other than saying *yes sir*, which is what is most probably expected as part of the military discourse from a recruit rifleman in a situation like this, it is likely that he will suffer the consequences. To put it differently, this type of discourse can be defined as a specialized discourse type (Warren, 2006) and specialized discourse types do not have the *naturalness* of un-specialized discourse types such as conversation (Warren, 2006). For the reasons mentioned, the discourse types required by this study should be defined and discussed for their advantages and disadvantages.

Warren (2006) cites from various studies and gives examples of specialized discourse types: bureaucratic encounters, interviews, business transactions, business meetings, telephone conversations, courtroom discourse, service encounters, workplace discourse, classroom talk, news interviews, academic discourse, university oral research presentations, academic seminars, public speaking, genetic counselling, nurse/patient discourse and doctor/patient discourse consultations. He argues that there is a risk in concentrating too much on a specialized discourse; the findings and generalizations may not fully apply to the matrix of communicative practices and procedures which are socially organized, since specialized discourse events are a 'subset' of conversation (p. 4). The solution therefore is to define conversation as a speech event.

Analysts should make informed decisions about the type of discourse, since the inherent characteristics of a discourse can have different effects, both at the extraction and the analysis level. For example, Cameron (2001:10) argues that one distinctive component of conversation is that the spoken interactions in conversation are not prototypical. For example, when an employer calls an employee who has been late to work to 'have a conversation,' the employee would not expect to chat, as in having a conversation, but would perceive the irony. Analysts who work with such subtleties cannot ignore the effect or take the characteristics of discourse type for granted.

The definitions of conversation vary greatly; however, as Warren (2006) points out, they range from 'casual talk in everyday settings, to being equivalent to any form of spoken interaction' (p. 6). For example, Beattie (1983:49) examines conversation through 'university supervisions, tutorials and seminars, telephone calls, and televised practical interviews;' Black (1988:433) analyzes conversation through 'a televised political interview, friends chatting, and telephone calls to a radio talk show,' whereas Aijmer (1996:5) does it through face-to-face conversation, interviews, public speeches and new broadcasts. Such a broad definition of conversation may well indicate a common approach not to define conversation as distinct from other discourse types. Pomerantz and Fehr (1997:64–65) claim that while there are those who make a distinction between conversation as informal talk and talk occurring in formal talk, for a conversation analyst who focuses on 'conduct and action in both contexts, a priori distinction between the two is regarded as analytically unnecessary.' Having said this, however, Warren (2006:7) cautions against classifying conversation as a particular genre or register, citing Fillmore (1981):

> I would argue that the most straightforward principles of pragmatics or contextualization are to be found in the nature of conversational language, the language of people who are looking at each other or who are otherwise sharing some current experience and in which the hearer processes instantaneously what the speaker says. I believe that once the syntax, semantics and pragmatics of these basic types of discourse have been mastered, other types of discourse can be usefully described in terms of their deviation from such a base. (Fillmore, 1981:65)

Since defining conversation is a difficult task, Warren (2006) undertakes the task of describing its components in detail. The first component is whether or not a conversation should include ritualized exchanges, e.g. 'how are you?/fine thanks' and, what the length and the content of it would be. Both Goffman (1971) and Donaldson (1979) claim that a conversation should go beyond a ritualized exchange and that it must involve some exchange of information. As implied through the *exchange of information*, at least two participants taking turns should be involved.

Wilson (1987, 1989) argues that a conversation can only be defined through an 'equal distribution of speaker rights' (1987:96). This claim is different to participants taking equal turns: 'It is rather recognition of the fact that in conversation, speakers have equal rights in terms of initiating talk, interrupting, responding, and deciding not to do any of these' (Warren, 2006:8). Wilson (1989) claims that the 'speaker rights theory' (SRT) is what distinguishes conversation from other types of discourse. This theory describes best the type of discourse used and therefore the speech events discussed and analysed in this study will be termed *conversation* since in this type of discourse there are not designated speakers controlling to a greater or a lesser extent the speaker rights of other participants. With this view in mind, the analysis of impoliteness carried out in this study is not similar to Bousfield's (2008) study since his data come from specialized discourse such as the army training, where the participants do not have equal rights in the discourse.

Warren (2006) explains that:

> When it is claimed that the participants in conversation are of equal status, this does not mean that one can never converse with one's employer, for example. What is meant is that for the duration of a conversation, the external status set aside, and for the purposes of conducting the conversation, the participants are deemed to be of equal status. In this way the participants perceive themselves to be of equal status for the purposes of holding a conversation. This distinguishes conversation from specialized discourse types in which the status of participants is unequal, which in turn has consequences for the resulting discourse ... Even if in reality a particular conversation is dominated verbally by one or more of the participants, the responsibility for the discourse remains shared. Moreover, the participants in a conversation can only share responsibility for it if they perceive themselves to be of equal status. This is not the case in specialized discourse types in which it is the speaker(s) who is designated as dominant and who has the ultimate responsibility for the discourse. (p. 9)

Another component in the definition of conversation is open-endedness. Crystal and Davy (1969) point out the inexplicitness, randomness and lack of planning; Sinclair and Coulthard (1975), Cheepen and Monaghan (1990), and Tsui (1994) emphasize topic shifts, reciprocity and thus the spontaneity of conversation, as opposed to other types of discourse. Cameron (2001:10) also argues that one distinctive component of conversation is that the spoken interactions in conversation are not prototypical and that is the reason why when an employer wants to 'have a conversation' with an employee who has been late to work, it is perceived as ironic. Biber (1988:71) states that in conversation – especially in face-to-face conversation – 'the interactional focus is primary, usually overshadowing the informational focus' and that what characterizes a conversation is a high degree of interaction and goal negotiability as well as a considerable effort at maintaining a relationship. Since the focus of this study is impoliteness in spoken interaction, the dynamism of spoken interaction – with the abovementioned features of conversation (the inexplicitness, randomness and lack of planning, reciprocity and spontaneity) – is best captured with 'conversation' as the discourse type. Therefore, 'conversation' was selected as the discourse type for this study rather than other specialized discourse types.

2.5 Conversation Analysis

Wooffitt (2005) gives a detailed a detailed review of how Conversation Analysis started and how it is different from discourse analysis. The relevant parts are summarized below.

Conversation analysis (CA) started with pioneering research carried out by Harvey Sacks (Schegloff, 1972). The research began with a puzzle. The Los Angeles Suicide Prevention Centre had observed that if the callers gave their name to the staff speaking to on the phone at the prevention centre, they were more likely to identify themselves and disclose their identity information. This, in turn, helped the staff to take necessary actions immediately. The puzzle for them, then, was to get the callers to give their name, and this is how the research looking into the conversations was initiated. However, for Sacks, as Schegloff notes, the main issue became how to decide the point in the discourse in which a caller was not telling their name. He had to listen to the recordings of the telephone calls made to the organization and since he was working with real data, he had to develop analytical tools. He observed that there are norms concerning where in conversation certain kinds of activities should happen, and that there are slots in interaction in which specific actions are expected. Therefore, he decided to analyse the structure generated by these norms and utterances, and the actions utterances perform. Utterance activities that happen in pairs, for instance, were good examples to analyse. He realized that greeting, question-answer, and invitation-response utterances generally followed each other. In addition, if an inappropriate sequence followed, such as a question being asked and no answer offered, then a breakdown was likely to happen in the expectations that underpinned the interpersonal interaction.

Sacks was not the only researcher who was interested in the actions utterances perform. Austin developed his theory of Speech Acts (1962). However, they departed greatly in their selection of data; Austin focused on specific types of sentences, and so constructed examples, whereas Sacks worked on recordings of real-life interaction. Moreover, by arguing that intuition alone should not lead the researcher to anticipate the sequence of utterances, Sacks maintained that even what appears to be accidental, ungrammatical or irrelevant might be of inter-actional importance. This in turn meant an unfiltered transcription of spoken words and non-lexical components. A system was devised for the transcription conventions including properties of turn-taking, such as simultaneous speech events or gaps within and between turns, and properties of the production of talk, such as emphasis, volume, speed of delivery and sound stretching. However, this does not mean that every transcription follows the conventions to the same degree, but a CA transcript captures details that would be missed by a more conventional transcript. Wooffitt (2005:12) gives the following as an example of a CA transcript:

```
 1  E:  hh something re:d. ehrm:: i-looks like it might be a
 2      porcupines with lots of spines standing hhh standing up
 3  S:  yeah ·hh
 4  E:  and then a frog= a frog's face peering over something
 5      (0.8)
 6  E:  hh a ghost? Coming out of a door:or a chai:r (0.5) like a mirror. (.)
 7      in a funny house
 8  S:  yeah=
 9  E:  =hh shapes (0.3) ahr:: are in this funny house
10      and shapes look like ehm  ↑ bunny rabbits with weird ears
11 S:  yeah (ch) hhuh huh ·hhh
12 E:  then you said sheep lots of sheep
13 S:  ·hhhh (g)oads of sheep (pf)ah didn't know what
14      it was (hi-) ·h hhh (k) huh uh ((smiley voice))
15 E:                  ok(h)a(h)y ((smiley voice))
16      (0.5)
17 E:  huh
18      (3.5)
19 E:  okay ·hh something in the ceiling
20      ((continues))
```

In this transcription, for example, the subject's turns in lines 3, 8 and 11 are included because 'even a minimal turn consisting only of one word can signal the speaker's understanding of the ongoing interaction, and thereby facilitate or constrain the range of possible next turns other speakers may produce' (Wooffitt, 2005:12). The non-lexical items such as 'er' and 'erm' were claimed by various studies to perform delicate interactional tasks such as establishing continued speakership rights by indicating that the current turn might still be going on (cited in Wooffitt, 2005:12 from Jefferson 1984; Schegloff, 1981). Still, Wooffitt (2005) warns the researchers against committing a fallacy; although a careful transcription of what takes place in a conversation is very important as a methodological procedure, CA goes beyond the study of transcripts. 'It seeks to make sense of those events of which the transcription is a representation. The transcript is merely an aid (albeit a valuable one) in the analysis of the events recorded on tape' (p. 13).

At this point, it becomes crucial to examine the approach CA takes towards interpreting the *representation* mentioned above. It is closely linked to the empirical orientation of discursive psychology which looks into the relationship between language and the mind or, 'the instances of language in which cognitive states or mental processes seem to have an importance for the participants' (Wooffitt, 2005:113). Wooffitt (2005), by citing other scholars, describes discursive psychology as 'reflecting the concerns of Wittgensteinian philosophy (Wittgenstein, 1953) and ethnomethodological sociology' (Coulter, 1979, 1989), and seeking to 'analyze reports of mental states, and discourse in which mental states become relevant, as social actions oriented to interactional and inferential concerns' (p. 113). In other words, in its simplest form, discursive psychology tries to answer the question: in what ways are references to and descriptions of mental states, and a cognitivist vocabulary, used to perform social actions?

Let us consider the state of thinking. Wooffitt (2005:117) gives the following extract from Atkinson and Drew (1979:58):

    1 B: Uh if you'd care to come over and
    2   visit a little while this morning
    3   I'll give you a cup of coffee
    4 A: hehh Well that's awfully sweet of you,
    5   I don't think I can make it this morning
    6   hh uhm I am running an ad in the paper and and uh I
    7   have to stay near the phone.

To the invitation for coffee coming from B, A's reply is 'I don't think I can make it this morning.' By using the 'I don't think (X)' structure, A refuses B's offer. However, A does it in such a way that it adjusts the strong impact of a blunt refusal, which would sound insensitive, and by displaying an uncertain or a tentative condition of the action manages concerns such as face.

Talk in interaction is complex to analyse and so CA could not escape criticism for its methodological, analytical approach in interpreting the representation displayed by the transcript. The two major criticisms can be summarized as follows: (1) CA does not contribute to the sociological queries such as the relationship between power and inequality, disadvantage and gender, ethnicity or class; and (2) by focusing on the technical or sequential orientation of everyday communication, it disregards wider issues such as historical, cultural and political contexts that words are invoked by. These criticisms appeared in the late 1990s in the published debates between Emanuel Schegloff, Margaret Wetherell and Michael Billig (Wooffitt, 2005:158). For example, Billig (1999a, 1999b) analyses CA rhetoric, and argues that what CA does is contrary to what it claims to do; CA claims to begin the analysis of data without any prior assumptions and to analyse the talk-in-interaction in its own terms; however, it imposes its own interpretation by offering an explanation through technical tools such as 'paired action sequences' or 'repairs'. Moreover, Billig argues that CA is politically naive since CA refers to the people who talk as members or participants, and this assumes people have equal status in interactions. With this assumption, CA masks the asymmetries in terms of power and social injustices in social interactions. The example Billig (1999a) gives to support his argument is the 'talk' in the context of a rape, between the rapist and the victim: 'One might imagine that the talk, in the course of a rape ... had been recorded and transcribed. One can imagine the rapist threatening and verbally abusing the victim, who in turn pleads ... how should their talk be analyzed?' (pp. 554–555).

In fact this example was prompted by the writing of Schegloff (1997), where he analysed a telephone conversation between a man and a woman. In this conversation, there were instances of the man starting to speak while the woman was speaking. With the use of this example, Schegloff warned against simplifying the matter of interruptions to reflect the inequality of power and status between the man and the woman. He proposed that these interruptive instances in fact had a function: to carry on the sequential implications of a particular type of socially organized activity and offering and responding to assessments. An interpretation based on gendered discourse would have been misleading in this case.

Billig's (1999a) criticism illustrated by the example of rape was responded to in detail by Schegloff (1999); however, in summary Schegloff pointed out that CA explores 'the way a turn-taking system permits of biases in the way rights, obligations and opportunities to talk are differentially allocated amongst participants' and that CA does not *presume* a society where people are equal – rather it *allows* for such a society:

> Rape, abuse, battering, etc. do not exist in some other world, or some special sector of this world. They are intricate into the texture of everyday life for those who live with them. How else are we to understand their explosive emergence where they happen if not by examining ordinary interaction with tools appropriate to it, and seeing how they can lead to such outcomes ... If interaction is produced within a matrix of turns organized into sequences, etc., and if it is from those that motives and intentions are inferred, identities made relevant, stances embodied and interpreted, etc, how else –when confronted

by the record of singular episodes – are we to understand their genesis and course, how else try to understand what an unwilling participant can do to manage that course to safer outcomes, how else try to understand how others might intervene to detoxify those settings? (Schegloff, 1999:561–562)

Although Billig (1999a, 1999b) criticized CA for its theoretical orientation, elsewhere, he tends to agree with its analytical approach to transcription to explore talk in interaction. 'The transcripts should contain as much accurate information as possible about the talk. Care should also be taken over the transcripts, because for most practical purposes, the transcripts provide the material for the analysis' (Billig, 1997:46–47). However, as was pointed out by Wooffitt (2005:164), he departs significantly from CA in terms of his interpretation of transcribing when 'he says that he uses three dots "..." to indicate *interruption*' (Billig, 1997:46). Wooffitt (2005) puts it beautifully:

> [Billig's] claim that three dots – or indeed any symbol – can indicate 'inter-ruption' is problematic. CA tries to avoid characterizing interactional events with 'common sense' or 'vernacular' terms which impute motive, intent or significance to the participants. This is because broadly, CA embodies the ethnomethodological claim that it's the participants' understanding of what is happening is important, not what the analyst thinks is happening. Consequently, value-laden terms like 'interruption' are avoided. (p. 164)

When it comes to transcribing talk-in interaction and developing a database with these transcriptions, a corpus is eventually generated. Similar to what CA deals with, which is real language, corpus linguistics deals with real world texts. Corpus linguistics can be described as the study of language expressed in samples (corpora) or 'real world' text. The approach runs counter to Noam Chomsky's view that real language is full of performance-related errors. According to this perspective, language studies require careful analysis of small speech samples obtained in a highly controlled laboratory setting. Corpus linguistics, on the other hand, relies on real language with its so-called performance errors to produce reliable conclusions.

Although the origins of corpus linguistics and the idea of searching for words and phrases in multiple contexts date back to as early as the thirteenth century (McCarthy and O'Keeffe, 2010:3), it was in the 1960s that the notion of corpus linguistics grew and technological developments brought the digitization of many documents (Tognini-Bonelli, 2010:15). The first electronic corpus of written language, called the Brown Corpus and compiled by Henry Kucera and Nelson Francis, is a carefully compiled selection of American English (Tognini-Bonelli,

2010: 15), totalling approximately one million words extracted from a wide variety of sources. With the help of the developments in technology over the years, new corpora have been created in different sizes and modalities. Scholars interested in the contrastive analysis of languages have begun using corpora for various reasons, two of which are that it is easy to access real-language samples and that such samples can readily be obtained from any language constituting the object of study. More importantly, with the development of technology, computer-mediated corpora made it possible to categorize various forms and genres of language, such as talk in interaction, political speeches, and business meetings are accessible in transcribed and annotated material.

CA, with its procedural method of data collection, transcription and its aim, is closely related to corpus linguistics. CA aims at developing 'a new form of naturalistic observational sociology that could handle in formal ways the details of actual conduct' (see Wooffitt, 2005:165). In principle, it seeks to make the data available to the other researchers who want to study it again to see what they could make of it, and agree or disagree with the interpretation. Sacks put it as the following in one of his lectures:

> It was not from any large interest or from some theoretical formulation of what should be studied that I started with tape-recorded conversation, but simply because I could get my hands on it and I could study it again and again, and also consequentially, because others could look at what I had studied and make of it what they could, if, for example, they wanted to be able to disagree with me. (Sacks, 1984:26)

Despite similarities between CA and corpus linguistics, corpus linguistics has been associated with various different methods and as a result, some of the practices carried out through corpora analysis depart hugely from the theoretical orientation of CA. Still, corpus linguistics has recently been discussed in terms of its theoretical underpinnings towards the data it deals with. As explained in the following section, CA and corpus driven linguistics are parallel and they are both of fundamental importance for this study for the reasons discussed below.

2.6 Corpus Driven Linguistics

Römer (2005, p.7) explains that 'corpus linguistics is usually referred to as a methodology or as one of the possible data-gathering options a linguist can choose from when she or he needs evidence (alongside with informant asking or relying on her or his intuition).' However, she refers to corpus driven linguistics (CDL) as 'a new theory emerging from corpus linguistics' (p. 7) and puts forward her reasons as to why it is possible to refer to CDL as an emerging *theory*. This viewpoint goes against descriptions of what corpus linguistics in general is. For example, Kennedy (1998:7) considers it 'misleading' to suggest that corpus linguistics is a theory of language similar to other theories of language, such as transformational grammar, or even that 'it is a new and separate branch of linguistics.' Meyer (2004: xi) states that 'corpus linguistics is more of a way of doing linguistics ... than a separate paradigm within linguistics.' The disagreement as to what corpus linguistics is or is not is perhaps the best indication that in corpus linguistics studies, a terminological distinction should be drawn and theoretical considerations can thus be clarified. CDL is characterized with an entirely 'corpus-generated model of language' as opposed to corpus based linguistics (CBL), 'in which corpora are analysed quanti-tatively and qualitatively on the basis of theoretical preconceptions, possibly in conjunction with noncorpus data' (Mukherjee, 2004:115). The distinction has been outlined and discussed in detail in Tognini-Bonelli (2001) and Aarts (2002).

Römer (2005) lays out the results of some corpus studies and the researcher is left with surprising findings which do not fit into existing frameworks. For instance, Mindt carried out studies on future expressions in English (1985, 1987, 1991, and 1992) and claimed that corpus linguistics brings out findings that require linguists to redefine linguistic classes, regroup cases or reclassify them (Mindt, 1991:194). As a study presenting a good example of the same findings Römer (2005:7) gives the COBUILD project at the University of Birmingham. The researchers, who studied natural data in a corpus, came to the understanding that the findings of their research clashed with the existing theory with which they began their study. The natural data necessitated a reconsideration of the traditional division of the language system into grammar and lexis. For instance, with *want*, which is always followed by a *to* infinitive, the division of the language system into grammar and lexis proved rather inadequate since the structure *want to* could occur both for the systems of grammar or lexis and that, in fact, lexis and grammatical structures are closely related to each other. Römer (2005) explains that the authors Hunston and Francis (2000) came to the conclusion that the language patterns within their pattern grammar approach were used 'with a restricted set of lexical items, and each lexical item occur[red] with a restricted set of patterns' (p. 3). Römer (2005) then adds that the reason these researchers were able to form new insights was due to the fact that they took the data on board and, rather than verifying a theoretical framework that was pre-formulated, they followed the data to formulate a thesis.

It is researchers' approach to the data that distinguishes CDL from CBL; whether the data are used to verify, through statistical significance, a pre-formulated framework or theory or to reach new findings in light of the findings of the natural data corpus linguistics supply. Römer (2005) in her chapter, 'The theoretical basis of the study: corpora, contexts and didactics,' points out that the researchers should explicitly clarify their approach to data analysis since there is usually 'an interrelation between object, method, and theory in any field of study which ought to be critically reflected by any researcher (see e.g. Bald 1995:104), and that changes in the object and method side are likely to result in changes on the theoretical side too' (Hunston and Francis 2000:2509; Stubbs, 1996:232). It is with this aim in mind that for this study a distinction between CDL and CBL is made, and it is maintained that for this study that CDL is the underlying theoretical approach to impoliteness and corpus linguistics.

Römer (2005) is among many scholars who distinguish between CDL and CBL, although the term CDL might not have been used explicitly by all researchers who followed a CDL. CBL has been used as a general term to refer to any study that deals with corpus data regardless of whether the study is corpus-informed or corpus-inspired (Römer 2005:9). Due to the lack of distinction, it is difficult to give examples of the studies within a CDL or CBL framework since researchers do not explicitly present their approach. Tognini-Bonelli (1996:54) postulates that '[a] corpus can be used in different ways in order to validate, exemplify, or build up a language theory.' Tognini-Bonelli (1996) describes a corpus-based approach as 'a type of methodology where the commitment to the data as a whole is not ultimately very strict or systematic' (p. 65) by explaining that researchers make use of the corpus to prove a certain hypothesis or to 'exemplify existing theories' which are usually pre-formulated or driven by fixed categories in mind (p. 55). The implication of the corpus-based approach is then that the researchers do not consider altering the pre-formulated theory despite significant differences the data may offer towards a reformulation of the thesis. This implication also gives a hint as to why corpus linguistics has been associated with 'frequency data, attested illustrative examples, or with answers to questions of grammaticality or acceptability' and why researchers who study corpus linguistics are regarded as 'instrumentalist[s]' who use 'corpora as instruments alongside other research strategies and other types of data' (Römer, 2005:9). Despite the methodological perspective adopted, the design of the data has a great influence on the analysis and interpretation of data.

Römer (2005:22–23) asserts that CDL and CBL can be regarded as two different opposing disciplines within corpus linguistics, as their stance towards the following three questions differs fundamentally; how they respond makes it more obvious why CDL is 'more theory-prone' than CBL:

1. What is the status of the data and how and when (i.e., which stage in the research) is the corpus approached?
2. Does corpus annotational material, i.e., any kind of information which can be added to the plain text (e.g. part-of-speech tags) have positive or negative effects?
3. Do we as researchers have to allow alterations of how the [the language] system [is theorized to be] and should we be prepared to change existing theories in the light of corpus evidence?

In relation to the first question concerning the status of the data, the analyst, within the understanding of CDL, has to look into the data very closely, and the data is at the heart of formulating a framework given that they may signal a revision of existing theory, which is less likely to happen in CBL studies. This is similar to CA's orientation towards the data. CA works with the conversation very carefully so as not to skip any detail such as overlaps and pauses, since even what appears to be accidental, ungrammatical, or irrelevant might be of interactional importance. Also, as Wooffitt (2005) points out '[CA] it seeks to make sense of those events of which the transcription is a representation. The transcript is merely an aid (albeit a valuable one) in the analysis of the events recorded on tape' (p. 13). That is why CA takes precautionary steps to transcribe the data in a way that it represents the actual conversation without imposing any interpretations. Similarly, CDL is cautionary against annotations because they may have an effect on the analysis. Both deal with real language data with the implication that theories should be based on real data findings and revised according to the findings.

In terms of the second question concerning the effect of annotational material on the analysis of the data, for studies carried out within the scope of CBL, analysts usually 'favour' the annotation (Römer 2005:9). In other words, since they do the research to verify their theory and usually look for quantification, categorized, or annotated material in a corpus, CBL works well for their aims. In fact, annotation, which is any kind of information that is added to the plain text, can be a very useful tool for all corpus studies, as was argued by McEnery and Wilson (2001:32): 'the utility of the corpus is considerably increased by the provision of annotation' (cited in Römer, 2005:9). Still, analysts have to be alert as to whether the annotated material has a positive or negative effect on the study as Römer (2005) explains:

> [t]he annotation of text means an abstraction of the data to certain categories (e.g. word classes). These categories seem to be more important than the actual data and the actual meaning of a lexical item may be obscured in this annotational process. Corpus-based linguists are thus further away from their data than corpus driven linguists. (p. 10)

The essential point with annotated material studies driven by CDL, then, is that the researcher should have an awareness of how to make use of annotated material at every stage of the study from extraction to the analysis. It requires a conscious theorizing as to foresee how annotations would expand or limit the study. A researcher who has adopted CDL does not take for granted what a corpus offers in terms of annotation. On the contrary, she/he should be prepared to sort out the necessary annotated information – the use of which would enrich the study – from other annotated information, which in some cases may cause predispositions and interfere with how the stages of research unfold. This approach to annotation is very similar to what CA tries to avoid, as mentioned earlier: 'CA embodies the ethnomethodological claim that it's the participants' understanding of what is happening that is important, not what the analyst thinks is happening. Consequently, value-laden terms like "interruption" are avoided' (Wooffitt, 2005:164).

CHAPTER 3

A Methodological Perspective to Studying Impoliteness: Research Design and Corpora

3.1 An Overview

Corpus linguistics is traditionally used as a method for lexicographic studies, studies about aspects of grammar and is increasingly used in different areas such as language teaching and learning discourse analysis, literary stylistics, forensic linguistics, speech technology (McCarthy and O'Keeffe, 2010). It is also used for pragmatics research, as much as the corpus used lends itself to the analysis of language. Since investigating the pragmatic aspects of language requires spontaneity and authenticity in data, a corpus of transcribed spoken interaction can be ideal for the researcher. However, a study linking corpus linguistics with pragmatics has to go beyond 'traditional' corpus linguistics (Schmidt and Wörner, 2009:2) for the following reasons. First, spontaneous interaction is a 'multi-party interaction' from which unpredictable changes arise between the roles of the participants and therefore the data in the corpus must be able to represent both the sequential and the simultaneous actions produced by the participants. Second, pragmatic analysis has to go beyond analysing syntactic and lexical properties of speech since it is an 'integrative enterprise' and paralinguistic phenomena (like laughing or pauses) and suprasegmental features (like intonation and voice quality) are important.

For pragmatics, context plays an especially important role and is a complex notion as it has a number of levels (Schmidt and Wörner, 2009:2). The first level is the interactional, with which one can analyse the context of a certain utterance, who it was uttered by, which turn it preceded and followed, and what other behavioural data do, such as an accompanying gesture. The second level is the situational context which refers to more general circumstances such as time and location, spatial arrangements of participants, and the topic and occasion of the interaction. The third level is ethnographic metadata (i.e., any kind of biographic information such as age or social status) about the participants and the broader cultural setting of the communication. Therefore, a study of pragmatics such as an impoliteness study, for which data come from a corpus, has to go beyond frequency analysis, which is customary in traditional corpus linguistics.

The constructionist approach, which is in line with what studies of pragmatics requires from corpus linguistics researchers as discussed above, maintains that meaning is negotiated, and indeed 'co-constituted' in interaction (Arundale, 2006a:196). This acknowledgment in turn leads to an adoption of a certain kind of analytic methodology when analysing spoken corpora. Such methodology should be in line with conversation analysis in utterance interpretation (Jurafsky, 2004), and with an epistemological approach that recognizes that it is the researcher who hypothesizes that a particular linguistic variable is a marker of a certain type of interaction and linguistic performance based on findings in the literature. However, it should not be disregarded that it is ultimately texts that throw out what variables actually emerge in the discourse (see Teubert, 2005). This point of view in corpus studies is essential, given the fact that the analyst is not a participant or a participant observer of the interaction. In line with this data-driven approach to investigating language use (Tognini-Bonelli, 2001), a corpus driven approach to impoliteness is exploratory and therefore the steps in such research are not linear but cyclic.

Although she adopts a different methodological perspective, Taylor (2011) points out that the adoption of any particular methodology raises questions about the sequential order of research: is the resulting analysis primarily data driven or hypothesis testing (p. 214)? She gives examples of studies of corpus work and impoliteness and shows that there is a range of categorization between the most data-driven to the most deductive. In this book, it is illustrated that a study of impoliteness demands a corpus driven approach (Tognini-Bonelli, 2001) especially if other notions such as discourse prosody (Stubbs, 2001) or semantic prosody (Sinclair, 1998; Stubbs 2002, Louw, 2000) are taken into consideration in identifying impoliteness in spoken corpora. Following such a methodology allows the researcher to go beyond standard procedures such as exploration of concordance outputs and frequency information and to move from clause discourse to extended discourse, which is essential to arrive at more insightful findings on the impoliteness phenomenon.

3.2 Research Design

Any study which aims to analyse impoliteness in corpora has to have two layers: the extraction level and the analysis level. The reason why impoliteness studies should have these two levels is to minimize the degree of subjectivity in extracting impoliteness, thus preventing epistemological fallacies in the analysis. Watts (2003:9) points out that impoliteness is a complex notion that is difficult to define: 'It is a term that is struggled over at present, has been struggled over in the past and will, in all probability, continue to be struggled over in the future.' It is essential to clarify the method for extracting incidences of impoliteness since interpretations of impoliteness vary from person to person, and context to context. The other reason why a clear method must be applied for extracting impoliteness is that, since it is a broad concept, the method for the extraction will eventually guide the researcher to develop an operational construct of impoliteness. Table 3.1 illustrates the study levels proposed and followed in the present study:

Table 3.1. The research levels of the study

1. EXTRACTION	Discursive Approach	Cue-based Approach
	Metapragmatic comments Reactive Response	Conventionalized impoliteness formulae (Culpeper 2010; 2011b) Non-conventionalized implicational impoliteness (2011b) Conversation management tools (e.g. turn-taking, pauses, etc.) Verbal and non-verbal forms signalling interpersonal conflict (e.g. change in structural patterns such as turn-taking, topic change, repetition, seeking disagreement) Semantic Prosody
2. ANALYSIS		

As illustrated in Table 3.1, metapragmatic comments and reactive responses come under the heading *discursive approach*. Conventionalized impoliteness formulae, non-conventionalized implicational impoliteness and verbal and non-verbal forms signalling interpersonal conflict come under the heading cue-based approach. The discursive approach is characterized by its emphasis on how participants in interaction perceive politeness. With this emphasis, this school of researchers (Eelen 2001; Mills 2003; Watts 2003; Watts, Ide, and Ehlich, 2005; Locher, 2004; Locher and Watts, 2005) criticize the essentialist view that the notion of politeness is the same across cultures, which has been reinforced with Brown and Levinson's politeness theory. Since metapragmatic comments and reactive responses open a window as to how interactants perceive the politeness phenomena, they are listed under the discursive approach. The discursive approach has been criticized for its emphasis on politeness and it was argued that it raised questions about the validity of researchers' analysis (Haugh, 2007). Therefore, it is necessary to adopt an analytical approach that complements the discursive approach for what it is lacking in. The cue-based approach is what is proposed in this study to complement the discursive approach.

It is assumed that the conventionalized impoliteness formulae, non-conventionalized implicational impoliteness, conversational management tools (e.g. turn-taking, pauses, etc.), verbal and non-verbal forms signalling interpersonal conflict (e.g. change in structural patterns such as turn taking, topic change, repetition, seeking disagreement) and semantic prosody could create an inclusive model to compensate for what might be neglected by the discursive approach. However, the boundary between the discursive and cue-based approaches is not clear-cut. In conversation, which has a dynamic nature, metapragmatic comments can function as the co-text for creating a context for non-conventionalized implicational impoliteness. In other words, what metapragmatic comments supply in co-text, which is characterized by the discursive approach, may signal interpersonal conflict through the change in structural patterns and so be used as cues to interpret context-driven implicational impoliteness. Ruhi (2008) states:

> [h]uman communication is 'intentional' in the wide sense – in our (mental) acts of attributing properties to people and their acts. Viewed from this perspective, politeness phenomena may be better investigated as attributions directed towards (linguistic) behaviour. (p. 290)

Along with this line of thought that attributions directed towards (linguistic) behaviour reflect politeness phenomena, it is assumed that conventionalized impoliteness formulae (Culpeper 2010; 2011b) and non-conventionalized implicational impoliteness (Culpeper, 2011b) will give significant clues leading to impoliteness.

Other linguistic and paralinguistic forms are taken into consideration since impoliteness is very much linked to context and co-text and linguistic expressions per se do not warrant an interpretation that an incidence is impolite. Reactive responses, patterns signalling interpersonal conflict (e.g. change in structural patterns such as turn-taking, topic change, repetition, seeking for disagreement) and conversational management tools (e.g. turn-taking, pauses, etc.) are among the linguistic and paralinguistic forms. Since the notion of face is closely related to the studies of politeness and impoliteness phenomena, considerations have been made regarding how the notion of face might be at a play at the extraction level, especially with incidences of non-conventionalized implicational impoliteness. Ruhi (2010:2131) points out that an alternative research method, which seeks to bring the 'background' events into discussion, is required:

> Face and facework have been described as permeating interaction such that interlocutors cannot but attend to face (see, e.g., Spencer-Oatey, 2007; Terkourafi, 2007). However, accounting for face in a manner that corresponds to participant interpretations is a complex task, as face and self-presentational concerns are very often 'background' events (Ruhi, 2008; Schlenker and Pontari, 2000; Spencer-Oatey, 2007). Furthermore, short and/or long-term interactional goals and understandings of the social interaction order, which interact with the interpersonal dimension of talk, may not be easily discernible in talk-in-interaction (Hak, 1995). It thus behoves researchers to render analyses accountable in a manner that does justice to the multifaceted nature of face and participant interpretations. Enhancing theory and research methodology research in this regard in studies on face is crucial, as understanding how people construe the interaction underway is as important as how such interaction is constructed. (Hammersley, 2003)

Therefore, the clues the background events in context and co-text supply about what might generate impoliteness are also taken consideration. For example, Extract 1 from the BNC discussed in Chapter 4 presents a situation where membership categorization (Sacks, 1989; Ruhi, 2010), which is a background event, played a role in generating a conflict which is perceived as impolite.

Once again, because of the fact that impoliteness is difficult to extract and define, it is foreseen that a large and a representative bank of data is needed to be able to reach conclusive findings. Therefore, the BNC, which is a fairly large, representative corpus, and the STC, which is representative in terms of variety of interactions and demographic sampling but relatively limited in size, have been selected. CDL and CBL approaches to data influence the research stages (Tognini-Bonelli, 1996; Römer, 2005; Schmidt and Wörner, 2009); that is why implications of corpus driven and corpus-based approaches are discussed and evaluated for the research purposes of this study and the corpus driven approach has been chosen.

Römer (2005) refers to CDL as 'a new theory emerging from corpus linguistics' (p. 7) and puts forward her reasons for why it is possible to refer to CDL as an emerging *theory* (emphasis mine). As part of the endeavour to avoid epistemological fallacies, rather than forming a theory in the beginning of the analysis and verifying a (pre-formulated) theory, the researcher, who approaches the data within the framework of a corpus driven approach, will end up with informed insights as to what research questions and theory or framework she should analyse the data with, once the extraction level is completed.

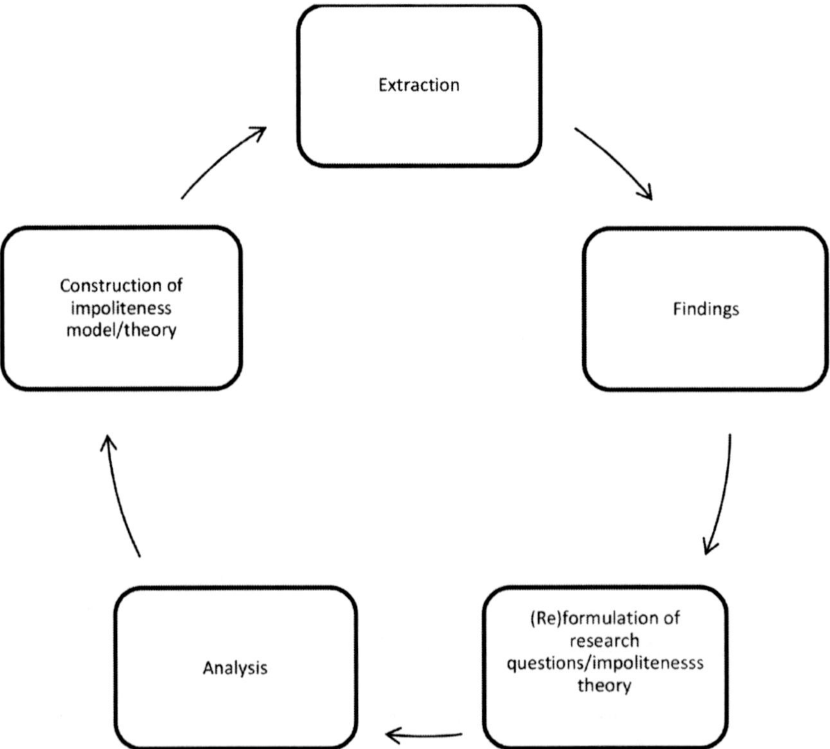

Figure 3.1. Cyclic research pattern

This cyclic process, i.e., going backwards from collated data to develop the theory or the framework which the analysis level should be applied to later studies, is of fundamental importance for impoliteness research carried out in corpus linguistics since the natural data a corpus provides will always offer new findings that do not fit the pre-formulated assumptions. The findings will inevitably bring out issues that have not been closely linked or discussed in detail in the literature. Therefore, the cyclic process of going backwards from collated data to develop a theory should be applied both among different and within single studies. Within a single study, the cyclic approach requires tentativeness in terms of the research questions the analyst starts the study with. Perceiving the research questions as tentative means that the researcher is willing to revise the questions later as the study unfolds. Rühlemann (2007:1) describes this state as an 'open mind' to contribute to the linguistic discussion of the data he explores. It is fundamental in the corpus driven approach applied in studies with natural data, because if the findings from the data do not fit any existing theories, they will in fact be bringing new dimensions to be explored and revealing answers to questions which the analyst did not have in mind in the beginning.

The research stages then are as follows: the data are extracted and the methodology of extraction is described in detail. Since a corpus driven approach has been adopted for this study, in light of the findings gathered from the extraction level, existing theories of impoliteness have been revisited and new theoretical dimensions are theorized. The analysis level has been carried out within this new theoretical framework and contrastive analysis of impoliteness in two languages will be offered.

3.3 Research Questions

The research questions, which are still tentative at this stage since they could be revised depending on what the data will bring out, are as follows, categorized under the relevant study levels.

Layer 1: Extraction:

(a) What methodology can be devised for impoliteness to be extracted in conversation across languages, which in the case of this study are British English and Turkish?

(b) What do findings at this level of the study tell the researcher about what impoliteness is?

Layer 2: Analysis

1. For Spoken British English in Conversation:
   (a) What triggers impoliteness in interaction among speakers of British English?
   (b) What impoliteness strategies are employed in interaction by speakers of British English?
   (c) How is impoliteness countered in interaction by speakers of British English?
   (d) What is the role of countering strategies in relation to face in interaction employed by speakers of British English?

2. For Spoken Turkish in Conversation:
   (a) What triggers impoliteness in interaction among speakers of Turkish?
   (b) What impoliteness strategies are employed by speakers of Turkish?
   (c) How is impoliteness countered in interaction carried out by speakers of Turkish?
   (d) What is the role of countering strategies in relation to face in interaction employed by speakers of Turkish?

3. For the contrastive analysis of British English and Turkish:
   (a) What are the implications of the study for impoliteness and face theory?

Figure 3.2 gives a visual illustration of the layers and the research questions.

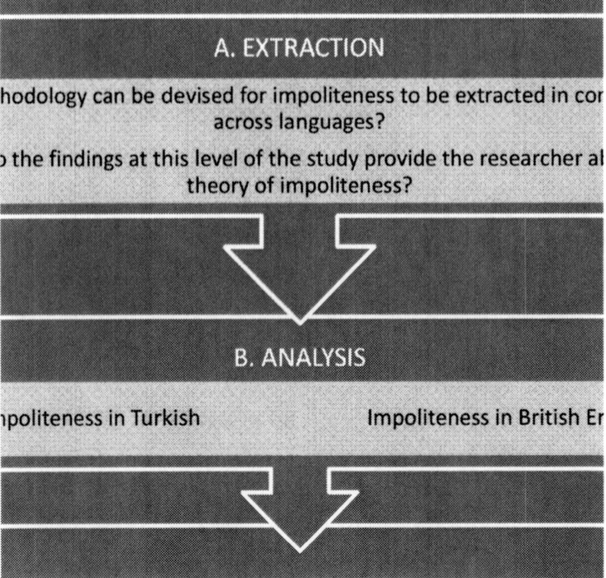

Figure 3.2. Research questions and layers

3.4 The Corpora

This study analyzes impoliteness in spoken conversation for English and Turkish in corpora. The data sources are BNC for English and STC (Ruhi, Eyrılmaz, and Acar, 2012) for Turkish. There are various reasons why these corpora have been decided upon. Fraser and Nolen (1981) claim that, '[n]o sentence is inherently polite or impolite. We often take certain expressions to be impolite, but it is not the expressions themselves but the conditions under which they are used that determine the judgment of politeness' (p. 96). Terkourafi (2005a) puts forward that, in order not to be left with 'the minute descriptions of individual encounters' that 'do not add up to an explanatory theory of the phenomena under study' (p. 245), the analyst attempts to arrive at generalizations by looking into relatively large-scale data. The acknowledgment that it is difficult to judge what is impolite (and so the analyst needs large-scale data to increase the predictive value of the study) requires taking an informed decision about the selection of the data sources. The reason for selecting BNC was mainly because the corpus provides a large data source and is representative of British English. This is also true of the spoken subcorpus, which is the main focus in the present study. Biber (1993/2004) defines representativeness as 'the extent to which a sample includes the full range of variability in population' (p. 174). For researchers, it has been the sample size, sampling theory and transcription which are considered to be the most important issues for representativeness of a corpus. Biber (1993/2004), on the other hand, claims that a corpus design can be evaluated to be representative of a language in terms of two points: (1) the range of text types in a population, and (2) the range of linguistic distribution in the population. The section below on the BNC and the spoken subcorpus lay out an overview of why the BNC is considered to be a representative corpus.

The reason for selecting STC as the corpus is rather straightforward: it is the only spoken corpus in Turkish. Until 2009, when METU published the METU Turkish Corpus (Say, Zeyrek, Oflazer, and Özge, 2004) of two million words of post-1990 written Turkish samples, no corpus was available for the Turkish language. The words of the Turkish Corpus were taken from 10 different genres. At most two samples from each source were used. It should not be surprising that the scholars undertook the mission of expanding the Turkish corpora by creating a spoken Turkish corpus, which to date has not been fully published. The STC has been in process since 2009, and its purpose is to collate interactions of present-day Turkish of one million words of face-to-face or mediated interactions that are linguistically analysed. This study will be the first extensive study carried out on this spoken corpus. The Demo and Sample versions of STC were published in 2010 and can be accessed at http://stc.org. The access to the unpublished data used in the study has been provided by Prof. Dr. Şükriye Ruhi. The author contributed transcriptions to access unpublished STC files. Although STC is not comparable with BNC in terms of the size, it is representative of the language as the information given on STC in the following sections demonstrates.

3.4.1 British National Corpus (BNC)

The BNC XML Edition, which is the full BNC and the edition used for this study, is a 100-million word collection of samples of both written and spoken language of British English of the late twentieth century. There are two subset products of the BNC XML Edition, namely the BNC Baby and the BNC Sampler. The full BNC XML Edition can be defined as a monolingual, synchronic, general corpus. The written part makes up 90% and the spoken 10% of the corpus. The spoken part includes transcriptions of both scripted speech and unscripted informal conversations. Biber (1993/2004) has pointed out that constructing a spoken corpus that represents a language is more complicated. There are no catalogues or bibliographies of spoken texts. Since speakers are constantly adding to the number of spoken texts in everyday conversations, identifying an adequate sampling frame is difficult. However, without a prior analysis of parameters of speech within a language, such a task is impossible. Therefore, it is not wrong to say that with spoken language there are no obvious objective measures that can be used to define the target population or construct a sampling frame. In order to address this issue, in the construction of the spoken corpus of BNC, an alternative approach was adopted for approximately half of the spoken part of the corpus: demographic sampling (Burnard, 2007). The sampling frame was defined in terms of the language production of the population of British English speakers in the United Kingdom. In other words, the issue of representativeness was addressed by sampling a spread of language producers in terms of age, gender, social group, and region, and recording their language output over a set period of time.

The details of demographic sampling are as the follows: through random location sampling, individuals from across the United Kingdom were asked for a personal interview and 124 people above the age of 15 were recruited (Burnard, 2007). They were given a portable recorder to record their conversations over a period of a week. Priority was given to recruiting an equal number of men and women, from each of six age groups, from all social classes. Additional recordings were gathered by a project from the University of Bergen COLT Teenager Language Project for the BNC by respondents below 16. An initial pilot study was carried out to predict future problems about data gathering and transcriptions and some problems were addressed before the actual projects started. Since the placement day of the recruits varied, recordings were made on different days including weekends, which added to the variety of conversations. Furthermore, recruits were given a log to take notes of the participants for each conversation as well as date, time, and setting. A range of subjects from different age-groups, social class, sex, and region were selected to ensure better sampling.

In order to make the data as close as possible to natural and spontaneous speech, there was an attempt to record the conversations unobtrusively (Burnard, 2007). Since, in many cases the parties involved in speech were aware that they were being recorded, some initial unnaturalness was noted but found to fade away by the experts who were in charge of constructing the corpus. All the names of the participants were removed from the log to ensure confidentiality. If the participants learned that they were being recorded after the fact and if they were unhappy about their conversation, the conversations were erased. Overall, 700 recordings were gathered and the number of speakers was about 1,000. A complementary context-governed approach was adopted and before the conversations were recorded a priori linguistically motivated division was made and a typology was created of four categories: educational, business, public/institutional, and leisure. The context and text types are outlined in Table 3.2.

Table 3.2. The BNC context category

Context Category	Text type
Educational and informative	Lectures, talks, educational demonstrations, news commentaries, classroom interaction
Business	Company talks and interviews, trade union talks, sales demonstration, business meetings, consultations
Public or institutional	Political speeches, sermons, public/government talks, council and religious meetings, parliamentary and legal proceedings
Leisure	Speeches, sports commentaries, talks to clubs, broadcast shows and phone-ins, club meetings.

Table 3.3 gives percentages of the context categories. Leisure, with its types of speech, is assumed to give the closest discourse type or genre defined to be the focus of this study in conversation. It is noteworthy that Leisure makes up 25% of the spoken context, which indicates a fairly good size as a databank.

Table 3.3. The BNC spoken context

	Text	w-units	%	s-units	%
Educational/Informative	169	1646380	26.65	118987	27.83
Business	129	1282416	20.76	107366	25.11
Public/Institutional	262	1672658	27.08	96500	22.57
Leisure	195	1574442	25.49	104670	24.48

Another point of interest is that almost 85% of the spoken context is dialogue, which adds to the richness of the databank (Table 3.4).

Table 3.4. The BNC spoken subcorpus interaction type

	texts	w-units	%	s-units	%
Monologue	207	1562017	15.00	92619	8.92
Dialogue	701	8847834	84.99	945461	91.07

The richer in dialogues the databank is, the better the chances are to arrive at conversations fulfilling the purpose of this study. Conversation can be defined differently, however, as Warren (2006) points out it ranges from 'casual talk in everyday settings, to being equivalent to any form of spoken interaction' (p. 6). Both Goffman (1971) and Donaldson (1979) claim that a conversation should go beyond a ritualized exchange and that it must involve some exchange of information. For an exchange of information, at least two participants taking turns should be involved in conversation. Table 3.4 on 'interaction type' gives an estimation of dialogue as 701 texts, and w-units, 8847834 and s-units 945461, which is a fairly large sample of corpus to arrive at conclusions on impoliteness in conversation.

Until very recently, as of 17 July 2012, the BNC spoken subcorpus has been monomodal. It offered only the transcriptions of the sound recordings, although it was possible to reach the original tapes deposited at the National Sound Archives of British Library and from the University of Bergen for the Bergen Corpus of London Teenage Corpus, which is a part of the BNC. However, using the sound files was still problematic since the library catalogue was not informative enough and the quality of the recordings and did not allow the researchers to do a sound analysis. The British Library Sound Archive and Oxford University Phonetics Laboratory worked on digitizing all the tapes in 2009–2010 and released a sampler of the BNC spoken subcorpus at http://www.phon.ox.ac.uk/SpokenBNC, by John Coleman, Ladan Baghai-Ravary, John Pybus, and Sergio Grau (2012). On the sampler, the conversations were encoded as Praat Textgrid files, so now the subcorpus lends itself to a more in-depth analysis, especially if the sample conversations on the sampler website are of interest to the researchers. Some sound files are also made available through COLT: the Bergen Corpus of London Teenage Language on a CD-ROM in mp3 format and Longman distributed as audio cassettes, Cassette Sleeve images, during the collection process. However, for this study only the transcriptions of the conversations were used mainly for two reasons. First, the released audio files on the sampler conversations website are not necessarily the extracted conversations for the analysis. Two, since the audio files have been released only recently, they could not be included in the extraction level of the study.

Since it is only transcriptions of conversations used for the study, another component of the BNC that is referred to in Section 1.5 briefly and needs to be clarified further now is the transcription conventions and to what extent they were looked into for the extraction and discussion of the analysis. According to The Text Encoding Initiative (TEI), a spoken text may contain:

> [u]tterances, pauses, vocalized but non-lexical phenomena such as coughs, kinesic (non-verbal, non-lexical) phenomena such as gestures, entirely non-linguistic incidents occurring during and possibly influencing the course of speech, writing, regarded as a special class of incident in that it can be transcribed, for example captions or overheads displayed during a lecture, shifts or changes in vocal quality (TEI retrieved at http://www.tei-c.org/index.xml)

TEI is a consortium that aims to develop and maintain a standard for the representation of texts in digital form. It designs a set of guidelines which specify encoding methods for machine-readable texts, mainly in the field of the humanities, social sciences and linguistics. Since 1994, the TEI Guidelines have been widely used both by institutions such as libraries, museums and publishers, and individual scholars to present texts for online research.

In the speech representation below written by the TEI guidelines, we understand that the utterance 'this is just delicious,' indicated by < u who = "#jan" >. This is just delicious < /u > , belongs to Jan. just as he says it, the telephone rings indicated by < incident > < desc > telephone rings < /desc > < /incident > , and the other speaker Ann says, 'I'll get it' indicated by < u who = "#ann" > I'll get it < /u > . Tom, the other speaker says 'I used to smoke a lot' but between the utterances 'I used to' and 'smoke a lot,' he coughs, which is indicated by < u who = "#tom" > I used to < vocal > < desc > cough < /desc > < /vocal > smoke a lot < /u > :

```
<u who="#jan">This is just delicious</u>
<incident>
<desc>telephone rings</desc>
</incident>
<u who="#ann">I'll get it</u>
<u who="#tom">I used to <vocal>
<desc>cough</desc>
</vocal> smoke a lot</u>
```

The BNC has also used the TEI guidelines to represent speech phenomena both with the speech phenomena they encoded in the corpus and the elements they used to mark the speech phenomena. In the texts transcribed for the BNC, encoders marked the following phenomena:

> voice quality (e.g. whispering, laughing, etc., both as discrete events and as changes in voice quality affecting passages within an utterance)
> non-verbal but vocalised sounds (e. g. coughs, humming noises, etc.)
> non-verbal and non-vocal events (e.g. passing lorries, animal noises, and other matters considered worthy of note)
> significant pauses (e.g. silence, within or between utterances, longer than was judged normal for the speaker or speakers)
> unclear passages (inaudible or incomprehensible utterances or passages)
> speech management phenomena (e.g. truncation, false starts, and correction)
> overlap (points at which more than one speaker was active)

> (Burnard, 2007 [2000]:33)

The elements used to mark these phenomena are listed below in alphabetical order:

> < event > any non-verbal and non-vocal event (such as a door slamming) occurring during a conversation and regarded as worthy of note. Attributes include:
>> **desc** description of the event
>> **dur** duration of the event in seconds

> < pause > a marked pause during or between utterances. Attributes include:
>> **dur** duration of the pause in seconds.

< shift > a marked change in voice quality for any one speaker. Attributes include:

> **new** description of the voice quality after the shift

< trunc > a word or phrase which has been truncated during speech

< unclear > a point in a spoken text at which it is unclear what is happening, e.g. who is speaking or what is being said. Attributes include:

> **dur** the duration of the passage in seconds
>
> **who** the person or group responsible for the unclear piece of speech

< vocal > a non-linguistic but communicative sound made by one of the participants in a spoken text. Attributes include:

> **desc** the kind of sound made
>
> **dur** duration of the sound in seconds

(Burnard, 2007 [2000]:33)

The value of the **dur** attribute is normally specified only if it is greater than 5 seconds, and its accuracy is only approximate. All of these elements may appear anywhere within transcription, except for the < trunc > element.

The following example shows an event, several pauses and a patch of unclear speech:

```
<u who=d00011>
<s n=00011>
<event desc="radio on"><w PNP><pause dur=34>You
<w VVD>got<w TO0>ta <unclear><w NN1>Radio
<w CRD>Two <w PRP>with <w DT0>that <c PUN>.
<s n=00012>
<pause dur=6><w AJ0>Bloody <w NN1>pirate
<w NN1>station <w VM0>would<w XX0>n't
<w PNP>you <c PUN>?
</u>
```

Alignment of overlapping speech is also among the speech phenomena the BNC marks. The elements used to mark alignment of speech are:

< align > defines an alignment map used to synchronize points within a spoken text

< loc > a synchronization point within an alignment map to which other elements may refer

< ptr > an empty tag pointing from one part of a text to some other element. Attributes include:

> **target** supplies the identifier of some other element in a text; for alignment, specifically, a < loc > element within an alignment

For example, in the following conventional script, while two speakers are speaking, speaker W0014's attempt to take the floor has not been successful:

W0001: Poor old Luxembourg's beaten. You, you've, you've absolutely just gone straight over it -
W0014: (interrupting) I haven't.
W0001: (at the same time) and forgotten the poor little country

The transcription below demonstrates how the mechanisms are used to indicate what is happening in the speech event:

```
<u who=w0014>
<s n=00011>
<w AJ0>Poor <w AJ0>old <w NP0>Luxembourg' < w VBZ > s < w
AJ0-VVN > beaten < c PUN > .
<s n=00012>
<w PNP>You <w PNP>you<w VHB>'ve < w PNP > you < w VHB >
've < w AV0 > absolutely < w AV0 > just
<w VVN>gone <w AV0>straight <ptr target=P1> <w PRP>over <w
PNP>it <ptr target=P2>
</u>
<u who=w0001>
<s n=00013>
<ptr target=P1> <w PNP>I <w VHB>haven<w XX0>'t < c PUN > .
< ptr
target=P2/>
</u>
<u who=w0014>
<s n=00014>
<w CJC>and <w VVN>forgotten <w AT0>the <w AJ0>poor <w
AJ0>little
<w NN1>country<c PUN>.
</u>
```

Burnard (2007 [2000]) explains the procedure they followed to transcribe the example above:

> [f]or each point of synchrony, i.e. at each place where the number of simultaneous utterances, events, vocals etc. increases or decreases, a <loc> element is defined within an <align> element, which appears at the start of the enclosing <div>, if any. At each place to be synchronised within the text, a <ptr> element is inserted. The target (target) attributes of these <ptr> elements are then used to specify the identifier of the <loc> with which each is to be synchronized. (pp. 35–36)

Overall, the BNC offers a variety of opportunities to study conversation with a thorough representation the speech phenomena conventions in transcription as well as a conventional script, in which the speech phenomena is not indicated except for a couple of nuances such as capitalization of letters in script, laughter in parentheses, etc. Despite the thorough representation of speech phenomena in the BNC, the conventional script is used for the purpose of this study. During different stages of the study, relevant information supplied by the BNC, such as age group, social class, sex, and information in the form of annotated material, are referred to and made use of as cues when they signalled a further interpretation, which is in line with the CA methodology. The restrictive impact of not using the transcribed speech through conventions explained above on the analysis level is discussed in detail in Section 1.5.

3.4.2 Turkish Spoken Corpus (STC)

All conversations on STC (Ruhi, Eyrılmaz, and Acar, 2012) were transcribed according to the conventions of HIAT (Halbinterpretative Arbeitstranskriptionen – 'semi-interpretative working transcriptions'). HIAT is a transcription conversion tool which uses EXMARaLDA Partitur-Editor (http://annotation.exmaralda. org/index.php/HIAT-DOS_(Review)). Below is a screenshot of a sample conversation from STC transcribed with EXMARaLDA Partitur-Editor.

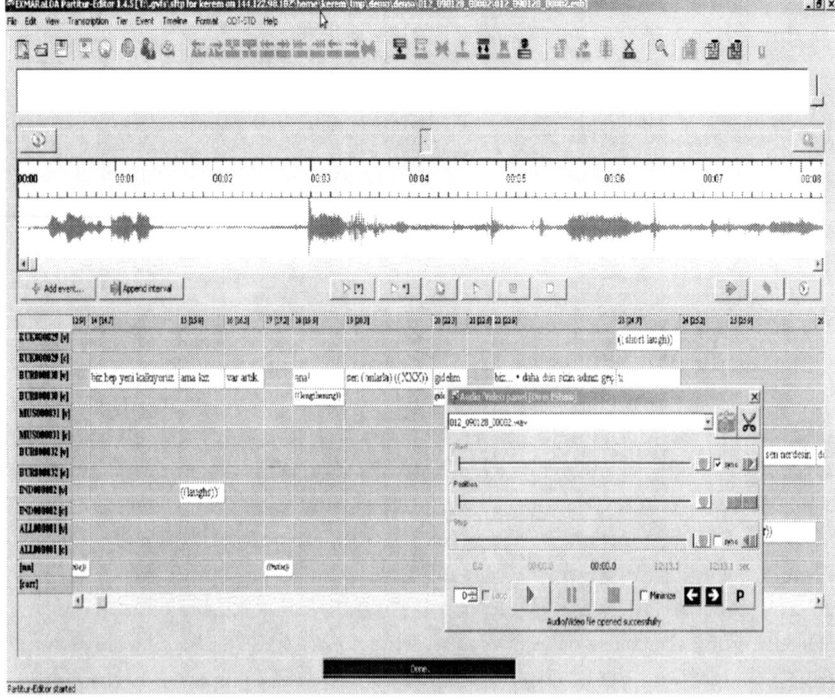

Figure 3.3. The STC Partitur Editor
Source: STC User Manual

The STC EXMARaLDA Partitur-Editor provides a variety of functions (Ruhi, Hatipoğlu, Eröz-Tuğa, and Işık-Güler, et al. 2010a). EXMARaLDA Partitur Editor enables transcribing language in the layout of a musical score (German: *Partitur*) notation that represents 'multi-party, multi-level, and multi-modal descriptions of spontaneous interaction' (Schmidt and Wörner, 2009:5). Different lines mark different speakers on a sheet showing their utterances time-aligned all at once and it illustrates the overlaps with utterances marked from start to end horizontally, aligned with vertical boxes of turn-taking and annotation. With EXMARaLDA Partitur-Editor, it is possible to put descriptions of data through tiers, which are unlimited in principle and can be reordered or deleted at any time during the transcription (Schmidt and Wörner, 2009:5). The transcriptions in the STC provide speaker 'verbal' (v) tiers, speaker 'comment' (c) tiers, nn-tier (background sound and actions), ALL (collective speech) and IND (individual unidentifiable speaker tier). The STC supplies different formats (e.g. [TEI], [Praat], [Folker], RTF), which provide different nuances for different purposes. For this study, the data used is in RTF file. For all the excerpts that will be discussed from STC, the musical score format in RTF file is used. RTF allows a detailed discussion of conversational conventions, co-text and context by providing details of overlaps, turn-taking, and other clues provided by the annotations. An example is given below, discussed in Chapter 4 as Extract 1, of the format retrieved from RTF file. The translation is provided, by the author, in a translation row in Table 3.5 utterances indicated with Trans.

Table 3.5. The RTF format used for the STC extracts

ASI000037 [v]		((0.6)) ben iki...			son sınıfta almıştım.
Trans.	I bought it ... when I was my final year at the university.				
IND000002 [v]				hayır.	
Trans.	no.				

The described musical score that the STC offers provides a visual layout for alignment of speech or overlaps and other notation concerning more clues for issues such as interruption and turn-taking patterns, the analysis of which was not possible in the BNC because conventional script format is used for the study. The script used for BNC examples is in the form of speaker X's utterance followed by speaker Y's utterance, with no visual representation of alignment of speech as in the following:

> (PSO3T) I didn't. It's just ever so cold.
> (PSO3S) Quite cold is the phrase.
> (PSO3T) What did you say?
> (PSO3S) I said quite cold is the phrase, not ever so cold.

While transcribing speech, focus was given to the representation of orthography, interjections and utterance initializers, fillers, variation in lexemes and pronunciation, mispronunciation and slips of the tongue, pauses and silences, and utterance boundaries. The utterance boundary signs used are given in Table 3.6.

Table 3.6. The STC utterance boundary signs and their functions

Symbols	Uses
Full stop (.)	The full stop is used to indicate declarative utterances and other utterances that have falling intonation.
Question Mark (?)	The question mark is used for all types of questions, including utterances that are syntactically declarative but functionally a question. The question mark is used for backchannels that are interrogative.
Exclamation Mark (!)	Excluding all forms of questions, the exclamation mark is used to mark utterances that have an exclamatory function, utterances that have a rising intonation, and greetings and vocatives uttered loudly.
Cut-off Sign (...)	The cut-off sign is used for utterances that are not completed by the speaker or where the speaker's turn is interrupted.
Repair (/)	Repairs occur in utterances where a speaker corrects, changes a word, or restarts an utterance, without changing the syntactic structure of the utterance.
Ligature sign for latching (‿)	The ligature sign (‿) is used for latching. It shows that the speaker did not leave an audible pause between two utterances.
Hyphen (-)	The hyphen (-) is used for multi-syllable non-lexicalized interjections and other types of semi-lexicalized units such as agreement markers (e.g. o-oo-oh!; a-a!; hı-hı).
Superscript dot (•)	The superscript dot is used for non-lexicalized backchannels (e.g. hı-hı, haa, hm, etc.) and paralinguistic features that form a distinct intonation contour (e.g. ((laughs)) •).

The table below gives a partial list of interjections and their explanations taken from the STC transcription guide (Ruhi, Hatipoğlu, Eröz-Tuğa, and Işık-Güler, 2010b) which is available on request through http://std.metu.edu.tr. Table 3.7 presents the variety of the interjections that appear in the STC extractions discussed in Chapter 4 and demonstrates the complexity of translating them with the subtleties explained in the English translation column. Special words such as

Table 3.7. Sample interjections in the STC

Turkish interjections	Explanation/English translation
a!/aa!	*For surprise*
a-a! /a-ah!	*Two syllables; for surprise or disagreement*
aboo!	*For surprise*
ah!	*Criticizing, as in 'ah! pek de alçakgönüllüyüz'*
ah!/aah!	*For strong wish, pity, sadness, etc.*
aha!	*Uttered to draw attention to something, for something surprising, or in the sense of 'Oh, I understand'*
ay!/ayy!	*As in 'ay ben olsam', 'Ayy! Ne güzel!', 'ay bilmiyorum ne olacak', indicating surprise, anxiety, etc.*
ay!	*Ugh! (to mark distaste); as in 'ay! ne kadar yapmacıksınız'*
be!	*As in 'gelsene be!'*
cık cık cık (multiple cık sound)	*Write as many cık's as you hear to show disapproval, resentment, and concern etc. (as in 'cık cık cık, nasıl yaparsın böyle'; 'cık cık cık, nasıl da hemen vazo kırıldı')*
ee!	*Weell!*
eh! /eeh! /ehh!	*well (in the sense of 'sort of' or to indicate (partial) agreement); as in 'eh! fena değil', 'eh! neyse öyle olsun bakalım'*
eh ama (yani)!	*Indicating anger*
Hadi	*As in 'hadi canım sen de!'*
Hah	*come off it! (as in 'hah! başladı yine'); or showing approval/agreement (as in 'hah! şöyle adam ol'/ 'hah öyle demek istedim')*
hii!	*For strong surprise, fear, excitement*
o/oo!	*For surprise, noticing something, showing appreciation* *Write as two syllables if heard as 'o-oo'*
of! (oof!, ooff!, öf!, ööf!)	*For boredom, frustration, dislike of an imposition*
o-oo-oh!	*Usually indicates depreciation; as in 'o-oo-oh! çok gördük böylesini'*
şş/şşt!	To silence people or to get people's attention
Tıh	*An utterance-initial sound. Uttered often like a click sound or smacking of lips/the tongue at the beginning of utterances.* NOTE: *Do not confuse this sound with 'cık', which signals disagreement, criticism, or means no'.*
Ya	*As in 'ya bi gelsene'*
(saçmalama) yaa!	*'Oh don't talk nonsense'*
yaa!	*Really!/Oh really!*
yo! /yoo!	Meaning: no

'*şey*' (e.g. in the STC Extract 4), which can be 'a lexical filler, a part of a repaired unit, and a part of a pragmatic unit starting an utterance etc.' (Ruhi, Hatipoğlu, Eröz-Tuğa, and Işık-Güler, 2010b:44) add to the complexity. However, the audio files of the STC extracts are available to interpret the nuances in the tone of the speakers, which has been of a useful tool for translating special items such as interjections, backchannels or fillers.

Similar to the BNC, the STC supplies metadata files on bibliographic information such as when the conversation was recorded, what context category or genre it falls into, relations between the speakers, and the location that the conversation was recorded. Below is an example of a conversation extracted from STC (see Spoken Turkish Corpus demo version user guide):

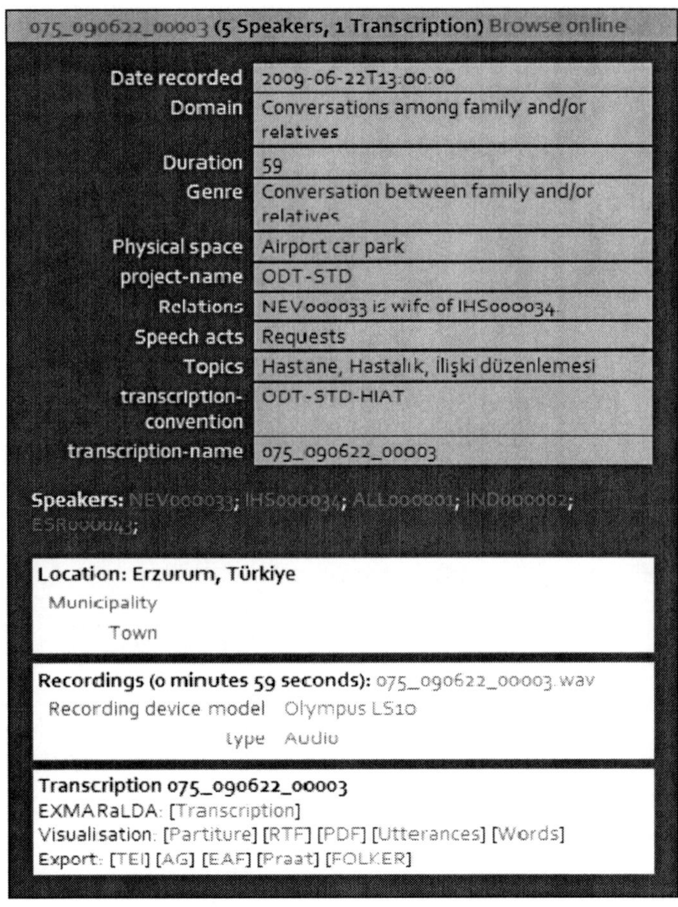

Figure 3.4. The STC metadata
Source: STC User Manual

Moreover, the dialogues, listed in terms of both speech acts and the context in which they take place, indicate that STC, similar to BNC spoken subcorpus, supplies data in the discourse type defined as conversation (Warren, 2006).

In terms of the representativeness of Turkish spoken interaction, STC offers a detailed analysis of sampling in terms of the context of the conversations (e.g. shopping, meeting with friends, family meetings); and demographic sampling (e.g. gender, age, city the speakers are from) (Ruhi, Hatipoğlu, Eröz-Tuğa, and Işık-Güler 2010b). The domain and genre distribution the project is aiming at publishing can be retrieved from http://std.metu.edu.tr/tanitim-surumunun-temel-ozellikleri/: (family/relative gatherings, 25%; work, 20%; education, 15%; Radio/TV broadcast, 15%; friend/acquaintances gathering, 12%; getting service, 5%; conversations with friends and family; 4%, other, 4%):

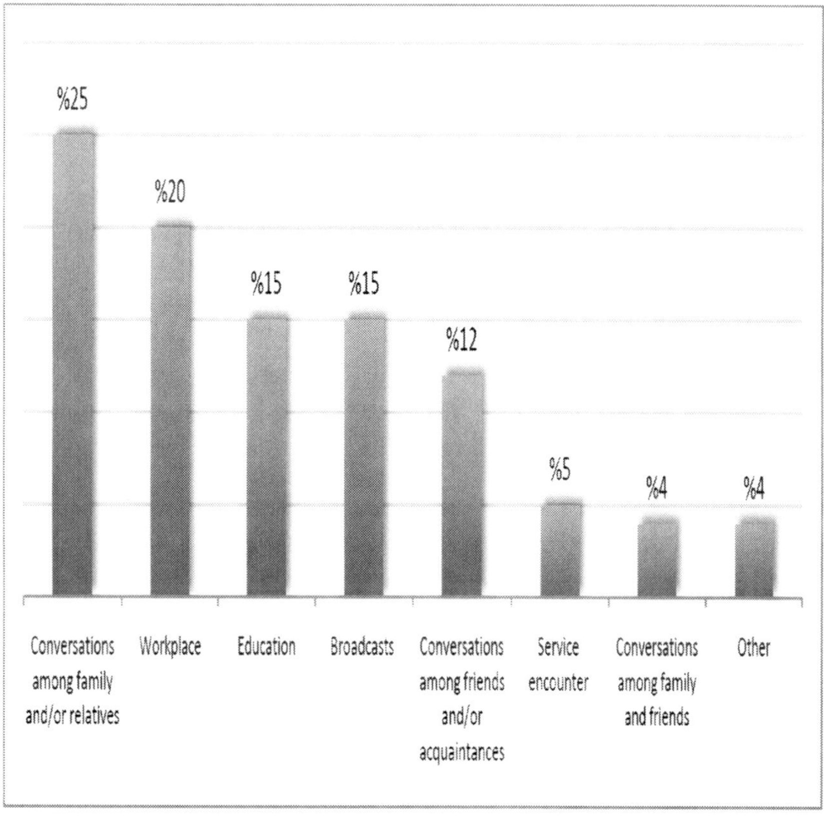

Figure 3.5. Planned Domain Distribution in the STC
Source: STC main features

Further information given on the STC and its features are discussed in relation to the methodological perspective and study levels in this chapter. During the different stages of the study, relevant information supplied by the STC, relations between the speakers, *and* overlapping speech and annotations are referred to and made use of in interpreting data, which is in line with the CA methodology.

3.5 Annotations and the corpora

Annotation can be described as the practice of adding a note to text in a general sense. These notes can take a variety of forms such as comments, footnotes, tags, or links. In designing a corpus, a system needs to be decided upon as to what to add to the actual words interlocutors are uttering. In transcribing conversations, annotating material can be a relatively simple act if more discernible aspects (e.g. who an utterance belongs to, what the duration of a pause is between two utterances). It can also be very complex, especially when annotation comes as a commentary (e.g. in cases where a participant has a humorous tone, or is shouting angrily) from the transcriber. Similar to the transcriber, a researcher who is working with transcribed and annotated texts needs to be alert to present nuances. Römer (2005:22–23) cautions us against being unaware of the effect of annotated material if we are aiming at studying data within the CBL approach. A detailed review has been given in section 2.6. This section discusses how annotations in the STC and the BNC are approached and how they were used or purposely disregarded.

The annotations regarding the voice quality in the BNC are indicated in the transcription at the points where the speaker's voices change. Although 156 different descriptions of voice quality are used in the transcriptions, the BNC User Reference Guide (Burnard, 2007) lists the following ones, which are used more than 10 times in the whole corpus: 'laughing, reading, singing, shouting, whispering, yawning, sighing, mimicking, spelling, crying, screaming, whining, whingeing, praying, reading bible, reading newspaper, reading+laughing, reading book, on telephone.' In the STC, the qualities of speech are annotated under three different categories through a comment tier, verbal tier and nn-tier. In addition to the annotations given in Table 3.9, the two qualities *((change in tone of voice))* and *((empathetically))* are used to mark the emotive tone of voice and special discursive emphases (Ruhi, Hatipoğlu, Eröz-Tuğa, and Işık-Güler, 2010b: 25). When the annotations for speech quality are compared in the two corpora in terms of their suitability as clues for extracting and analyzing impoliteness, it is observed that the annotations they both offer can be interpreted as clues backed up with linguistic clues present in the text. However, since the STC is transcribed with EXMARaLDA Partitur-Editor and following the annotations in the comment tier in the STC in musical score files provides a visually easier system (see Figure 3.3 for illustration), working with the STC has been more feasible for the purposes of this study. Schmidt and Wörner (2009) explain that:

> The EXMARaLDA Partitur-Editor is a tool for inputting, editing and outputting transcriptions in musical score (German: Partitur) notation. Among the established forms of transcript layout (vertical 'line-for-line' notation, column notation, musical score notation, see Edwards 1993), musical score notation (cf. Ehlich and Rehbein 1976) is the one which best meets requirements for representing multi-party, multi-level, and multi-modal descriptions of spontaneous interaction. (p.5)

They maintain that pragmatics inevitably deals with different linguistic levels in which the syntactic and lexical properties of speech are recorded with paralinguistic phenomena (e.g. laughing, pauses) and suprasegemental characteristics (such as intonation and voice quality) and '[t]he data structure must therefore also be able to accommodate and distinguish descriptions on different levels' (p.3). Elsewhere, Schmidt (2010:3) gives the following as an example of a transcript used in discourse analysis:

> X [nv]*left hand up*
> X [v]Yes, • • sure. But ((cough)) how exactly? Oh, well!
> X [de]Ja, • • klar. Aber ((hustet)) wie genau?
> Y [nv]*Eyebrows raised*
> Y [v]Well, I th/ ehm I mean ... I don't know

Schmidt (2010:3) then explains the details of how this transcript can be read as a representation of a conversational exchange between two speakers:

- the temporal structure of the speakers' verbal and non-verbal behaviour is represented in the arrangement of the corresponding descriptions in a 'musical score';
- speaker turns are segmented into utterances, words, pauses (represented by two bold dots) and non-phonological material (the 'cough' of speaker X);
- utterances are qualified with respect to their speech act qualities (assertive, interrogative, etc.), and interrupted utterances are marked as such;
- within utterances, speech act augments (like 'well') and repair sequences consisting of a reparandum, an intervention and a reparans (such as 'I th/' – 'ehm' – 'I mean') are identified;
- stressed syllables (like 'how') are marked;
- for some of the utterances a translation into German is provided.

Except for the last point about translations of utterances into another language since the STC is Turkish monolingual, all the other points Schmidt (2010) mentions above are valid for the STC.

In order to illustrate and better explain the stance taken towards the use of annotations in the transcribed data, a discussion of an extracted conversation from the STC, 113_090404_00004 is given below in a text format, which is different from how the STC extracts are given in the analysis section. In the analysis section, musical scores of the extracts are used. However, for the sole purpose of illustrating the role of annotations in this section, the text format organized in a table has been chosen to make it easier to follow the Turkish with English translation. In this

Table 3.8. The STC annotations and impoliteness in Extract 1

ASI	*son sınıfta almıştım.*	I bought it in my final year at university.
BAD	‿*bu o zaman bayağı para ver ya o zaman o almıştı yaa.*	she had spent a lot of money at the time really
ASI	*sene iki bin/*	the year two thousand/
ASI	*sene iki bin altı.*	the year two thousand six.
BAD	*di mi? seni öyle hatırlıyorum ben.*	right? I remember you (doing) that.
ASI	*evet. üç yüz on milyona almıştım kısaca. **((short laugh))***	yes. I had bought it for three hundred million in short. ***((short laugh))***
IND	*konuşuyorlar.*	chatting.
BAD	*((0.8)) ben de üç yüze aldım.*	((0.8)) I bought it for three hundred as well.
OZG	*ben de çalışmaya başlayınca alacağım.*	I am going to buy one when I start working.
DER	*çok hava atmana gerek yok.*	you don't need to show off so much.
ASI	*((1.5)) sizi çekelim biz de arkadaşlar.*	((1.5)) let's take photographs of you, friends.
DER	*yo beni çekmeyin.*	no, don't include me.
ASI	*çekebiliriz.*	we can.
BAD	*((0.1)) bişey diyeceğim.*	((0.1)) I am going to say something.
OZG	*niye sen çekme. sen bi yeme. sen bi içme.*	why, don't take. just don't eat. just don't drink.
BAD	*sana bi geçireceğim zaten ((XXX)).*	I am going to slap/hit you now (XXX)).
OZG	*ne oluyor ya Allah Allah. ((0.3)) marjinal.*	what is happening, Gosh. ((0.3)) marjinal.

conversation, there are five participants: ASI00003, BAD000036, IND000002, OZG000035, DER000038 (henceforth; ASI, BAD, IND, OZG, and DER). In Table 3.8, the first column indicates the speaker taking a turn, the second column is the Turkish utterance, and the last column on the right gives the English translation. The annotation that will be discussed is in bold.

In this conversation, the annotation in bold was used to interpret the meaning of the utterances. The impoliteness is triggered when DER said to ASI, 'you don't have to show off so much,' (*çok hava atmana gerek yok)*, which is a pointed criticism and personalized negative assertion. The reason why DER thinks ASI is showing off is because ASI has taken too much time to give details about the camera. First, she says 'I bought it in my final year at university,' then encouraged by the BAD's comment, 'she had spent a lot of money at the time really. Right? I remember you (doing) that,' she gives the exact year and the amount of money she had spent for the camera taking her time, as the repetition of the phrase the year indicates, in the conversation, 'The year two thousand,' trying to remember exactly, 'the year two thousand six,' 'Yes. I bought it for three hundred million in short.' followed by a '((short laugh)).' By completing her turn by saying 'in short,' she is signalling that she is aware that her turn on the details of when she bought the camera and how much she paid for it have taken too much time from the conversation. She then gives a short laugh as she might be thinking of what she had just said, 'in short,' and might have found it contradictory since she is aware she has flouted the maxim of quantity in two ways both by giving the exact year and the exact price. At this point the annotation *((short laugh))* is of high importance as it expands the interpretation by providing a cue which would not be available to the analyst otherwise, if not supplied by the annotations. In this case not making use of the annotation would take away from the soundness of the interpretation.

Table 3.9 summarizes frequently-used annotations in the STC. Annotations of this kind which are beyond the level of certain fixed categories, such as word classes, offer an indispensable asset for the researchers as they give rich clues at a glance for the potential of a variety of study focuses, which would otherwise take a long time for the researchers to come to see those clues themselves, probably an equal amount of time that the corpus designers spend on the annotations. The last annotation 'pro' in the comment tier refers to 'pronunciation' and it is used when a word with the same spelling in Turkish and in a foreign language is pronounced with its foreign language pronunciation (Ruhi et al. 2010b).

Table 3.9. Frequently used annotations in the STC

(c) Comment tier	(v) Verbal tier	(nn) nn-tier
Loudly	laughs	noise
slowly	short laugh	traffic noise
softly	laughter	TV/radio noise
stuttering	clears throat	clatter of tableware
syllabifying	sighs	voices in the background
whispers	coughs	
fast	sneezes	footsteps
lengthening	hiccups	microphone noise
laughing	kissing	silence
coughing	inhales	
eating	exhales	
shouting	sings	
humorous tone	sniffs	
list intonation		
pro		

Regardless of the rich material, an analyst who does not consciously evaluate her/his approach to the annotated material and decide on what annotations would be helpful and what would be misleading may start with a predisposition towards the data and follow the framework of the CBL. For instance, another type of annotated material the STC provides is the speech acts found in conversations (Table 3.10).

Table 3.10. Speech acts in the STC

Advising
Apology
Asking about well being
Asking for advice
Asking for opinion
Asking for permission
Compliance (as a response to a request)
Criticizing
Declarative
Greetings
Insults
Inviting
Leave taking
Offering
Other expressives
Promising
Refusals (as a response to a request)
Representative
Requests
Thanking
Well wishes/Congratulations

The window in Table 3.11 shows how recordings are annotated in relation to speech acts and categorized in STC.

Table 3.11. Speech acts and conversation categories in the STC

Speech act	In Communication(s)
Advising	069_090610_00015 • 061_090622_00020 • 116_090206_00018
Apology	012_090128_00002 • 117_090310_00019
Asking about well being	072_090913_00006 • 012_090128_00002 • 024_091113_00031
Asking for advice	024_091113_00031
Asking for opinion	072_090913_00006 • 021_090501_00013 • 116_090206_00018 • 119_090123_00029 • 119_090501_00026
Asking for permission	012_090128_00002
Compliance (as a response to a request)	115_090323_00017
Criticizing	012_090128_00002 • 117_090310_00019 • 072_090618_00005 • 061_090622_00020 • 118_090321_00021
Greetings	012_090128_00002 • 075_090629_00023 • 116_090206_00018 • 119_090531_00075
Insults	117_090310_00019
Inviting	012_090128_00002
Leave-taking	117_090310_00019 • 118_090321_00021 • 072_090913_00006 • 069_090610_00015 • 024_091113_00031 • 061_090622_00020 • 119_090123_00029 • 119_090501_00026 • 119_090531_00075
Offering	118_090321_00021 • 075_090629_00023 • 021_090501_00013 • 061_090622_00020 • 012_090128_00002 • 116_090206_00018 • 072_090913_00006 • 075_090627_00035
Refusals (as a response to a request)	117_090310_00019 • 024_091113_00031 • 061_090622_00020
Representative	072_090618_00005 • 069_090610_00015 • 119_090531_00075
Requests	075_090622_00003 • 012_090128_00002 • 117_090310_00019 • 069_090610_00015 • 021_090501_00013 • 072_090618_00005 • 061_090622_00020 • 116_090206_00018 • 115_090323_00017
Thanking	117_090310_00019 • 118_090321_00021 • 061_090622_00020 • 116_090206_00018 • 115_090323_00017
Well wishes/ congratulations	072_090913_00006 • 061_090622_00020 • 116_090206_00018 • 118_090321_00021

If the analysts take for granted the annotations regarding speech acts, theorizing that certain speech acts are potentially more viable to extract impoliteness, it is a given that he/she should focus on conversations listed below criticizing, insults, refusals and perhaps apologies. However, by taking a more cautionary step towards extraction as suggested by the CDL, the analyst is able to reach more insightful and inclusive data which do not come under the presupposed headings such as criticizing, insults, refusals, and apology, but can be found under a variety of speech acts. Still, it is not always the analyst making a decision whether or not to use an annotation. Data encoding and transcription schemes can determine how accessible annotations are. Especially when extracting the material requires a complex task due to encoding, the focus of a study may not allow for a discussion of annotations. This was the case with certain points for this study.

Since data encoding and transcription schemes are different for the BNC and the STC, annotations that indicate nonverbal, paralinguistic forms existing in data retrieved from the corpora differed depending on the corpus. Non-verbal forms such as structural patterns and a change in the pattern in conversation (e.g. turn-taking, overlaps, topic retention, repetition signalling a potential for impoliteness, continuous disagreements), metadata features such as the relationship of speakers, or paralinguistic forms such as, prosodic aspects (e.g. pauses and rises in intonation or pitch) or annotations describing the utterance (e.g. speaker laughing, yawning) played a major role in interpreting the data as far as the corpora the BNC and the STC allowed. However, not all the data the corpora offered were used to the same extent due to certain limitations.

For the BNC, paralinguistic phenomena such as pauses, speech management phenomena (e.g. truncation, false starts, correction), and overlaps in the data were disregarded due to the complexity of data retrieval. BNC offers two different formats to retrieve data; one, Extensible Markup Language (XML henceforth) and two, the 'fancy' format which is closer to a conventional script. Figure 3.6 shows a screenshot from the corpus the BNC of a hit in XML for the conversation discussed as BNC Extract 1 in Section 4.2. XML is the format through which alignment in speech is given in the BNC and the circled instances show how speech events aligning appear on the screenshot.

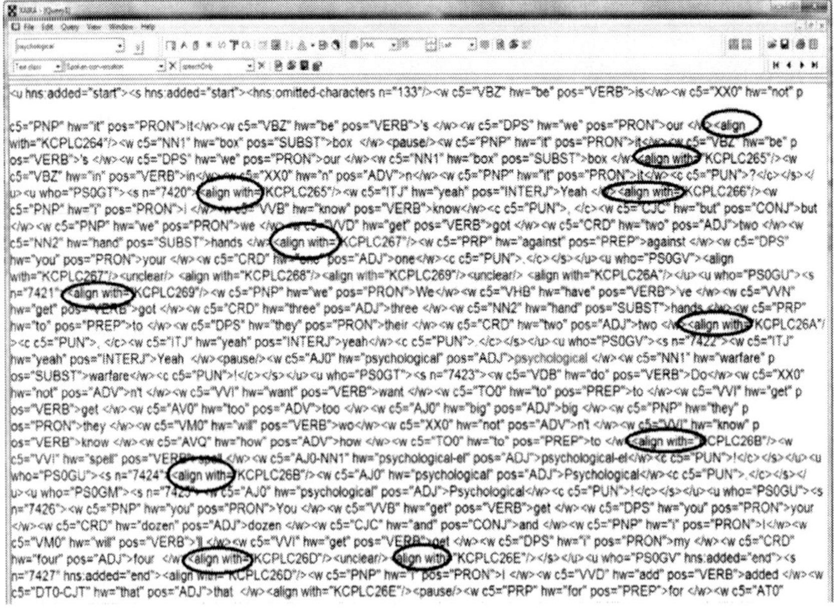

Figure 3.6. Alignment of speech in the BNC
Source: XAira (BNC-XML)

If a researcher wants to include alignment of speech into his/her discussion of overlaps for their potential for impoliteness, he/she must find a systematic way of making sense of numerous 'align with' marks circled in Figure 3.6. Besides, he/she must come up with a way of presenting that to the readers. The focus of that intent would be then re-encoding the corpus data. Therefore, although XML format supplies information about the alignment of speech, which may give important clues about overlaps and interruptions signalling a potential for impoliteness, 'fancy' format is preferred due to the complex process of the data comprehension required. Figure 3.7 shows a screenshot of the fancy format for the same conversation given in Figure 3.6.

<> isn't [KCPLC263] [...] .
<PS0GU> [KCPLC263] It's our [KCPLC264] box [P] it's our box [KCPLC265] innit?
<PS0GT> [KCPLC265] Yeah [KCPLC266] I know, but we got two hands [KCPLC267] against your one
<PS0GV> [KCPLC267] [...] [KCPLC268] [KCPLC269] [...] [KCPLC26A]
<PS0GU> [KCPLC269] We've got three hands to their two [KCPLC26A] , yeah
<PS0GV> Yeah [P] psychological warfare!
<PS0GT> Don't want to get too big they won't know how to [KCPLC26B] spell psychological-el!
<PS0GU> [KCPLC26B] Psychological.
<PS0GM> Psychological!
<PS0GU> You get your dozen and I'll get my four [KCPLC26D] [...] [KCPLC26E]
<PS0GV> [KCPLC26D] I added that [KCPLC26E] [P] for the old tape, you know?

Figure 3.7. 'Fancy' format in the BNC
Source: XAira (BNC-XML)

In order not to work from screenshots, what appeared in the screen (Figure 3.7) has been transcribed once more (see below) to use paper space economically. When paralinguistic information was present in the 'fancy' format as annotations (e.g. laughing, yawning), they were taken into consideration in interpretation.

(PSOGU) We've got three hands to their two, yeah.
(PSOGV) Yeah psychological warfare!
(PSOGT) Don't want to get too big they won't know how to spell psychological-el!
(PSOG) Psychological.
(PSOGM) Psychological!
(PSOGU) You get your dozen and I'll get my four
(PSOGV) I added that for the old tape, you know?

3.6 Extraction and the corpora

This section gives detailed information about various extraction methods tried on the BNC and the STC. Initially, a variety of queries had to be run for both corpora to detect metapragmatic comments and conventionalized impoliteness formulae as well as non-conventionalized implicational impoliteness. In order to collect conversations from the BNC that involve impoliteness, a variety of query methods were used. Initially, word and collocation queries were run for a list of taboo words such as *sodding, fucking, shit* and conventionalized phrases such as *bugger off* and *shut up* in the spoken subcorpus with the text type selected as spoken conversation. Most words for queries came from a study by Millwood-Hargrave (2000) cited by Culpeper (2011b) (Table 3.12).

Table 3.12. Words and offensiveness in Britain in the year 2000

Rank-ordered 1–15		Rank ordered 15–28	
1.	Cunt	15.	Spastic
2.	Motherfucker	16.	Slag
3.	Fuck	17.	Shit
4.	Wanker	18.	Dickhead
5.	Nigger	19.	Pissed off
6.	Bastard	20.	Arse
7.	Prick	21.	Bugger
8.	Bollocks	22.	Balls
9.	Arsehole	23.	Jew
10.	Paki	24.	Sodding
11.	Shag	25.	Jesus Christ
12.	Whore	26.	Crap
13.	Twat	27.	Bloody
14.	Piss off	28.	God

However, through such queries, it was found that occurrences that signal impoliteness in conversation were displayed as separate hits, not contextualized in the conversation in which they took place. Bearing in mind that not all conventional utterances are conventionalized formulae and conventionalized impoliteness formulae are closely linked to the idea of co-occurrence regularities between language forms and specific contexts, as explained above through the illustration of what *cunt* meant for a student, it was apparent that individual hits on the display menu did not serve the purpose of extracting the incidences of impoliteness. The display in the window shown in Figure 3.8 illustrates the hits the corpus gives after running a query for *bugger off*.

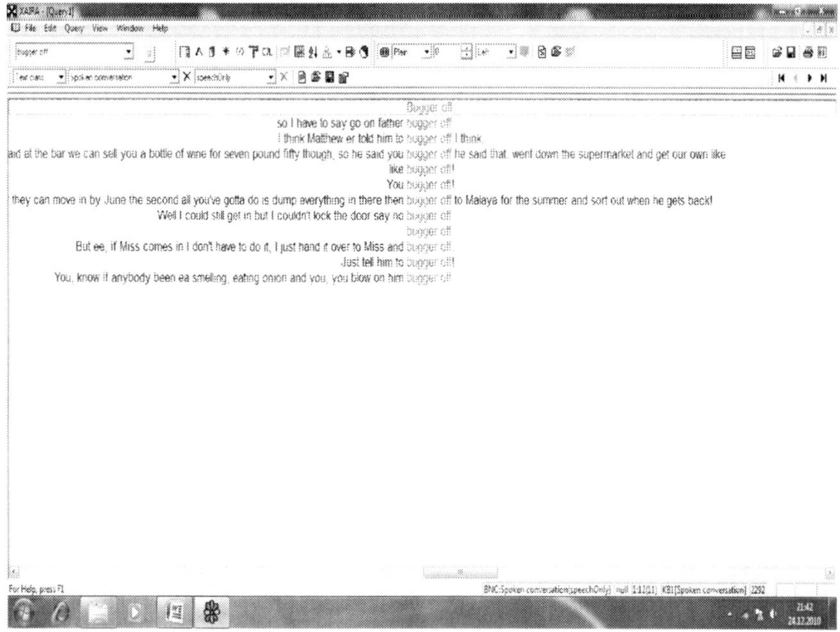

Figure 3.8. Display window of hits in the BNC
Source: Xaira (BNC-XML)

Although each hit can be analysed in terms of the source, bibliographic data, and non-verbal clues in XML query, the word and phrase query did not serve the purpose of the study for the reason explained above. The scope of this study demanded a different type of query for the reason that the research questions required an analysis of the whole conversation in which the occurrences took place since how the conversation evolved determined the impoliteness strategies preferred by the speakers and hearers.

In order to reach the whole conversation where an occurrence took place, the following search method has been used. On the BNC main query window, there are two columns that list all the texts and information about these texts such as its type, e.g. whether it is spoken or written. In these columns, the texts are titled with three digit alpha-numerical codes. Spoken conversations are listed between KBX to KEX. Each text given a three-digit name was recorded by a different person and varies in terms of the duration it was recorded for and the number of the conversations it included. From the list, each spoken text recorded by a different person is selected, one by one, and using the bibliographic data and browse option the conversations were downloaded to a Word document. Approximately 500 conversations were downloaded. Among these conversations, the ones which could include instances of impoliteness were gathered through word query in Word by the use of the 'find in the document' option and occurrences were highlighted. Then the conversations were printed and were extensively read to get a sense of the context. At this stage, the data appeared as the following:

Conversation Extract 1

We've got three hands to their two, yeah.
Yeah psychological warfare!
Don't want to get too big they won't know how to spell psychological-el!
Psychological.
Psychological!
You get your dozen and I'll get my four
I added that for the old tape, you know?
Did you?
Mm rather than being monosyllabic.
Monosyllabic oh!
Oh God, not.
Right let's keep this under control!
This is stupid!
Yeah, it is a bit!
Well ain't you nothing?
What if I have!
Excuse me!
I got my er you know
Outside, two minutes!
No problem.

Parts indicating a potential for impoliteness were highlighted and focused upon while reading extensively. Through the extensive reading, additional clues were taken into consideration in order to be able to pick the signals for impoliteness. For instance, imperatives, repetitive instructions, confrontational language (e.g. excuse me!), and language to disagree were taken into consideration. It is noteworthy to explain the series of steps taken to identify the speaker and reach the utterances that come before and after the utterance of that speaker. In order to get the necessary additional information about which utterances belonged to which speaker, in the BNC, a word or a phrase from the text is put into the query box and from the number of hits the one that came within the larger phrase in which it existed was selected. For instance, from Conversation Extract 1, the phrase selected, 'psychological warfare' (which is italicized above in the Conversation Extract 1), is run in the BNC and the findings are displayed in the screen shot below. In the hit screen below, the fourth hit, 'Yeah psychological warfare!' is the phrase that needs to be tracked down to reach the speakers.

Figure 3.9. The BNC hits for 'psychological warfare'
Source: XAira (BNC-XML)

When this hit is selected on the screen, the format box is set to 'fancy1' and the scope box is increased to high as it gives the conversation, which in this case is 20 as the screen shot shows in Figure 3.10.

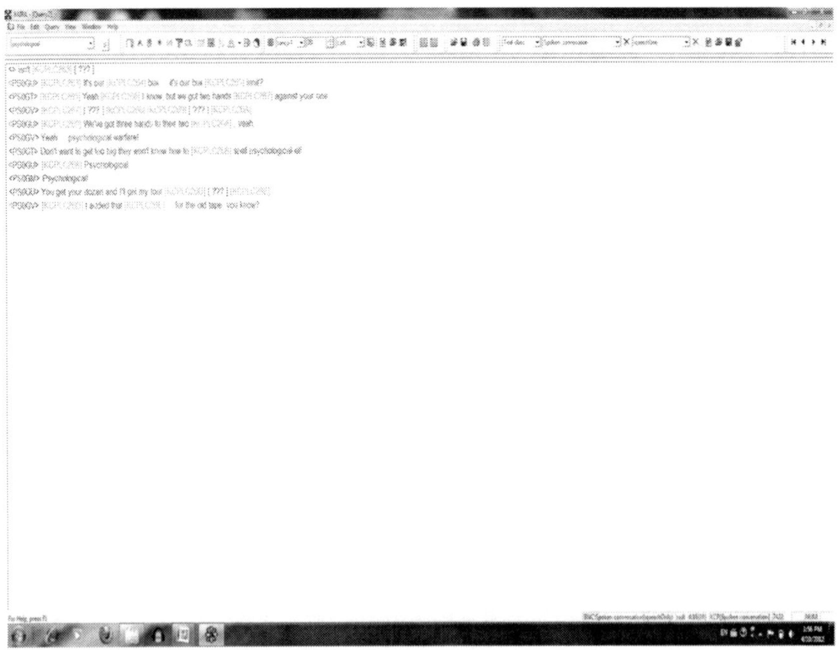

Figure 3.10. The BNC Format Used for Extracts
Source: Xaira (BNC-XML)

When 'the highest scope' did not show the necessary part of the conversation on the screen for the analysis, another phrase is selected on the screen from the bottom or top depending on whether the beginning or the end of the conversation is being tracked, and the same series of steps were followed. Each time, the screen shots were saved in Jpeg format since BNC software did not allow Word copy/paste function. Then parts were put in order and for practicality purposes, rather than putting Jpeg files together one after other, a text for further discussion has been created as follows:

> (PSOGU) We've got three hands to their two, yeah.
> (PSOGV) Yeah psychological warfare!
> (PSOGT) Don't want to get too big they won't know how to spell psychological-el!
> (PSOG) Psychological.
> (PSOGM) Psychological!
> (PSOGU) You get your dozen and I'll get my four
> (PSOGV) I added that for the old tape, you know?

Once the conventionalized linguistic expressions were picked, the incidences of impoliteness were categorized under the types (Culpeper 2010, 2011b): insult, personalized negative assertions, challenging or unpalatable questions and/or presuppositions, condescension, message enforcers, dismissals, silencers, threats, negative expressives (e.g. curses, ill-wishes). An advantage of categorizing the impoliteness incidences as such is that while comparing British English and Turkish, the types, not the linguistic expressions, provided a framework for the contrastive analysis. The linguistic expressions were focused on with the consideration that semantic analysis was necessary so as not to ignore subtleties such as discourse or semantic prosody, the latter of which is discussed in more detail in Chapter 4.

A similar method of searching for keywords or phrases was followed for extracting incidences of impoliteness in the STC. The recorded data were listened to in order to pick similar linguistic expressions in British English brought out by Millwood-Hargrave (2000) with the acknowledgment that expressions could differ in two languages. There have been a number of studies in Turkish on the function of slang and swear words. For instance, Aydın (2006) studied the humoristic function of slang and swear-words in the Turkish movie entitled G.O.R.A. She maintained that despite the fact that the slang and swear words and expressions used in the movie are generally associated with negative meanings and perceived as insults during real interactions if uttered, in the movie they are perceived as highly entertaining. Below is a list of some slang and swear-words and expressions she mentioned from the movie:

> *ibneler* (faggots), *pezevenk* (pimp), *yalama* (ponce), *grup indirimi (grup seks kastedilerek), girdi mi?* ("got the group discount?," "group discount" meaning group sex), *hepinizi yapıcam* ((I) will fuck all of you), *her yerden alıyo musun?*((do you) get fucked from everywhere?),*gırtlağa dayanmak* (having had enough), *uzatmak* (going on and on), *yavşamak* (being slimy), *kafası iyi olmak* (being drunk), *götünden uydurmak* (pulling out of someone's arse), *ne mal olduğunu göstermek* (showing what a bastard someone is*)*, *ulan* (asshole), *lan* (jerk), *kafana sıçiyim* ((I) will shit on your head), *amına koyim* ((I) will fuck your pussy), *siktir* (fuck off), *ananı sikim* ((I) will fuck your mother), *gerzek* (cretin), *pislik* (dirt), *hayvan* (animal), *aptal* (moron), *maymun* (monkey), *geri zekâlı* (retard), *dingil* (shaft), *dandik* (lousy), *eşşoğlu eşşek* (son of a bitch) , *bunak* (insane)

Another study, carried out by Güneş (2009) examined the spelling of slang and swear words and expressions in cartoon magazines and various Internet sites. She pointed out that although in general, in written language, spelling rules are applied in writing these words, alterations are made to the spelling of such words in cartoon magazines and Internet sites due to censoring factors. Some examples she gave from the cartoon magazines and sites for the slang and swear words are: *pezemenk, ipne, ananı!, orsbu, orrspu çocuu, hastir, eşşeoğlueşşek, amuğaa goduumun, bok satıyor, sıçtık, puştmuşsun lan.* Most words and expressions in Aydın's (2006) and Güneş's (2009) studies overlap, indicating that these are commonly used and accepted as slang and swear words in Turkish. Although it is not possible to arrive at conclusions about the rank of offensiveness of these words, it is assumed that a list of these words would function well for carrying out the word query for extraction in Turkish as Millwood-Hargrave (2000)'s list used for word query in British English.

In cases where linguistic expressions differed from slang and swear words and expressions, the incidences were checked against the types (Culpeper 2010, 2011b), which are insult, pointed criticisms/complaints, challenging or unpalatable questions and/or presuppositions, condescension, message enforcers, dismissals, silencers, threats, negative expressives (e.g. curses, ill-wishes). For instance, the linguistic expressions *hadi len yok artık* (no way dude) or *pes yani* ('oh no!' as refusal of belief in) in a conversation in Turkish may function as a silencer although one might argue that these expressions do not have equivalences in Culpeper's conventionalized impoliteness formulae as actual linguistic expressions. Nevertheless, the types of conventionalized formulae; insult, personalized negative assertions, challenging or unpalatable questions and/or presuppositions, condescension, message enforcers, dismissals, silencers, threats, and negative expressives (e.g. curses, ill-wishes), are assumed to be cross-linguistically applicable for extracting impoliteness. In addition, the dialogues were scanned through an initial word query, collocation query and question sentences and tags query, query for imperatives and possible queries that allow for searching for prosodic nuances. For the word query, Işık-Güler's (2008) dissertation findings about strongly-associated concepts with KABA (impolite) in Turkish were used, with the acknowledgment that concepts strongly associated with IMPOLITE in British English do not necessarily match the concepts with KABA in Turkish. Among the lexical items that she finds to be strongly associated with KABA and which will be used for the word query for this study are: *düşüncesiz,* 'inconsiderate,' *saygısız,* 'disrespectful,' *nezaketsiz,* 'tactless,' *küstahlık*; 'arrogance,' *patavatsızlık*; 'indiscretion,' *kırıcı*; 'offending,' *bencil*; 'selfish,' *çirkin*; 'ugly,' *cahil,* 'ignorant,' *empati kuramayan*; 'cannot empathize.' Furthermore, taboo words (e.g. *fucking*) were regarded as cues that may indicate a metapragmatic comment or an utterance that may turn out to be conventionalized impoliteness formulae or non-conventionalized implicational impoliteness.

Studies attempting to bring out the semantic mapping of politeness-related terms were conducted by other scholars. Pizziconi (2007) used lexeme analysis as an explorative technique to describe structured representations of politeness. Her lexeme analysis findings indicate that 'the resources – the conceptual constraints and possibilities – afforded to language users by their repertoires are fairly similar (in the basic sense of fundamental judgments about cognitive and affective distinctions that users can make), but they also offer different expressive possibilities (or they facilitate them) with regard to the preference for detail in 'informal,' 'friendly,' nuances of English, and 'reserved,' 'modest' nuances in Japanese. It is in line with this finding that the lexical items Işık-Güler (2008) proposes to be strongly associated with impoliteness in Turkish have been used for this study for the word query to extract impoliteness.

Special attention was given to semantic prosody. Semantic prosody is a term that is used in many ways with different emphases over the years (Sinclair, 1987, 1991; Louw, 1993, 2000; Bublitz, 1996; Tognini-Bonelli, 2001; Hunston and Thompson, 1999; Hunston, 2002, 2007; Partington, 1998, 2004a; Stubbs, 1995, 2001; Hoey, 2005). Sinclair (1996:87–88) defines semantic prosody as follows:

> A semantic prosody ... is attitudinal, and on the pragmatic side of the semantics/pragmatics continuum. It is thus capable of a wide range of realization, because in pragmatic expressions the normal semantic values of the words are not necessarily relevant. But once noticed among the variety of expressions, it is immediately clear that the semantic prosody has a leading role to play in the integration of an item with its surroundings. It expresses something close to the 'function' of an item – it shows how the rest of the item is to be interpreted functionally.

Hunston and Thompson (1999:38) emphasize the importance of immediate surroundings as well as the hidden evaluative quality of semantic prosody, which is of particular importance in Louw (1993, 2000):

> The notion of semantic prosody (or pragmatic meaning) is that a given word or phrase may occur most frequently in the context of other words or phrases which are predominantly positive or negative in their evaluative orientation [...] As a result, the given word takes on an association with the positive, or, more usually, the negative, and this association can be exploited by speakers to express evaluative meaning covertly.

Stewart (2010), who gives a summary of many approaches to semantic prosody and raises critical questions about discussions formed around the concept, also points out that although most definitions and descriptions present semantic prosody as 'a type of meaning,' there is a close relationship between 'semantic prosody and the process or phenomenon from which it derives' (p.19). He cites Gavioli (2005:46), who defines semantic prosody as 'the way in which words and expressions create an aura of meaning capable of affecting words around them.' Although brief, the given information underlies what is central to the concept of semantic prosody in this study: it shows an evaluative orientation and it applies to the unit of meaning, which is larger than a single word and indicates a process that is not necessarily diachronic. In order to illustrate how semantic prosody plays a role in evaluating metapragmatic comments and conventionalized and non-conventionalized implicational impoliteness, an example from the STC (conversation number 113_090404_00004) is given. In the extract, the first column from the right marks the speaker (ex. OZG000035), [v] refers to the verbal tier, and [c] refers to the comment tier. Unless the row gives the comment tier, after each row a new row was inserted below to provide the translation. In the discussion of the excerpt, semantic nuances are given especially when they play a role for semantic prosody and are crucial for the discussion of extracted impoliteness.

Extract 1. 113_090404_00004

ASI000037 [v]		((0.6)) ben iki...			son sınıfta almıştım.
Trans.	I two ... I bought (it) (when I was) in my final year at university.				
IND000002 [v]				hayır.	
Trans.	No.				

BAD000036 [v]	((1.0)) ha evet. ⌣bu o zaman bayağı para ver	ya o zaman o
Trans.	yeah, right. she spent a lot of money at the time	
ASI000037 [v]		sene iki bin/
Trans.	the year two thousand/	

BAD000036 [v]	al	mıştı yaa.		di mi? • seni öyle hatırlıyorum
Trans.	(she) bought (it), yeah. right? I remember you (doing) that.			
ASI000037 [v]			sene iki bin altı.	
Trans.	year two thousand six.			

OZG000035 [v]		((1.4)) e ben son sınıfım. hala yok.	((0.1)) ki o zo/ o
Trans.	I'm in the final year (of university). I still don't have (one). And the last		
BAD000036 [v]	ben.		
Trans.	I.		

OZG000035 [v]	son sınıfla bu son sınıf arasında fark var. ⌐artık her yer
Trans.	year of university in those days and now are different. now, (there are)

OZG000035 [v]	fotoğraf makinesi yani.	((0.2)) eskiden çok yoktu.	
Trans.	cameras everywhere, I mean. didn't use to be many in the past.		
ASI000037 [v]			evet. üç
Trans.	yes. I		

BAD000036 [v]			((0.8)) ben
Trans.	I		
ASI000037 [v]	yüz on milyona almıştım kısaca.	((short laugh))˙	
Trans.	bought (it) for three hundred million, in short.		

OZG000035 [v]		Ben	de çalışmaya başlayınca	alacağım.	
Trans.	I'll buy (one) too when I start working.				
BAD000036 [v]	de üç yüze al	dım.			
Trans.	bought it for three hundred as well.				
DER000038 [v]					çok
Trans.	(so much)				

ASI000037 [v]		((1.5)) sizi çekelim biz de
Trans.	let's take (a picture) of you	
DER000038 [v]	hava atmana gerek yok.	
Trans.	(you) don't have to show off so much.	

OZG000035 [v]							niye sen
Trans.	why, you						
BAD000036 [v]					((0.1))	bişey	
Trans.	something						
ASI000037 [v]	arkadaşlar.		çeke	biliriz.			
Trans.	friends. (we) can take						
DER000038 [v]		yo beni çek	meyin.				
Trans.	no, don't include me.						

OZG000035 [v]		çekme. sen bi yeme. sen bi içme.		ne	oluyor
Trans.	don't take (one). just don't eat. just don't drink. what's happening				
BAD000036 [v]	diyeceğim.			sa	na bi
Trans.	I'll say (something). (you) now				

OZG000035 [v]		ya Allah Allah.	((0.3)) marjinal.	
Trans.	Oh, God. marjınal.			
BAD000036 [v]	geçireceğim	zaten ((XXX)).		((0.8)) flaşını
Trans.	I will hit/slap you right now. (the flash)			

BAD000036 [v]	açalım mı?		
Trans.	Shall we switch on the flash?		
DER000038 [v]			((0.5)) tamam çekin ya
Trans.	oh well, ok, take (a picture)		

In this extract, the utterance from BAD000036 '*sana bi geçireceğim zaten ((XXX))*' is translated as 'I am going to hit/slap you right now' because the semantic prosody in the utterance *(sana bi geçireceğim)* required it. The verb *geçir–* has the following denotative meanings in Turkish: to migrate, to impose, to enter, to pass, to cover, to fit, to fix, to screw to gear, to pass through, to squeeze, to penetrate, to undergo, to convey, to pass over. The question then is, what, in the discourse, triggers this negative evaluation of the utterance (*sana bi geçireceğim zaten ((XXX))*,' which is then considered a threat, or a conventionalized impoliteness formula (Culpeper, 2010). In order to find what generates the semantic prosody, first the verb *-geçir* and the closest lexical item *bi* to it in the utterance are semantically examined. Since *bi* is a phonologically attenuated form of *bir*, the indefinite article/number one in Turkish, a dictionary analysis has been conducted for the item *bir* as well. Then a corpus analysis is run on the METU Turkish Corpus (Say, Zeyrek, Oflazer, and Özge, 2004) to examine the relationship between *geçir-* and *bi*. After carrying out these analyses, it is concluded that (see Section 4.3) the use of '*bi*' triggers a negative evaluation in the utterance *(sana bi geçireceğim)* by quantifying the verb *geçir-* and emphasising the activity. The negative evaluation is intensified through a personalization effect by the use of 'sana,' which is a case of an overt use of pronoun that could be omitted in a pro-drop language. Further discussion on the extract and the role of semantic prosody appears in section 4.3 but it has been discussed here briefly so that its role in extracting impoliteness in corpora can be explained. What is highlighted here for the extraction method is that, in addition to conventionalized impoliteness formulae, cues for implicational impoliteness such as semantic prosody were tracked down for both British English and Turkish to compensate for the incidences of impoliteness which could have been missed otherwise because they did not fall into what might have been named as conventionalized impoliteness formulae.

3.7 Methodological issues: The discursive, cue-based and cyclic approaches

The previous sections on impoliteness theories and CDL suggest the following analytical procedures. These are touched upon briefly in Chapter 2 but are detailed in this section. In extracting and at times simultaneously analysing impoliteness events in conversation, metapragmatic comments, conventionalized impoliteness formulae and cues for non-conventionalized implicational impoliteness present in the co-text and context together with other nuances such as semantic prosody are taken into consideration. This means that bearing in mind that 'neither the expression nor the context guarantee an interpretation of (im)politeness' (Culpeper 2010:3237), the conversations which are selected as containing impoliteness were examined discursively, for metapragmatic comments existing in the co-text, as well as having been looked at through the cues existing both in the co-text and context to detect conventionalized impoliteness formulae and non-conventionalized implicational impoliteness. This cycle of looking at conversations to extract impoliteness events has two steps:

1. Study the co-text, what linguistic expressions come before and after utterances, for *metapragmatic comments* (e.g. 'you're rude,' 'what she did was rude').

2.   Study the co-text, for *conventionalized impoliteness formulae*, (e.g. 'you are such a hypocrite,' 'Shut up!') and context, what is beyond the linguistic expressions for *non-conventionalized implicational impoliteness* (e.g. the relationship of speakers such as parent-child, prosodic aspects such as pauses, and rise in intonation and pitch.)

Step 1 characterizes the discursive approach and Step 2, the cue-based approach (see Table 2.1 for visual illustration).

The reason why two approaches are applied together at the extraction level is because the methodological issues brought up about the discursive approach made it necessary to complement it with another approach that is considered to be more fine-grained. The distinction between politeness1 (first-order politeness) and politeness2 (second-order politeness) is a cornerstone of the discursive approach (Haugh, 2007). After making this distinction, the researchers following the discursive approach argued that politeness research should focus on what people perceived politeness to be (first-order politeness) and that a focus on politeness2 lacked utility since scientific notions of politeness would be normative. The discursive approach has been proposed by researchers who follow a postmodern paradigm (Eelen, 2001; Mills, 2003; Watts, 2003; Watts et al., 2005; Locher, 2004; Locher and Watts, 2005). The point these researchers agree on is that there needs to be a shift from the emphasis on the attempt to construct a model of politeness to predict when politeness is expected to the emphasis of how participants in interaction perceive politeness. When politeness is regarded as 'a slippery ultimately indefinable quality of interaction' (Watts et al., 2005: xiii), as Haugh (2007) notes, there is a hint of giving much less importance to the notion of politeness itself as a focus of research (Locher, 2006:251). The postmodern, discursive approach to politeness does not aim to pursue the descriptive theory of politeness (Watts, 2003:142) or to develop a universal, cross-cultural theory of politeness (Locher and Watts 2005:16). The focus of politeness researchers should be on broader issues of interpersonal interaction or on *relational work* as Locher and Watts (2005) refer to. With this emphasis, this school of researchers is attempting to defy the essentialist view that the notion of politeness is universal.

However, the discursive approach also has received criticisms. For example, Haugh (2007) argues that while the attempt to shift the emphasis may look valid, there are some consequences of adopting the discursive approach: it does not only abandon the pursuit of a priori predictive theory of politeness but it also objects to any attempts of developing a universal, cross-culturally valid theory of politeness. He then raises a question: if a theory of politeness is neither necessary nor desirable, what is the role of politeness research as a field of study given that it cannot be carried out within the research traditions? Therefore, he discusses in detail the discursive approach and its epistemological and ontological challenges. As for the ontological challenges the discursive approach holds, Haugh (2007) argues that 'the discursive approach places a considerable burden on the validity of the analyst's interpreting of the interaction' (p. 302). If the analyst's role is not to impose a theoretical view of politeness as suggested by the discursive approach, but rather to explicate the participants' understandings or perceptions of politeness, then it raises questions regarding the status of the researcher in relation to the participants (p. 303). In other words, if the analyst is to avoid making generalizations for the aim of not being normative, then the analyst's job becomes purely a report of participants' evaluation of impoliteness occurring within a particular context at a particular time. Therefore, since generalizations are not to be made, these studies would be reporting *potential* instances of (im)politeness. To put it differently, with the discursive approach, the analyst should not make an interpretation about what is impolite, since its validity is questionable. Then, as Haugh (2007) argues, what might have been accomplished by a study carried out by a discursive approach, which questions the validity of the analyst's interpretation, is questionable.

Despite these criticisms, the discursive approach plays an important role in this study as discussed in Section 1.3 in relation to the Foucauldian move Mills (2009) is suggesting. The discursive approach emphasizes emic analysis, which is referred to as politeness1 or the lay person's view. It is fundamental for the extraction level as explained in step 1: study the co-text, what linguistic expressions come before and after utterances, for *metapragmatic comments* (e.g. 'you're rude,' 'what she did was rude') which fall into the discursive approach of analysing impoliteness and its focus is impoliteness1. It provides 'an analysis of the means by which these supposed norms are held in place, or are asserted to be norms in the first place; that is, we analyse the discursive mechanisms by which cultural stereotypes about language are developed and circulated' (Foucault, [1969] 1972 cited in Mills, 2009:1048). However, addressing the same criticisms Haugh (2007) points out, the present study is not categorized under the discursive approach. Studying the co-text (for *conventionalized impoliteness formulae* for expressions such as 'you are such a hypocrite' or 'shut up!') and the context (for *non-conventionalized implicational impoliteness* with the clues such as the relationship of the speakers (such as parent-child), and prosodic aspects such as pauses and rise in intonation and pitch to go beyond the linguistic expressions is the aim of Step 2 in the present study. With this step, this approach will facilitate reaching generalizations to explain impoliteness theoretically. The second step then offers an etic analysis and leads to politeness2, with the utmost attention given to the cues so as not to impose the researchers' interpretation to the data. This is where, both theoretically and in practice, the approach in this study complements the discursive approach: Watts (2003:11) argues that 'scientific notions of politeness (which should be non-normative) cannot be part of a study of social interaction (normative by definition)' and by implication, that politeness research should be on first-order politeness. However, in this study, in the pursuit of developing a methodological framework to extract and analyse impoliteness across two languages in order to explain impoliteness phenomena, analytical validity and utility are formed with caution so that the researcher's interpretation is not imposed on the data.

Despite the fact that Step 1 and Step 2 are numbered linearly, it is impossible for the researcher to analyse the data linearly. Owing to the dynamic nature of conversation, metapragmatic comments can function as the co-text for creating a context for non-conventionalized implicational impoliteness. Examining what metapragmatic comments supply in co-text (as is characteristic of the discursive approach) may signal interpersonal conflict through the change in structural patterns and so be used as cues to interpret context-driven implicational impoliteness. It is impossible to decide where the boundaries of discursive approach end and cue-based approach starts for the theoretical discussion. A study of impoliteness is only possible where these two approaches are taken into consideration together and applied simultaneously.

This study presents an example of such a methodology in a data set consisting of both Turkish and British English in conversation. As Culpeper (2010) points out, the focus of the discursive approach is on the *micro*: the focus is on 'participants' situated and dynamic evaluations of politeness, not shared conventionalized politeness forms of politeness' (p. 3235). In addition, to address the issue Terkourafi (2005a) puts forward (i.e., not to be left with 'the minute descriptions of individual encounters' that 'do not add up to an explanatory theory of the phenomena under study' (p. 245), the analyst attempts to arrive at generalizations by looking into relatively large-scale data. Moreover, the analysts apply the cue-based approach, in which the listener is also assumed to have used different cues in the input to help decide how to build an interpretation (Jurafsky, 2004) and look for co-occurrence regularities to reach conclusions. It is in this way that the discursive and cue-based approaches are combined to address politeness1 and politeness2.

Furthermore, this study follows the corpus driven approach, which demands that the approach to impoliteness be exploratory and data-driven. Therefore, it aims to present how the linear steps of research should be replaced by a cyclic pattern. As discussed in this chapter, the cyclic approach to research requires exploration rather than verification. The researcher who approaches the data within the framework of the CDL approach will take a different route from forming a theory in the beginning of the analysis and verifying that (pre-formulated and existing) theory. She/he will start with tentative questions and a review of existing theories but once the extraction level is completed, she/he will revise the research questions and reconsider the existing theory in the light of the new insights. The insights may answer different research questions from what the research started out with and may bring out new theoretical models and implications. Therefore, the research questions need to be revisited and theoretical issues the insights bring forth should be included in the discussion of existing theories This cyclic process, i.e., going backwards from collated data to develop the theory or the framework of the analysis level to be applied is of fundamental importance for impoliteness research carried out in corpus linguistics since the natural data a corpus offers will always bring out new findings that do not fit the pre-formulated assumptions. The cyclic process of going backwards from collated data to develop a theory requires *tentativeness* in terms of the research questions with which the analyst starts the study. Considering the research questions *tentative* means that the researcher is willing to revise the questions later as the study unfolds. It is fundamental in a corpus driven approach applied in studies with natural data since if/when the findings from the data do not fit any existing theories, they will in fact be bringing new dimensions to be explored and reveal answers to questions which the analysts did not have in mind in the beginning. Therefore the research questions are revisited in Chapter 5 and discussed further in the light of insights the analyst thinks is happening. Consequently, value-laden terms like "interruption" are avoided' (Wooffitt, 2005:164).

CHAPTER 4

Impoliteness in Conversation: British English and Turkish

4.1 An Overview

This chapter analyzes the data of and about impoliteness extracted from the BNC and the STC. The extracts were selected through the method explained in detail in Chapter 3. Since this study is corpus driven, while analysing the extracts, no one singular theory or model was adopted. The data are discussed in light of extant concepts and theories on impoliteness and notions and concepts raised by the data analysis in relation to existing theories have been examined as the data required. Additional analytical methods, such as corpus and semantic analysis are employed where a further exploration is necessary. For instance, the discussion of *bi* in Turkish in an extract pulled from the STC required a frequency analysis of the context from a different corpus. Since the BNC and the STC are different types of corpora (see Section 3.4), the format of the extracts are different. Therefore, the extracts are discussed as much as the corpora allowed (see Section 1.5).

4.2 Impoliteness in the BNC

In this section, the examples that are extracted from the BNC will be discussed and analysed. The analysis, which is corpus driven, will be related to the discussion of impoliteness in the field and, later in the following chapter, will be compared to the data extracted from the STC to theorize about what impoliteness models should take into consideration.

In the extract below, the participants are playing cards and they are aware that they are being recorded. Considering the procedure with which the BNC data were collected and that participants were informed either in the beginning or after being recorded that their speech would be transcribed, the utterance 'I added that for the old tape, you know?' makes it obvious that in the context above, the participants already knew they were being recorded. This piece of information is noteworthy as it serves an important function for PSOGV to save face later in the conversation. When the background information supplied by the co-text is analysed, it is clear that PSOGU and PSOGT are playing as partners against PSOGV and PSOGM.

Extract 1.

(Text ID: KCP, conversations recorded by PSOGM)

(PSOGU) We've got three hands to their two, yeah.
(PSOGV) Yeah psychological warfare!
(PSOGT) Don't want to get too big they won't know how to spell psychological-el!
(PSOGU) Psychological.
(PSOGM) Psychological!
(PSOGU) You get your dozen and I'll get my four
(PSOGV) I added that for the old tape, you know?
(PSOGT) Did you?
(PSOGV) Mm rather than being monosyllabic.
(PSOGT) Monosyllabic... oh!... Oh God, not [???]
(PSOGM) [laugh]
(PSOGV) Right let's keep this under control!

An interesting conversation takes place as PSOGV likens the competition in the game to psychological warfare. PSOGT, who is a member of the other team, returns the comment with 'Don't want to get too big they won't know how to spell psychological-el,' which sounds to the other two players as if it was meant to refer to PSOGU and PSOGM since they both respond with 'psychological.' What has been described above is illustrated below with a visual schema in a sequence (1, 2, 3). PSOGU, PSOGT PSOGV, PSOGM are represented by U, T, V, M respectively in the bubbles of the two teams and the speech bubbles filled in with the participants' utterances.

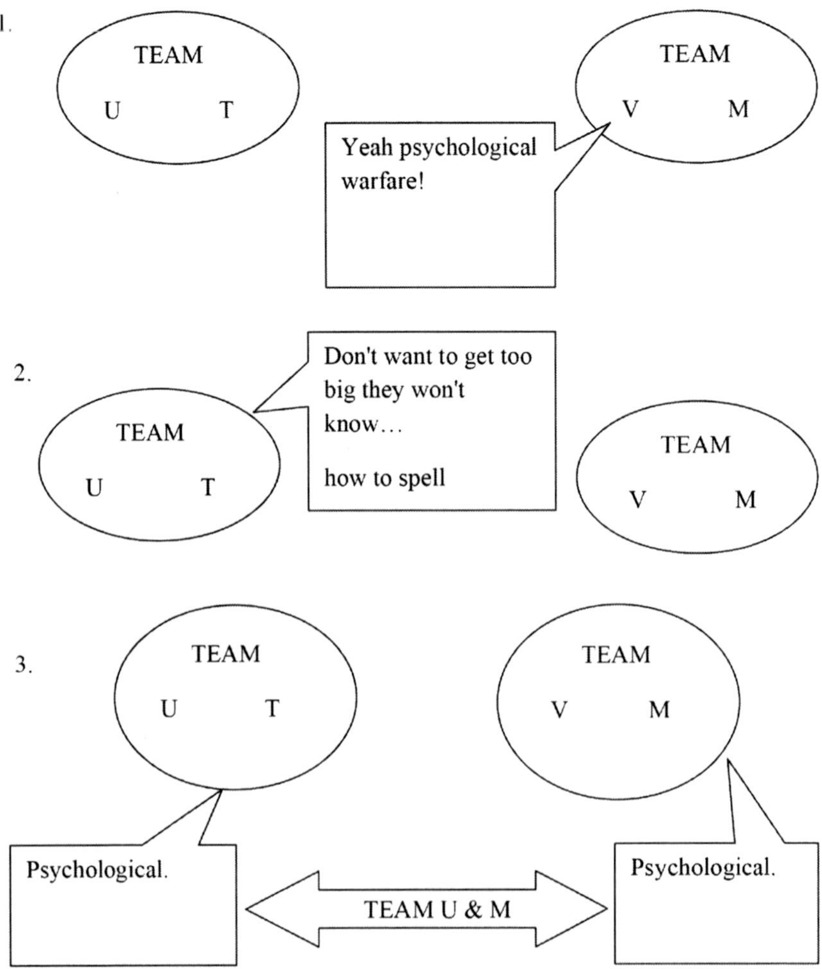

Figure 4.1. Membership categorization and face unfolding in interaction

What is noteworthy here is that V and T are members of different teams and are expected to behave in accordance with their team partners. However, V's comment in 1 triggers a comment from T, which in turn reveals that T and V have made an alignment and have formed an alliance. Therefore, when U replied in 3 with the utterance 'psychological', it confirms that T's comment with pronoun 'they' was perceived to have been addressed to U and M. M joins in with U and forms another alliance against team V and T. In other words, the expected behaviour shaped by the commitment of the membership of a team in the beginning is redefined and reconstituted as the interaction unfolds and the turning point is 2, in the sequence illustrated above. PSOGV is the first speaker to mention the word psychological, 'Yeah psychological warfare!' When PSOGT replies, 'Don't want to get too big they won't know how to spell psychological-el!' the utterance is ambiguous as 'they' could refer to 'the people who are recording and will later be transcribing' or to the other two participants PSOGU and PSOGM, who are most probably in the other group playing cards. 'Getting too big' implies that the subject of the utterance is already very big, in an idiomatic sense, compared with what it is directed at, and creates a scalar relationship. With the intensifier 'too,' the utterance widens the distance; however, this distance is not flat but scalar and hierarchical. That is why indicating that spelling the word psychological would be too hard for 'them' is an insult. PSOGU and PSOGM's rejoinder, 'they won't know how to spell psycho-logical-el!' by repeating the word psychological (most probably spelling the word) is to prove that they know how to spell it. The fact that they wanted to prove they can spell the word indicates that for them, in the utterance, 'they won't know how to spell psychological-el!' the pronoun 'they' refers to PSOGU and PSOGM themselves and not the BNC transcribers. When PSOGV realizes how PSOGU and PSOGM took the comment, she/he attempts to clarify why she/he used the word psychological, which is apparently not expected to be used in this context, by saying 'I added that for the old tape, you know,' which is meant to clarify the ambiguity of what 'they' referred to, that is, to the transcribers.

The misunderstanding with the pronoun 'they' creates a different frame for indexicality and creates a different membership organization which in turn pushes PSOGV to point out what 'they' in fact meant to refer to 'the old tape.' This correction offered, in fact, functions as a metapragmatic comment to repair the face attack PSOGV encountered after having performed: (1) violation of membership organization through an utterance which creates a different indexicality; and (2) an insult directed at two other members, which in turn damages his/her own face and so triggers an implicit apology, 'I added that for the old tape, you know.' This comment from PSOGV also serves the purpose of easing the tension present. At this point, PSOGT feels obliged to save his/her own face by saying 'Did you,' implying that he did not realize it and thus he said, 'they won't know how to spell psychological-el.'

The discussion on membership in this extract brings out two related concepts; indexicality and membership categorization, discussed in the literature in relation to face and impoliteness theories. Ruhi (2010) discusses the constitutive role of face in interaction and the role of indexicality. She (2010) argues that:

> [f]ace is a Janus-like indexical concept which categorizes the self-in-
> interaction, as it indexes and is indexed by (linguistic) acts, and features of
> underlying conceptualizations of social practices relevant to the interaction.
> According to this understanding of face, affective responses, such as pride,
> liking, solidarity, disassociation, embarrassment or resentment, and other
> orientations to face derive from (perceived) categorizations emerging in the
> unfolding interaction. (p. 2131)

Her argument is informed by Garfinkel (1967) and Sacks' (1986, 1989) proposals of indexicality and membership categorization. In her article, 'Face as indexical category in interaction,' Ruhi (2010) explains how Sacks (1989) describes membership categorization. It is 'a very central machinery of social organization' and that a person can be categorized in an indefinite number of ways (Sacks quoted in Ruhi 2010:2134). The example Ruhi (2010) gives from Sacks (1989:330, 335) to explain membership categorization further is a story produced by a two year-old baby: 'The baby cried. The mommy picked it up.' Here, 'crying' categorizes 'baby' as a 'stage in life,' but the category *baby* is also a categorization device in the notion of 'family' so that the 'mommy' is inferred to be 'the mommy of the baby' and this dynamic interpretation is a 'membership categorization device (MCD)' (see, Sacks, 1986). Ruhi (2010) examines photographs taken at a wedding ceremony together with the video recording as 'parallel documents,' illustrating background events for membership categorization and proposes that 'face is an inherently indexical concept that categorizes the social self in terms of its attributes *vis à vis* categorizing(s) of others' (p. 2144).

With the same line of thought in mind, Ruhi (2010) gives a further example from the field notes on face and (im)politeness in Turkish discourse before discussing how photographs show 'underlying social practices and participants' (linguistic) acts co-index each other, thereby rendering an accounting of face that is entrenched in features of situated interaction' (p. 2133). The example is a recon-structed dialogue between two participants, Aynur and Canan (names used as pseudonyms). Aynur and Canan are close friends and Canan, who has applied for a scholarship, breaks the good news to Aynur that she has won the scholarship. Aynur congratulates her by saying 'I am so happy for you' (*Senin adına çok sevindim*). Later at an interview, to a question prompted by Ruhi (2010), Aynur talks about her negative evaluations of Canan's reply, two of which are 'Canan wasn't really so happy' and 'Canan lacked warmth.' Ruhi (2010) points that:

> For Aynur, the expression indexes Canan's assessment of Aynur's accom-
> plishment, her affective response to this accomplishment, and her relationship
> to Aynur. Taking face to provisionally be related to self, Aynur's comments

suggest that her face was not constituted in the interaction in accordance with her understanding of what is appropriate in this setting. Given the fact that Aynur's comments crucially rely on her expectations, face becomes not only co-constituted but also constitutive of interaction. (pp. 2132–33)

Also based on Schlenker and Pontari's (2000) understanding of self-presentation, like Ruhi (2008), Spencer-Oatey (2007) pointed out this understanding has fundamental implications for studies on face and (im)politeness mainly because: (1) 'accounting for face in a manner that corresponds to participant interpretations is a complex task, as face and self-presentational concerns are very often background events' (Ruhi, 2010); (2) face is an indexical, categorical concept pointing to the self-in-interaction (Ruhi, 2005; Ruhi and Işık-Güler 2007, Ruhi, 2010); and (3) indexing features influence how participants make evaluations of face phenomena in interaction (Ruhi, 2010).

This example is also closely related to Spencer-Oatey's (2000) Equity and Association rights in her Rapport Management Model. Rapport management consists of three interconnected aspects: the management of face, the management of sociality rights and obligations and the management of interactional goals. For Spencer-Oatey, face is similar to how Goffman (1967:5) defines it: 'the positive social value a person effectively claims for himself [*sic*] by the line others assume he has taken during a particular contact' (quoted in Spencer-Oatey, 2000:13). The management of sociality rights and obligations are about social expectancies, meaning that they reflect people's concerns about fairness and appropriateness of behaviour. Interactional goals are the tasks people have when they interact with each other (Spencer-Oatey, 2000:14). What is important about perceived sociality rights and obligations is that people develop a sense of behavioural expectations and in cases where these expectations are met differently or not met at all, interpersonal relationships are influenced. She summarizes the bases of perceived sociality rights and obligations under three headings: (1) contractual/legal agreements and requirements; (2) explicit and implicit conceptualizations of roles and positions; (3) behavioural conventions, styles and protocols. She expands the last heading by giving an example: work groups, for instance, usually develop conventions for managing team meetings on issues such as who sits where and whether or not where they sit should depend on their status or role. Although the first basis, related to contractual/legal agreements and requirements, is more rigid, it is possible that these agreements and requirements were generated as a result of partial normative behaviour. Not surprisingly, the normative behaviour is what frequently or typically takes place in a context but these norms may not be arbitrary:

> They may reflect efficient strategies for handling practical demands, and they may also be manifestations of more deeply held values. For example, conventions in relation to *turn-taking and rights to talk* (emphasis mine) at business meetings are partly a reflection of the need to deal effectively with the matters at hand, but they are also likely to reflect more deeply-held beliefs about hierarchy and what is socially appropriate behaviour for a given role-relationship. In other words, people typically hold value-laden beliefs about the principles that should underpin interaction. (Spencer-Oatey, 2000:16)

Spencer-Oatey and Jiang (2003) call these beliefs Sociopragmatic Interactional Principles (SIPs), two of which are equity and association. These two principles are fundamental to expand on since they are the principles that link both Culpeper's (2010, 2011b) and Bousfield's (2008) models to Spencer-Oatey's Rapport Management model.

Spencer-Oatey (2000) describes equity as the fundamental belief that we expect to be treated fairly because we believe that 'we are all entitled to personal consideration from others, we are not unduly imposed upon, that we are not unfairly ordered about and that we are not taken advantage of or exploited' (p. 16). Two components of the equity principle are cost-benefit and autonomy-imposition. They reflect the extent to which we perceive the relationships as costly or imposing, with the basic assumption that costs and benefits and autonomy should be in balance. While equity is about the concept of fairness, association is about social involvement. There are two aspects of this principle: interactional involvement-detachment and affective involvement-detachment. The former is the belief that we are entitled to have an appropriate amount of conversational interaction with the others and the latter is the belief that we share an appropriate amount of concerns, feelings and interests.

In the extract when PSOGT replies, 'don't want to get too big, they won't know how to spell psychological-el!' the utterance 'don't want to get too big' brings to mind the idiomatic expression 'too big for your boots.' If someone is too big for his/her boots, it means he or she is conceited and has an exaggerated sense of his/her self-importance. As discussed above, 'getting too big' implies that the subject of the utterance is already full of himself/herself, in an idiomatic sense, compared with what the utterance is directed at, and creates a scalar relationship. With the intensifier 'too,' the utterance widens the distance but this distance is not flat but rather scalar and hierarchical. Therefore, indicating that spelling the word psychological would be too hard for 'them' is an insult for the people who are referred to. It is the reason why this utterance with its implications indicates a violation of the Equity Rights of the other members of the group because it is costly to their face in interaction. Another interesting point about the reply, 'Don't want to get too big, they won't know how to spell psychological-el!' is that it also forms a violation of the association rights as it detaches the people 'they' refer to and prevents their social involvement in the group. It is more than possible that the PSOGT becomes aware of the misunderstandings and makes the comment, 'I added that for the old tape, you know?' to restore the membership organization and repair the friction in interaction.

Overall, in this extract what is observed in terms of the research questions (i.e., what triggers impoliteness, what strategy is used, how is impoliteness countered, and the role of the countering strategy) is as follows. It seems that PSOGV and PSOGT, despite being in different teams while playing cards, form a new alliance against membership organization background assumptions, which triggers impoliteness along with the utterance 'don't want to get too big they won't know how to spell psychological-el,' which functions as an insult strategy. As a result of being insulted, PSOGU and PSOGM form a new alliance to protect themselves from the face attack and attempt to disprove the inadequacy implied by the insult while they both reply 'psychological.' This countering strategy in turns brings out an outcome as a repair strategy: PSOOGV says 'I added that for the old tape, you know?' and tries to repair the impoliteness perceived.

Extract 2.

(Text ID: KCP, conversations recorded by PSOGM)

This extract is a short piece of family conversation and the speakers are exchanging opinions on TV programs, which later turns into a discussion. Eventually the tension generates implicational impoliteness.

> (GU) She knew a lot of telly.
> (GU) Neighbours
> (GM) Oh!
> (GU) and bloody Coronation Street and all that crap!
> (GM) Ooh!
> (GT) Ooh!
> (GU) You'd hear all that!
> (GV) And don't say crap, that's a very good program!
> (GM) What is? I
> (GV) Coronation
> (GU) Coronation
> (GV) Str
> (GM) Oh what a load of dip!
> (GV) I lo, I've recorded whatever's on tonight, is it Eastenders?
> (GV) K Y T V I've got on tonight recorded that.
> (GU) S H I T more like!

GT laughs

> (GM) Yeah.
> (GV) K Y T V is very good, K Y T V.
> (GT) Hang on! *(laughing)*
> (GT) K Y T V, what's that?
> (GM) I didn't think you'd be a Coronation Street addict.
> (GT) No, I wouldn't!
> (GV) The best people are.
> (GV) Princess Anne.
> (GT) Well it is the biggest load of rubbish, people don't really live
> (GV) No, very good acting
> (GT) like that
> (GM) hmm
> (GV) No one said they did
> (GT) Well it isn't even good acting
> (GM) That's enough
> (GV) It's very good
> (GM) When we are on the

In this conversation when GU says that 'she knew a lot of telly' she is criticizing the person, which is why she gives the names of two programs and ends her comments with 'and all that crap', which functions as an intensifier for her dislike of the programs. When GV disagrees 'And don't say crap, that's a very good program!' she uses another modifier 'very good' to express how much she likes the program. The acronym for the name of the channel, KYTV, is mimicked by GU and echoed as SHIT in an offensive word 'shit.' This is how impoliteness comes to surface. However, GV replies 'K Y T V is very good, K Y T V' repeating the channel, reinforcing the acknowledgment, and echoing the mimicry SHIT back to its place. When the third speaker GT joins in and says 'No, I wouldn't!' be a *Coronation Street* addict, GV replies 'The best people are. Princess Anne.' GV implies that GU and GV are not among those best people, and thus, GV is impolite in return.

This example illustrates Culpeper's (2011b) second form-driven strategy for non-conventionalized implicational impoliteness: mimicry and echoic mention. He defines mimicry as 'a caricatured re-presentation' (p. 161). Referring to Goffman (1974:539), he points out that quoting is part of mimicry. When someone quotes 'too much,' for instance all the prosodic features of the speaker, the quoter becomes 'suspect' (p. 161). Culpeper (2011b) broadens Sperber and Wilson's (1995) mimicry and echoic mention and explains the tuning mimicry as such:

> First, on a recognition of the behaviour as an echo; second, on an identifi-
> cation of the source of the behaviour echoed, third, the recognition that
> the source of behaviour is a characteristic of the identity of the speaker who
> gave rise to it, and fourthly on a recognition that the speaker's attitude to the
> behaviour echoed is one of rejection or disapproval. (p. 161)

With this explanation in mind, the facts that in this conversation SHIT is spelled in letters s, h, i, t, just like the proper name for the TV channel, KYTV, and is written in capital letters in the script indicate that it is uttered to echo KYTV as SHIT TV and is uttered to reject the comment that the channel is good. It is an echoic mention and is an example of implicational impoliteness for taking the clues discussed into consideration. In this example, extracted from the BNC, which is a written corpus (as opposed to the STC which is bimodal, both with its written and audio components) the way the utterance SHIT is scripted provides enough context for the conclusion that the example reflects implicational impoliteness. This extract also exemplifies a case for face as an indexical concept (Ruhi, 2010). When the participant GU indexes the viewers of the program *Coronation Street* and the KYTV watchers under the same negative membership, GV adopts the tactic and indexes herself together with other viewers under a positive membership by saying the best people and Princess Anne are *Coronation Street* addicts.

However, this strategy does not seem to be effective to end the discussion since GT continues showing dislike to GV's taste repeatedly with 'people don't really live like that' and 'it isn't even good acting.' GV, in return tries to protect her face that has been attacked a couple of times so far and in front of other parties, responds with 'no one said they did' and 'no, very good acting' by offering counterarguments that did not really get GT to stop impoliteness. Interestingly, in the end, a third party, GM, who has agreed with GT that the program is bad by saying 'I didn't think you would be a *Coronation Street* addict' decides to end the impoliteness first very directly through a silencer 'that is enough' then by a topic change 'when we are on the (...).' This indicates that in interaction, participants try to protect their own faces when they encounter impoliteness; however, other participants who are witnessing the impoliteness may also want to stop impoliteness since they feel it is their face as well that is being attacked. A plausible explanation for this is that people want others to have a positive opinion of them, and not stopping impoliteness when they witness other people suffering from it gives a negative impression.

Overall, in this extract, impoliteness is triggered by showing strong dislike to someone's taste by the utterance 'SHIT TV more like,' which is a face attack. The strategy is insult, echoed and implied with the offensive word 'shit.' In return, to protect her face, GV, who is insulted follows the counter strategy of excluding herself from the members of the group by saying 'the best people are (*Coronation*

Street addicts)' and indexes herself with a new group of people,(e.g. 'Princess Anne') as well as putting forward two more counter arguments. However, the impoliteness is brought to an end by a third party who uses a silencer and offers a topic change followed by the impoliteness.

Extract 3.

(Text ID: KBB, conversations recorded by PSO35)

In this extract, a husband (PSO3S), and a wife (PSO3T) are having a daily conversation which gradually becomes tense and ends with impoliteness. In the end, PSO3T changes the topic by starting to talk about what Jackie bought: a Walkman. The rest of the conversation, which is not given here as part of the extraction discussed, gives away this information.

> (PSO3T) I shouldn't miss the pigeons all that much, I don't mind the blackbird and the thrush and the robin but and a few starlings but I don't like many pigeons about the garden.
> (PSO3S) They're too dirty.
> (PSO3T) They're not.
> (PSO3S) Yes they are.
> (PSO3T) Are you very bread hungry, toast hungry?
> (PSO3S) Oh no I'm not hungry at all
> (PSO3T) Well you should be.
> (PSO3S) [???]
> (PSO3T) Well you didn't have much after your dinner yesterday did you?
> (PSO3S) I don't know why you always have so many procedures [???] remain in [???] does it?
> (PSO3T) Don't be silly.
> (PSO3S) We're not going to go out at all then today?
> (PSO3T) Not in this fog. And I think it's freezing, the pantry was like an ice box.... I know there's no frost on the cars but it must still be cold.
> (PSO3S) What was like an ice box?
> (PSO3T) The pantry...I mean I
> (PSO3S) Well that's because the garage
> (PSO3T) I know I know but er
> (PSO3S) You must have had the window open.
> (PSO3T) I didn't. It's just ever so cold.
> (PSO3S) Quite cold is the phrase.
> (PSO3T) What did you say?
> (PSO3S) I said quite cold is the phrase, not ever so cold.
> (PSO3T) Is it? Oh. I stand corrected.

(PSO3S) You'll have to go back to the nursery.
(PSO3T) You, you'd like to go back to school. At your age.
(PSO3S) I'd show the kids a thing or two.
(PSO3T) You might… Apparently Jackie's got…
(PSO3S) What?

This conversation is interesting in that when the adjacency pairs are analysed, a very tense sequence comes up. Below is the chart that presents the pattern of the turns and the tension the sequence creates (Table 4.1).

Table 4.1. The analysis of adjacency pairs in the BNC Extract 3

Opinion (1)	I don't like many pigeons about the garden
Strong Opposite opinion (2)	They're too dirty.
Disagreement (3)	They're not.
Strong Disagreement (4)	Yes they are.
Change in topic, Strong assumption (5)	Are you very bread hungry, toast hungry?
Definite negative answer (6)	I'm not hungry at all.
Directive based on the strong assumption (7)	Well you should be.
Conventionalized impoliteness (8) (Culpeper 2010, 2011b) Unpalatable question	I don't know why you always have so many procedures [???] remain in [???] does it?
Conventionalized impoliteness (9) (Culpeper 2010, 2011b) Dismissal	Don't be silly.
Change in topic (10)	We're not going to go out at all then today?
Opinion (11)	I think it's freezing, the pantry was like an ice box
Directive based on a strong assumption (12)	You must have had the window open.
Disagreement (13)	I didn't. It's just ever so cold.
Change in topic (language correction to previous utterance)	Quite cold is the phrase.
Question	What did you say?
Answer	I said quite cold is the phrase, not ever so cold.
Opinion	Is it? Oh. I stand corrected.
opinion	You'll have to go back to the nursery.
Disagreement (with partial repeat)	You, you'd like to go back to school. At your age.
Agreement-	I'd show the kids a thing or two.
Agreement/change in topic	You might…Apparently Jackie's got…
Question	What?

The pattern in the sequence shows how the tension in the conversation rises Opinions are met by disagreements (see numbers 3, 4 in the chart); strong assumptions that the couple makes, directed at each other (see numbers 5, 7, 12) are dismissed with definite negative answers (6, 13) or impoliteness (8); and impoliteness is confronted with impoliteness (13) in return. The chart also presents, in italics, the words, such as 'too,' 'very,' 'not ... at all,' 'always,' and 'so many,' which modify the message and increase the tension by adding emphasis to utterances. For instance, the fact that PSO3S disagrees by using 'too' in the utterance 'They are too dirty' makes the disagreement a strong one. When PSO3S replies 'I'm not hungry at all,' 'at all' adds an intense definiteness to the negativity of the answer. The question 'Are you very bread hungry, toast hungry?' is in fact already formulated based on a strong assumption with modifier 'very' and presupposes that the person is at least hungry if not very hungry. The strong assumption that PSO3T is making with 'very' is replied by a strong negative answer with 'not at all,' which reminds us of impoliteness in mimicry and the echoic mention in implicational impoliteness (Culpeper, 2011b, see Section 2.2 for discussion). The extremity of 'very' is echoed back in 'not at all.' In this example, PSO3T's assumption that PSO3S is hungry and expressing that with the adverb qualifier 'very' (indicating a high degree to the assumption) is the echoed behaviour. PSO3S's reply – the echo – that he is not hungry and expressing that with the adverb qualifier 'not (hungry) at all' indicates a very high degree of negative response to the assumption made by PSO3T. The markedness of the echo lies in the exaggeration on the expression 'not ... at all,' but it is not at this point in the interaction that further inferencing comes into play. The implied echoed behaviour is that PSO3T always has so many procedures expressed in 'I don't know why you always have so many procedures' and it becomes clear when this utterance takes place. With 'always' in this utterance, we see that the echoer, PSO3S, thinks of the implied echoed behaviour as a characteristic of the echoed, PSO3T. Clearly, PSO3T recognizes the negative attitude and replies, 'Don't be silly.'

The tension increases even more with the instances of impoliteness which are realized through conventionalized impoliteness in 8 and 9 in the form of an unpalatable question, 'I don't know why you always have so many procedures [???] remain in [???] does it?' and a dismissal functioning as a silencer as well, 'Don't be silly.' After this point in the conversation, a more complex example of impoliteness takes place:

> (PSO3T) I didn't. It's just ever so cold.
> (PSO3S) Quite cold is the phrase.
> (PSO3T) What did you say?

(PSO3S) I said quite cold is the phrase, not ever so cold.
(PSO3T) Is it? Oh. I stand corrected.
(PSO3S) You'll have to go back to the nursery.
(PSO3T) You, you'd like to go back to school. At your age.
(PSO3S) I'd show the kids a thing or two. [laugh]
(PSO3T) You might ... Apparently Jackie's got ...
(PSO3S) What?

PSO3S corrects PSO3T by pointing out that the expression she uses is not the 'correct' expression by saying 'Quite cold is the phrase.' When PSO3S asks 'What did you say?' we understand that there is a breakdown in communication. The reasons for the breakdown could be various: PSO3S might not have heard what PSO3T just said; she might not have understood what he was referring to; she might be challenging him to say what he just said one more time. Since the context does not provide any clues to the issue, it is not possible to make an interpretation here. However, the following lines supply enough information on how she perceives what PSO3T said later. When PSO3T says 'I said quite cold is the phrase, not ever so cold' PSO3S replies, 'Is it? Oh. I stand corrected.' PSO3T is very direct in the way he repeats the correction and PSO3S replies, with a very formal expression of surprise, 'Is it? Oh. I stand corrected.'

'I stand corrected' is an expression used in the meaning of 'to be set right as after an error in a statement of fact; to admit having been in error' or 'used to admit that something you have said or done was wrong.' PSO3T's manner is quite direct and PSO3S's manner is quite formal in return. Both of the speakers' manner of speech, one being very direct in his correction and other being very formal in her reply, generates a style shift. A mismatch between the pragmatic context of speech, which is the context of a conversation between a husband and a wife at home, and the manner occurs. Therefore, it creates a case for convention-driven implicational impoliteness (Culpeper, 2011b). PSO3S carries on his pointed criticism by saying, 'You'll have to go back to the nursery' in a directive. In fact, how PSO3S replies to that directive 'You'll have to go back to the nursery' proves that implicational impoliteness has reached the target as PSO3T replies 'You, you'd like to go back to school. At your age.' PSO3T meets the impoliteness by being impolite and pointing out her husband's age, which is 82, as the bibliographic data analysis gives at the BNC. Eighty-two is not a common age to go to school and in fact PSO3T is reminding him the impossibility of it by pointing out, by implication, that he is too old. Again because age 82 is generally considered not to be the age of attending a school, giving this information is not relevant to the point she is making by, 'You, you'd like to go back to school.' On the contrary, this piece of information points to the opposite idea that he cannot go to the school. Therefore, it flouts the maxim of relation. Moreover, both speakers already know this information, so PSO3T also flouts the maxim of quantity. Therefore, interpreting the exchange requires a complex web of inferencing and poses a strong case for sarcasm, teasing and implicational impoliteness (Culpeper, 2011b).

In this extract, disagreement, verbalized in different forms, has a great impact on how the conversation unfolds and ends. While discussing what a disagreement is, Locher (2004) quotes Waldron and Applegate (1994:4): disagreement is 'a form of conflict, because verbal disagreements are taxing communication events, characterized by incompatible goals, negotiation and the need to coordinate self and other actions.' She continues by explaining how disagreements are noteworthy for face issues. Since a disagreement indicates a conflict on a content level, it has the potential to create face concerns because it is difficult 'to get one's point across without seeming self-righteous' (p. 94). However, the discussion on the function of disagreements takes a different direction over time. Locher and Watts (2005), Angouri and Locher (2012), and Sifianou (2012) draw attention to the fact that disagreements can serve a variety of functions, including the ensuring of sociability and intimacy. Disagreements may 'contribute to face-aggravating, face-maintaining or face-enhancing effects' and the suggested way of approaching the discussion of disagreement in impoliteness studies is to examine 'how disagreement is enacted and achieved and what the effects of different renditions might be' (Angouri and Locher, 2012:2). As briefly touched upon in Section 2.2, disagreement has also been discussed as an adjacency pair (Locher 2004:95), requiring a first and a second part and a sequence of offering opinions. The adjacency pairs may not be completed in two turns: Kotthoff (1993:195) points out that disagreements are not simply accepted or rejected. They are likely to create longer sequences. Usually speakers of the disagreement in an interaction follow it up with a further contribution, 'These change specifications of context so that ensuing disagreements may become more and more explicit without mitigation' (Kotthoff, 1993:195 cited in Sifianou, 2012: 4).

The pattern of adjacency pairs observed in the conversation is:

Opinion-opposition-disagreement
Change in topic
Question-answer-opinion
Change in topic
(Unpalatable) question-answer (dismissal)
Change in topic:
Opinion-opinion-disagreement
Change in topic

Question-answer-opinion-opinion-disagreement-(sarcastic)   agreement-(sarcastic) agreement
Change in topic
Question....

In this pattern, we observe that the disagreements end up with a change in the topic except after the last change of topic, where sarcasm and implicational impoliteness may be creating more reaction. In this conversation, turns are not followed up further by speakers; therefore, disagreements do not initiate longer sequences. On the contrary, since they are not accompanied by initiators such as hesitations, requests for clarification, partial repeats, etc., the sequences are cut short. This in turn gives an intense feeling to the conversation. Short sequences in the extract aggravate face, not so much due to the conflict in the content but due to the limited length managed by the speakers' initiation of topic change. The topic change here acts like a silencer and is used as a way of stopping further communication. Locher (2004) points out that disagreements may have restrictive power on the 'addressees' action-environment' due to their 'sequential position' (p. 95). This extract brings a new dimension to this insight. It is not only disagreements' sequential position that has a restrictive power; it is also whether they open up the stage for further communication by being accompanied by the mentioned devices to initiate further communication. Pomerantz (1984:70, 74) distinguishes between 'strong' and 'weak' disagreements. She explains that when disagreements are used in a position to react to what has taken place previously, 'weak disagreement can be accompanied by a delay of dispreferred messages through hesitations, "no talk," requests for clarification, partial repeats, other repair initiators, turn prefaces etc. while strong disagreement usually occurs without these devices' (quoted in Locher, 2004:95). This distinction is noteworthy for an argument: what Pomerantz (1984) characterizes as 'strong' disagreement followed up by a change in topic, and ending in short sequences, aggravates face more. The argument that no linguistic expression is inherently polite or impolite (Fraser and Nolen, 1981; Eelen, 2001; Terkourafi, 2001; Watts, 2003; Spencer-Oatey, 2005; Haugh, 2007; Ruhi, 2008; Culpeper, 2010) is also valid for speech acts. Speech acts are not inherently polite or impolite. Angouri and Locher (2012.2) point out that what we are interested in is the study of disagreement in the context and the effect of that context from a CA point of view too, rather than its mere existence. It is also noteworthy that the disagreements that unfold in the extract are very much like a tit for tat strategy: one disagreement is an aggravator for the next disagreement adjacency pair. This creates a spiralling of impoliteness which seems to be increasing with each spiral. Further studies would need to delve into the spiralling effect of disagreement, face aggravation and impoliteness.

Overall, in this extract, impoliteness is triggered by being critical to and showing dislike of one speaker's use of language '*quite cold* is the phrase.' However, it is aggravated by the tension created by disagreement followed by sudden topic changes and an unpalatable question preceding the criticism. The impoliteness strategy is an insult since '*quite cold* is the phrase' implies an inadequacy in using language. The counter strategy is an ironical acknowledgment 'I stand corrected' followed first by irony 'you might show kids a couple of things at your age' and then offering a topic change. As mentioned in Section 1.5, the data retrieved from the BNC have not been checked against sound files, which makes it difficult to assess the full nature of the 'tone' (jocular, mock impoliteness, etc.) in the interaction. However, considering that the only annotational clue about the voice quality given in the extract in the BNC is '[laugh]' after (PSO3S) following his own utterance 'I'd show the kids a thing or two,' it is hard to arrive at the possibility that jocular tone is present in the extract.

Extract 4.

(Text ID: KBE, conversations recorded by PSO4B)

The following excerpt is not an instance of impoliteness but a discussion of why it is not is fundamental. In this excerpt, what would normally be considered as the conventionalized impoliteness formula (Culpeper, 2010, 2011b) is not perceived as impolite as it does not cause any friction in the communication. In fact, it serves an opposite purpose, which is to show warmth and friendliness, and therefore politeness.

In a gathering at home, PSODM, 29, is the host and the wife, PSODN is the cousin, 29, and a housewife, and PSODP is a friend, 32, and a housewife. PSODM asks the cousin PSODN if she is going out on Friday night. PSODN explains that a friend of hers, whose son she looks after until her friend comes home from work, suggested going out to Cardiff with two other girls, Sandra and Alison. She says she is not sure if she wants to go out to Cardiff with Alison and Sandra being 'like that.' We understand from the excerpt that her reservations about going out with the girls come from her uneasiness about her weight.

> (PSODM) You going out tomorrow are you?
> (PSODN) Oh I don't know
> (PSODM) Do you go out on a Saturday now?
> (PSODN) No I don't do I? It's not that I t I my friend come[...] cos I do have her little boy now straight from school, she pays for him to have a taxi from Endrodenny down to my house and I do have him until she finishes work and she said oh coming out tomorrow? I said oh yeah! I mean I wouldn't've

minded if she said come up the house like and she mentioned Cardiff but I've gone so fat I don't wanna go!
(PSODP) [yawning] Oh don't be so stupid woman.
(PSODN) Honestly that's what I think, I just don't wanna
(PSODM) You always look smart
(PSODP) Yes she does.
(PSODN) I, yeah but I d I no I, I'm fat and I don't wanna go. And that's how I feel.
Cos then she said oh Sandra are you coming? I thought no there's Alison like that, there's Sandra like that I thought oh no. Can't handle it.
(PSODM) I've got to find my keys now to get in.
(PSODN) I don't know, I'll see how I feel.
(PSODM) Oh well

The exchange sequence I would like to discuss in this excerpt is the following:

(PSOND).... I've gone so fat I don't wanna go!
(PSODP) [yawning] Oh don't be so stupid woman.
(PSOND) Honestly that's what I think, I just don't wanna
(PSODM) You always look smart
(PSODP) Yes she does.
(PSOND) I, yeah but I d I no I, I'm fat and I don't wanna go.

When the exchange is taken at the surface level, one can say that because PSOND's comment '... I've gone so fat I don't wanna go!' is returned with by PSODP '[yawning] Oh don't be so stupid woman,' PSODP is being impolite. PSODP's utterance can be considered as a conventionalized impoliteness formula which fits into condescension (Culpeper, 2011b) as in: '– [that] ['s/is being] [babyish/childish/etc.].' However, as how the conversation unfolds indicate, '[yawning] Oh don't be so stupid woman,' is not perceived to be impolite by PSOND. The reply coming from PSOND is an elaboration on the comment PSOND had just made about herself: 'Honestly that's what I think, I just don't wanna.' There are at least two reasons why '[yawning] Oh don't be so stupid woman' might not have been perceived as impolite: (1) the negative assertion PSOND makes about herself is replied with PSODP's condescension and so it implies a positive meaning and does not function as an insult; and (2) PSODP is following the politeness rules as, in a way, she is expected to say something to make PSOND feel better; the absence of such behaviour would be perceived as impolite (Culpeper, 2011b) because it fits into context-driven implicational impoliteness.

What is also interesting here is that, of all the options PSODP could choose from (e.g. don't be stupid), she chooses to say 'don't be so stupid woman,' where both 'so' and 'woman' have important functions.

'So' increases the intensity of the message similar to the words 'too, very, not … at all, always, so many,' which added to the tension in Excerpt 3 (see the discussion above). If the utterance 'don't be so stupid woman' had been perceived as impolite by PSOND, 'so' would have created the same impact as the words in Excerpt 3 and increased tension. However, within the very context, the absence of 'so' could have created tension. PSOND's utterance '… I've gone so fat I don't wanna go!' which comes after a long explanation suggests that this is a sensitive issue for her and she is very emotional about her appearance, at least for the time being. This intensity of how she feels about her looks right now requires a similarly intense answer which has to emphasize and stress that her behaviour is unreasonable. In other words, in order not to respond with a lack of warmth and friendliness to such an intense way of expressing emotions, PSODP exaggerates her reply with 'so' to PSOND. Not using 'so' would be a mismatch of the context and create an absence of expected behaviour and be impolite.

The other lexical item mentioned above as having a very important function is '… woman.' 'Woman'[1] creates an effect: the comment is not directed at the person and not personalized. That is why 'don't be so stupid woman' does not fit into the insult; personalized negative vocative or assertion as conventionalized impoliteness formula Culpeper (2010, 2011b) identified. 'Woman' in the utterance 'Oh don't be so stupid woman' puts a distance between the speaker and the hearer and in this way secures a perception from the hearer that the comment 'stupid' is not an insult because it is not personalized as it would be in 'don't be so stupid,' addressed to the hearer directly through the implication of 'you.' The act of yawning accompanies the utterance and despite its importance, its pragmatic effect is hard to interpret. Selting (2012) examines complaint stories and various ways storytellers employ to mitigate their complaints, annoyance, and anger or indignation. She found that different gestures – even laughter and smiling – are used 'to make interpretable "helplessness" or "cheekiness"' (p. 412). Perhaps if the conversation had a visual recording, further interpretations could have been offered about the yawning; whether it is genuine or mimicked and to what effect it is used.

While discussing genuine versus mock impoliteness, Culpeper (2011b) focuses on 'conventionalized impoliteness formulae used in contexts where contextual expectations of politeness are very strong' (p. 207). He gives an example to illustrate such a case:

1. The effect of 'woman' can be different in different contexts for the very reason that it depersonalizes the person it addresses.

[Lawrence Dallaglio, former England Rugby captain, describing the very close family in which he grew up].

As Francesca and John left the house, she came back to give Mum a kiss and they said goodbye in the way they often did. 'Bye, you bitch,' Francesca said. 'Get out of here, go on, you bitch,' replied Mum.

It's in the Blood: My Life (2007),
from an extract given in *The Week*, 10/11/07

Culpeper (2011b:207) points out that in this example both a conventionalized insulting vocative, 'you bitch' and a conventionalized dismissal, 'get out of here' are used. However, this describes a loving family relationship as opposed to a hate situation and therefore this is at odds with the context. He explains that '... the recontextualisation of impoliteness in socially opposite contexts reinforces opposite effects, namely, affectionate, intimate bonds amongst individuals and the identity of that group' and that the example illustrates the use of mock impoliteness. This acknowledgment demands a discussion of contexts where impoliteness is normalized, legitimized or neutralized. In discussing these three different processes, Culpeper (2011b) states that normalization and legitimizing are similar in the sense that, for both of them, impoliteness is of a positive value. However, for legitimizing, an institutional structure is required such as in army training and/or interrogations (p. 216). Neutralization, on the other hand, is rather different from the others as in the case of mock impoliteness discussed earlier.

Watts (2003) discusses the neutralization process in relation to 'sanctioned aggressive face work' and states that certain types of interaction, such as those which take place between family members, close friends, or in competitive forms of interaction (such as in political debates or in hierarchical structures such as in the military services) are sanctioned and so 'neutralise face-threatening or face-damaging acts' (pp. 131–2). Culpeper (2011b) considers 'sanctioned' closely related to legitimizing but fundamentally different from neutralizing. He argues that in the military service for instance, in army training, impoliteness is legitimized but is not neutralized because natural data indicate that recruits still take offence, and that contestants report embarrassment and humiliation in *The Weakest Link*, which Culpeper (2011b) studied to collect data for impoliteness. The use of 'woman' in the extract above could also be reflective of the awareness that even in a context where an impoliteness formulae would be neutralized, the speaker of the utterance prefers to de-personalize the conventionalized impoliteness formulae against the risk of being perceived as impolite with the comment. The extract below illustrates a case where a conventionalized impoliteness formula does not become neutralized and therefore generates impoliteness.

Extract 5.

(Text ID: KBM, conversations recorded by PS1BL)

In extract 5, the conversation takes place among three friends who are students. They are talking about a deadline and the length of an assignment. It is understood from the co-text that the assignment is due after Easter but if it is to be handed in before, the paper will be marked and checked for the students to revise and submit after Easter. It should apparently cover six items, and as in one of the participants' comments below, each item should be expanded upon with approximately five hundred words. One of the participants, PS1BR, has decided to hand the assignment in the next day and get feedback before he submits its final version. When PS1BR says he/she has written one thousand words, PS1BL points out that it will not be enough and says 'You have wi write about five hundred words just to cover each point. You have to give loads and loads like.' PS1BR's reply to this is a conventionalized impoliteness formula; 'Fuck off!' PS1BL channels it back to the speaker PS1BL and directly addresses the speaker with the same conventionalized formula in the utterance 'You do!' with a more intense tone as in 'You do!' by implication 'you fuck off' is more personalized than 'Fuck off.' To this reply PS1BR's response 'Sod that!' is noteworthy since the response still includes another offensive word 'sod,' which is 23rd on the list of offensive words in the year 2000 (see Section 3.6 for list of offensive words from Millwood-Hargrave, 2000), but phrased in very depersonalized and distancing language as framed in pronoun 'that' in 'Sod that!'

> (PS1BN) Did we have to hand it in?
> (PS1BL) No. You hand it in before Easter if you want it marked and checked. But after Easter you just wanna hand it in and just sod it. I don't care.
> (PS1BN) I'll bring it after Easter. Just hand it in on time.
> (PS1BR) I'm gonna hand mine in tomorrow.
> (PS1BL) What the first? Bollocks!
> (PS1BR) Good as it'll ever be.
> (PS1BL) Six hundred words is nowhere near enough. Six thousand'll be about close enough. You should see what he says.
> (PS1BR) But I'm gonna one thousand
> (PS1BL) You a
> (PS1BR) words, but that's all I'm
> (PS1BL) yo
> (PS1BR) gonna do.
> (PS1BL) You have wi write about five hundred words just to cover each point. You have to give loads and loads like.

(PS1BR) Fuck off!
(PS1BL) You do!
(PS1BR) Sod that!
(PS1BL) have you do-
(PS1BN) What meat?
(PS1BL) [laugh]
(PS1BR) yeah well
(PS1BN) [laughing] [???] [???] put meat for one of his answers !
(PS1BL) [laugh]
(PS1BR) what?
(PS1BL) [laugh]
(PS1BN) about five points, he's just put meat.

Culpeper (2011b) elaborates on neutralizing and comments that even in situations where impoliteness is meant to function as mock impoliteness and is neutralized there is no guarantee that the target will not take offence. Culpeper (2011b:218) argues that neutralized impoliteness may still cause offence as impoliteness is difficult to see in context, which is what essentially neutralizes the negativity of impoliteness. He explains that a possible reason could be that people do not usually pay attention to the context since people have a tendency to pay more attention to negative stimuli, which in this case is the conventionalized impoliteness formula 'fuck off!'. Culpeper (2011b:218) cites Pratto and John (2005 [1991]) and reports that, '[they] argue that negative stimuli attract greater attention because of the inherent threat they pose, a prediction they label the 'automatic vigilance hypothesis':

> [People] assign relatively more value, importance, and weight to events that have negative, rather than positive, implications for them. In decision-making, potential costs are more influential than potential gains (e.g. Kahneman and Tversky, 1979). In impression formation, negative formation is weighted more heavily than positive information (e.g. Anderson, 1974; Fiske, 1980; Hamilton and Zanna, 1972). In non-verbal communication, perceivers are more responsive to negatively toned messages that are positive ones (Fordi, Lamb, Leavitt, and Donovan, 1978). Quite generally, then, 'losses loom larger than gains.' (Kahneman and Tversky, 1984:348, quoted in Culpeper, 2011b:218 from Pratto and John, (2005 [1991])

In other words, for mock impoliteness to occur, the context and the effects of what is included in the context (e.g. closeness of the participants, the poetic effect, etc.) compete with the impoliteness signal and neutralize it. Nevertheless, it is worth pointing out that there may be cases in which conventional impoliteness is taken as mock impoliteness or teasing and the target of the impoliteness still responds. In such cases, by responding, the target shows that they are competent speakers who can manage their face. However, at times, as is illustrated in the extract, the context and the effects of what is included fail to achieve the task of neutralizing impoliteness.

Overall, in this extract, what triggers impoliteness is the use of offensive language, 'fuck off,' which is itself impolite because it functions as an insult. The counter-strategy is impoliteness in the same phrase 'you do (fuck off)' in a more personalized form since it starts with 'you.' This strategy works and PS1BR depersonalizes the insult 'fuck off' with 'sod that' where 'that' adds a new direction to the insult and the impoliteness comes to a closure. The participants then start talking about the same topic in a jocular manner, indicated by the laughs in the following turns the speakers take.

Extract 6.

(Text ID: KPW, conversations recorded by PS58H)

Extract 5 illustrates a case where 'fuck off!' is interpreted as impolite and does not become neutralized. The reasons are first, that there are grounds to believe people have a tendency to pay much more attention to negative stimuli (Pratto and John, 2005 [1991]) and second, that the context and the effects included did not allow for a contrary interpretation (Culpeper, 2011b). In addition to the points about the discussion of what might have created a context in which the expression 'fuck off!' is not neutralized, another point is the frequency of the context the expression is normally used in.

The idea of the frequency of the context is closely related to schema theory and to the related concepts such as frames, scripts, and scenarios. Culpeper (2011b) summarizes a schema as 'a structured cluster of concepts containing relatively generic information derived from experience, and is stored in semantic long-term memory' (p. 14). Levinson's (1992 [1979]) 'activity type,' his notion of 'inferential schemata' (1992:97), and Schank and Abelson's (1977:41) script echoes a similar argument. Schank and Abelson (1977:41) define script as 'A structure that describes appropriate sequences of events in a particular context ... Scripts handle stylised everyday situations. Thus, a script is a predetermined, stereotyped sequence of actions that defines a well-known situation' (quoted in Culpeper, 2011b:196). When Terkourafi (2005b) characterizes conventionalization as 'a relationship between utterances and context, which is a correlate of the (statistical) frequency with which an expression is used in one's experience of a particular context' (p.

213), her focus is also on the frequency of the expression and the frame it creates in a person's memory.

The extract (text ID: KPW) below is a conversation exemplifying a situation where an expression such as 'shut up!' creates tension due to the frequency with which it is usually used. PS58J, who is 15 and a student, is speaking to her sister, who is 18 and also a student, at a gathering in a friend's house.

> (PS58J) [laugh] What was I saying? I said, yeah, it's me, er my sister said that erm she feels [laughs] a man in Olympus Sports, I said erm, on a poster playing basket ball and he looked like you. Are you sure it's not you? I said, are you sure it's not you? What are you doing there? He goes [...] oh shut up, like that. And er, he yeah, yeah [...] he told me he could play basketball [...] it must be right cos he's got a nice chest and he went what? Like that and he started laughing [laugh] He said yeah, cos he said he'd got, I, I don't know what I said [...] don't say shut up like that and I [...] [laugh] don't tell me to shut up like that!
> (PS6SM) Do I say that?
> (PS58J) You always talk to people like that, what are you talking about? You're just high and mighty
> (PS6SM) Don't talk to me like that! I don't, I don't appreciate the way you're talking to me!
> (PS58J) Okay [...] don't you know when I'm joking?
> (PS6SM) No, I don't when you're joking because you don't say shut up to me [...] for you to say shut up.
> (PS58J) [...] I wa you mean you don't know when I'm joking or being serious. I'm being serious now, anyway [...]
> (KPWPSUNK) [...]
> (PS58J) Who could that've been?
> (PS6SM) I haven't got a clue.

At the end of his exhaustive corpus analysis carried out in the Oxford English Corpus (see Chapter 3), Culpeper (2011b) indicates that the expression 'shut up' is a conventionalized impoliteness formula which functions as a silencer. In fact, the tension is reinforced and intensified by a couple of more linguistic mismatches with the context and in the end, one of the participants retaliates and the other one has to restore the interaction by saying he/she was joking. The following is the description of what took place.

One of the participants, PS58J, reports a past event and what she/he had said to another person at the time. While reporting what he/she said, PS58J, criticizing that person, says, 'I, I don't know what I said [...] don't say shut up like that and I [...] [laugh] don't tell me to shut up like that' which immediately gets PS6SM to react and she/he asks, 'Do I say that?' Apparently, the reply, 'You always talk to people like that, what are you talking about? You're just high and mighty,' PS6SM receives from PS58J is not what is expected because it is responded with disapproval by PS6SM: 'Don't talk to me like that! I don't, I don't appreciate the way you're talking to me!' In the utterance 'You always talk to people like that, what are you talking about? You're just high and mighty,' there are certain face-attacking strategies used. First, the utterance is personalized as it utilizes the second person pronoun 'you.' Second, the booster 'always' placed in a generalization in a pointed criticism implied by 'like that,' which has a negative meaning retrieved from the co-text. Third, this pointed criticism comes in an unpalatable question, 'what are you talking about?' All of these uses of strategies block the inference that PS58J claims to have intended; 'Okay [...] don't you know when I'm joking?'

PS6SM eventually reminds PS58J that 'shut up' is not used in a context like this and cannot function as a joke. In layman's terms, when PS6SM says, 'No, I don't know when you're joking because you don't say shut up to me [...] for you to say shut up,' he/she confirms Culpeper's (2010, 2011b) finding that 'shut up' is a silencer and dismissal. The metapragmatic comment coming from PS6SM indicates that the boundary between politeness1 and politeness2 is not as precise as it is argued. PS6SM's reminder that 'shut up' is not appropriate falls both under politeness1, as it is the speaker's evaluation, and under politeness2, as it brings a theoretical dimension to the evaluation. This example suggests that there is parallelism between the layman's concept and current theoretical model of impoliteness that it is the context (Culpeper, 2011b) that determines whether it is linguistic expressions that generate impoliteness.

Overall, in this extract, impoliteness is triggered through showing dislike of someone's behaviour. When PS6SM points out that what PS58J is criticizing is a characteristic of PS58J as well, 'you always talk to people like that, what are you talking about? You're just high and mighty,' PS58J perceives this to be impolite and reacts to this insult. The counter strategy PS58J follows is an implied warning: 'don't talk to me like that! I don't, I don't appreciate the way you're talking to me!' It is a bald-on directive, which is followed by an emotive negative assessment of the remark PS6SM has made. The warning has an effect on PS6SM because she/he says 'okay [...] don't you know when I'm joking?' which is a denial in order to change the topic. Then PS58J brings the impoliteness to an end by taking the theme in another direction – probably to a sound in the situation – 'who could that've been?'

Extract 7.

(Text ID: KPH, conversations recorded by PS55T)

The extract below is a good example of the emotions generated by being exposed to impoliteness. It illustrates the psychology of the person attacked, especially when coercive power is executed. The extract is a conversation between two participants, one of whom, KPHPSUNK, reports an incident of impoliteness; one of the professors of the school calls her *slut* because she was chewing, apparently not gum but sweets, giving the reason that it is rude to eat in public and such behaviour gives a bad reputation to the school because she looks like a slut. KPHPSUNK tells of the event to her parents and the parents ask her to go and tell the professor's wife. The wife calls her and asks her to go see the professor and the professor apologizes. The way he apologizes sounds odd to KPHPSUNK, as he says he did not mean to insult her; he used the word *slut* as in *slovenly woman*, which to KPHPSUNK does not sound any better than *slut*. Later, she continues to report that her father, having seen the professor, swore at him by saying 'that's that fucking arsehole that called you a slut isn't it?' adding that her father sounded funny.

(PS55T) Yeah. He's such an arsehole. But I can't believe when he s called you a slut.

(KPHLC) What!

((KPHPSUNK) Oh my God at swimming!

(KPHLC) Called you a slut?

(PS55T) She was chewing, okay, and

(KPHPSUNK) I wasn't chewing gum though, I was eating sweets

(PS55T) no you were like eating or something mm

(KPHPSUNK) yeah.

(PS55T) and he goes God you're such a slut or something, got really aggressive.

(KPHPSUNK) He goes don't you know it's rude to eat in public. You girls lower the school down, you look like a slut, yeah? And I was standing there going. Oh God, I would've crawled into a hole for the rest of my life.

(PS55T) I, I was standing next to her, I was going Jesus Christ!

(KPHPSUNK) I know, everyone was just going then erm I told my m my er parents and my parents said to me go and tell your house master so I told. What a shit. told his wife and his wife went and had a go at him. I would, yeah. and then, and then [gap name] came up to me and said erm

(KPHPSUNK) He didn't. if you if you go and see this afternoon erm he would like to speak to you and I was like he should come and speak to me . Yeah! Yeah. and erm

(PS55T) So you went and saw him?
(KPHPSUNK) so I went and saw him and he goes I didn't mean it as a slut as, as in a promiscuous woman
(KPHPSUNK) [laugh]
(KPHPSUNK) so he goes, no he goes I, I mean it as a slovenly woman, like you're
(KPHPSUNK) [scream]
(KPHPSUNK) so much better!
(KPHPSUNK) He goes I didn't mean to insult you, oh no sir, right, yeah!
(PS55T) slovenly from time to time, yeah.
(KPHPSUNK) And then he goes, he goes erm it's, it gets erm it really gets to me when I think people are chewing around school, I don't know what to do to stop people and I wasn't chewing, yes well it looked like chewing, but I wasn't chewing!
(KPHPSUNK) Oh God it was so pathetic. But just to call anyone a slut is just so rude.
(PS55T) It's just so rude, I know.
(KPHPSUNK) I know you don't, especially an adult in this school calling someone I know.
(PS55T) They're not adults in this school, don't worry.
(KPHPSUNK) Oh yeah,
(KPHPSUNK) My dad, do you know what my dad said? My dad was, my dad walked straight, just past him, was like where you are and my dad was where my feet are
(PS55T) Yeah?
(KPHPSUNK) and he goes that's that fucking arsehole that called you a slut isn't it?
(KPHPSUNK) [laugh]
(KPHPSUNK) And I was like
(KPHPSUNK) [laugh] [laughing] can you say it any louder dad [laugh]
(KPHPSUNK) as well like er [laughing] he sounds so funny.

This extract illustrates what Culpeper (2011b) defines as coercive impoliteness. In order to explain the type of politeness, he first refers to Tedeschi and Felson's (1994) definition of coercive action, which is closely related to the notion of coercive impoliteness. According to them, coercive action is:

> [a]n action taken with the intention of imposing harm on another person
> or forcing compliance. Actors engaged in coercive actions expect that their

behaviour will either harm the target or lead to compliance, and they value one of these proximate outcomes. The value they attach to compliance or harm to the target arises from their belief about the causal relationship between compliance or harm and terminal values. There are many values that might be pursued through coercive means. For example, actors might value harm to the target because they believe it will result in justice, or they might value the target's compliance because they believe it will lead to tangible benefits. (Tedeschi and Felson, 1994:168)

What is of interest about the concept of the coercive actions is that Tedeschi and Felson (1994) categorize them into three: threats, punishments and bodily force. The meaning of threat is wider than its common understanding; a threat can be contingent or noncontingent. If it is contingent, the statement of the source clearly states the intention to impose harm on the target in case of nonconformity. A noncontingent threat, on the other hand, includes anything that the source believes the target does not want, as in the statement 'If you don't do what I want, then I will do X.' In other words, that X in the threat is harm that is 'usually intended to frighten or humiliate the target person' as in 'If you don't do what I want I will harm you in some way' (p. 170). They also point out that the threat can be tacit and implied, and multiple strategies can be used as a threat such as facial expressions, bodily posture and the phrasing of a sentence. Once the tacit threat is perceived, it is likely to achieve the same outcome as an explicit or contingent threat. Culpeper (2011b) does not elaborate on the definition of threat in his study of conventionalized impoliteness formulae and does not make a distinction between contingent and noncontingent threats. However, an acknowledgment of the distinction requires a deeper analysis of threats as a category of conventionalized impoliteness formulae, as a wider pool of linguistic and non-linguistic items retrieved from the context could bring out essential information about what people perceive as impolite and what impoliteness is. In the extract above, we only have the participant's report and her friend's agreement on how it happened:

(PS55T) She was chewing, okay, and
(KPHPSUNK) I wasn't chewing gum though, I was eating sweets
(PS55T) no you were like eating or something mm
(KPHPSUNK) yeah.
(PS55T) and he goes God you're such a slut or something, got really aggressive.
(KPHPSUNK) He goes don't you know it's rude to eat in public. You girls lower the school down, you look like a slut, yeah? And I was standing there going .Oh God, I would've crawled into a hole for the rest of my life.

The conventionalized impoliteness formulae, 'God you're such a slut' reported to have been uttered by the professor, falls into the category of insult as a negative vocative (Culpeper, 2010, 2011b). Combined with aggressiveness, it could also be perceived as a noncontingent threat if the distinction drawn by Tedeschi and Felson (1994) is acknowledged. This point adds to the complexity of the methodological approach to extract impoliteness from a corpus as formulaic expressions with all their variety may still fail to point out an instance of impoliteness in a corpus unless the whole co-text and the context is taken into consideration.

The close relationship between insults in any form, such as a negative vocative in the extract, and notions of punishment and harm are important for understanding what is taking place in this extract. Tedeschi and Felson (1994) define punishment similarly to how Kleinig (1973) does; punishment is an action performed with the intention of imposing harm on another person. For Tedeschi (1970), there are different types of harm; physical harm, such as punching and stabbing, and deprivation of sources as in robbery and social harm. Social harm damages the social identity of a person by lowering their status. It can be executed through insults, reproaches, sarcasm and impolite behaviour and impoliteness. Negative evaluations, mild reproaches and disagreements may be perceived as identity attacks even when they are not intended to be (Tedeschi and Felson, 1994:171). In the extract above, the target of the impoliteness KPHPSUNK comments on how she felt after the moment she was likened to a slut by the professor: 'Oh God, I would've crawled into a hole for the rest of my life.' The emotion she feels is embarrassment; her social identity face is being attacked and as a result social harm is being imposed.

The insult in the form of a negative vocative functioned as punishment and generated social harm by attacking KPHPSUNK's social identity face. Spencer-Oatey (2002) defines social identity face as the following:

> We have a fundamental desire for people to acknowledge and uphold our social identities or roles, e.g. as group leader, valued customer, close friend. Social identity face is concerned with the value that we effectively claim for ourselves in terms of social or group roles, and is closely associated with our sense of public worth. (p. 540)

Social identity face is also closely related to the beliefs about socially appropriate behaviour, which are also related to two principles of interaction: equity and association. KPHPSUNK thinks that the teacher is violating both her equity and association rights because he is socially punishing and harming her. This creates an imbalance in the cost-benefit principle and brings out a costly result for her.

She feels so embarrassed that she wants to delay her interactional and affective involvement with the society (see the utterance 'Oh God, I would've crawled into a hole for the rest of my life'). She wants to detach herself from the society but this is not a voluntary action; it has been imposed on her to behave that way. Her freedom to choose is taken away from her and her actions are restricted. It is worth noting that she expresses this complex chain of the violation of her rights through the emotion embarrassment.

Spencer-Oatey (2011) pointed out that although the role of emotions have always been implicitly discussed in relation to politeness theory (Brown and Levinson 1987; Lakoff, 1989; Ide, 1989; Leech, 1983; Goffman, 1967), there has been little research on the role of emotions as Culpeper (2011b) and Ruhi (2009a) call attention to. In her study (2011), Spencer-Oatey addressed this issue and took a deeper look into emotion and impoliteness through explicit metapragmatic emotion labels in interview data she collected as a project manager of four groups of teachers of different backgrounds and nationalities, namely British and Chinese. She used Shaver et al.'s (1987) five basic emotion prototypes – love, joy, anger, sadness and fear – to group emotions expressed during interviews under politeness and impoliteness categories. She found that the prototype emotion sadness had the largest number of references. There were 13 emotion labels used under this prototype: disappointed, embarrassed, full of pity, unhappy, demotivated, uncomfortable, depressed, distant, aimless, ashamed, offended, hurt, and sorry. This extract also illustrates a case for the need to study the role of emotions and confirms Spencer-Oatey's (2011) finding that embarrassment is closely related to impoliteness. A similar argument came earlier from Goffman (1967:6–8); there are feelings attached to face, such as feeling good, bad, hurt, embarrassed and chagrined (quoted in Spencer-Oatey, 2011:3568). However, there is one important methodological difference between the points made here with the extract and Spencer-Oatey's (2011). As part of her analytical procedure, Spencer-Oatey (2011) only used 'explicit metapragmatic emotion labels' to avoid imposing the analyst's point of view to the data interpretation:

> Clearly, the interviewees could express their emotion in ways other than selecting an emotion label (e.g. through intonation or through recounting an incident that implied, but did not explicitly state, an emotional reaction), but since that entails more subjective analyst interpretation and my aim was to take a first order approach (Eelen, 2001; Watts et al., 1992), I focused only on instances of use of explicit metapragmatic emotion labels.

The comment in the extract 'Oh God, I would've crawled into a hole for the rest of my life' is not of the kind of metapragmatic label she had in mind for the analytical procedure. Nonetheless, if it is agreed that this comment is highly reflective of the emotion label *embarrassment*, the comment would be very valuable for the researcher. This example indicates that in studying naturally-occurring conversations, metapragmatic comments on emotions may not appear in the form of emotion labels but in the form of idioms, multi-word expressions and conventional or creative metaphors and metonymies.

Analysing conventional and creative metaphors and metonymies has been taken up as a method for analysis by scholars for different purposes in relation to (im)politeness. Ruhi and Işık-Güler (2007) investigated *yüz,* face and *gönül,* heart – roughly 'heart/mind/desire' – and examined metonymic and metaphorical expressions in the METU Turkish Corpus (Say, B., Zeyrek, D., Oflazer, K., and Özge, U., 2002) to investigate how conceptualization of face is related to the social person and self-presentation in a Turkish setting. Through the study on metonymic and metaphorical expressions and idioms, quoting Song (1998:102–3), they explain that they aimed at reaching 'cases of interpretive language use – that is, cases of metonymic and metaphorical metarepresentations of self that focus on "some property or value" and guide the "directions in which interpretation may proceed"' (Ruhi and Işık-Güler, 2007:7). Ruhi and Kádár (2011) compared the concept of face in Turkish and Chinese culture in the late nineteenth and early twentieth century, looking into five semantic/pragmatic domains: interpersonal, emotions, personality, situational and as body parts that earlier studies detailed (Ruhi, 2009a; Ruhi, 2009b, Ruhi and Işık-Güler, 2007). At the emotions level, for instance, for Turkish, they looked at the frequency of idiomatic uses of face such as *yüzü gülmek* (lit. 'to smile,' i.e., 'to become happy, be contended, satisfied'), *yüzünü ekşitmek* (lit. 'for one's face to become sour,' i.e., 'to show distaste, disgust on one's face'), *yüzü donmak* (lit. 'for one's face to freeze,' i.e., 'to be stunned'). In one recent study, Langlotz and Locher (2012) looked into how emotional stance was communicated in online disagreements. They analysed 120 English postings from the *Mailonline* both qualitatively and quantitatively examining how emotional stances were presented through conceptual implication, explicit expression and emotional description. They summarized their findings of the frequency of implied indexing of emotions, the direct expression of emotions and the description of emotions in the corpus according to argumentative moves in Figure 4.2.

	Total	Ratio per post overall (*n* = 120)	In disagreement	Ratio per disagreement post (*n* = 104)	In agreement	Ratio per agreement post (*n* = 19)	In extension	Ratio per extension post (*n* = 28)
Means of *implying* emotions								
Conceptual implications	90	0.8	63	0.6	11	0.6	16	0.6
Lexical connotations	75	0.6	49	0.5	9	0.5	17	0.6
Metaphors and their stylistic implications	30	0.3	23	0.2	4	0.2	3	0.1
Sarcasm	13	0.1	9	0.1	0	0	4	0.1
Irony	12	0.1	9	0.1	0	0	3	0.1
Word play	3	0	3	0	0	0	0	0
Total	223	1.9	156	1.5	24	1.3	43	1.5
Means of *expressing* emotions								
Exclamations	41	0.3	28	0.3	8	0.4	5	0.2
Intensification	35	0.3	24	0.2	6	0.3	5	0.2
Name calling	17	0.1	13	0.1	1	0.1	3	0.1
Verbalization of emotional reaction	17	0.1	11	0.1	5	0.3	1	0
Smileys	2	0	2	0		0	0	0
Interjections	2	0	1	0	1	0.1	0	0
Emotional construction	1	0	1	0		0	0	0
Total	115	1	80	0.8	21	1.1	14	0.5
Means of *describing* emotions								
Verbal descriptions/ascriptions of emotional states	30	0.3	20	0.2	3	0.2	7	0.3
Emotion words	10	0.1	8	0.1	1	0.1	1	0
Total	40	0.3	28	0.3	4	0.2	8	0.3
Overall total and ratio	378	3.2	264	2.5	49	2.6	65	2.2

Figure 4.2. The implied indexing of emotions, the direct expression of emotions and the description of emotions in the corpus according to argumentative moves.
Source: Langlotz, A. and Locher, M.A. 2012:12

In this figure, we see that *describing* emotions totalled 40 comments; *implying* emotions totalled 223 and *expressing* emotions totalled 115. *Describing* emotions was five and three times lower. For instance, metaphors and their stylistic implications came in at 0.3 while emotion words came in at 0.1 per post overall, which indicates there is a strong possibility that conflict talk, which has the potential to signal impoliteness, will include metaphors, metonymies and other forms of idiomatic multi-word expressions. One of the insights Spencer-Oatey (2011) reaches is that if it is not 'simply a reflection of this form of data collection,' (p. 3576) it is:

> The much larger number of metapragmatic emotion comments than (im)
> politeness comments could suggest that people's personal emotional reactions
> are more primary and critical than their evaluative judgments of others' (im)
> politeness, at least when reflecting on workplace teams. (p. 3576)

She then suggests further research to explore other possible explanations. However, further research focusing only on emotion labels would disregard the emotional reactions expressed through metaphors and metonymies. This means that CDL or indeed any methodological approach, needs to develop ways of extracting such expressions when investigating (im)politeness.

4.3 Impoliteness in the STC

In this section, the examples extracted from the STC will be discussed and analysed. The analysis, which is corpus driven, will be related to the discussion of impoliteness in the field and, later in the following chapter, will be compared with the data collated from the BNC (in the section above) and used to theorize what impoliteness models should be taken into consideration. As far as the data from the STC is concerned, a series of steps have been taken for readers' convenience. The closest possible translations of speaker utterances are provided in the row following the utterance. In cases where an utterance is annotated by a comment tier, the translation row comes after the comment tier so that readers can see to which parts of the utterance the annotations apply (see STC Extract 2). Since Turkish is a pro-drop language, the translations of dropped lexical items are given in parentheses in the translation. If the interjections, lexical and non-lexical backchannels in Turkish can be translated with their close equivalents, they have been translated. If not, the effect has been provided by an additional item such as an exclamation mark. When the information is relevant for the discussion, nuances have been pointed out in the text. In cases where a full name of a speaker is present as part of an utterance, the name has been replaced by the first three capital letters of the name (see STC Extract 4) in order to maintain the privacy of the speakers.

Extract 1:

The conversation, 113_090404_00004, takes place when the interactants are at a café taking photographs. There are four speakers ASI000037, BAD000036, IND000002, OZG000035, and DER000038 (ASI, BAD, IND, OZG and DER henceforth). ASI is the speaker who triggers impoliteness coming from OZG and BAD due to her irritating behaviour. The extract is a part of the conversation from 113_090404_00004 lasting 8 minutes and 12 seconds.

Extract 1. 113_090404_00004

ASI000037 [v]		((0.6)) ben iki ...			son sınıfta almıştım.
Trans.	I two ... I bought (it) (when I was) in my final year at university.				
IND000002 [v]				hayır.	
Trans.	No.				

BAD000036 [v]	((1.0)) ha evet. ⌐bu o zaman bayağı para ver			ya o zaman o
Trans.	yeah, right. she spent a lot of money at the time			
ASI000037 [v]				sene iki bin/
Trans.	the year two thousand/			

BAD000036 [v]	al	mıştı yaa.		di mi? • seni öyle hatırlıyorum
Trans.	(she) bought (it), yeah . right? I remember you (doing) that.			
ASI000037 [v]			sene iki bin altı.	
Trans.	year two thousand six.			

OZG000035 [v]		((1.4)) e ben son sınıfım. hala yok.	((0.1)) ki o zo/ o
Trans.	I'm in the final year (of university). I still don't have (one). And the last		
BAD000036 [v]	ben.		
Trans.	I.		

OZG000035 [v]	son sınıfla bu son sınıf arasında fark var. ⌐artık her yer
Trans.	year of university in those days and now are different. now, (there are)

OZG000035 [v]	fotoğraf makinesi yani.	((0.2)) eskiden çok yoktu.	
Trans.	cameras everywhere, I mean. didn't use to be many in the past.		
ASI000037 [v]			evet. Üç
Trans.	yes. I		

BAD000036 [v]			((0.8)) ben
Trans.	I		
ASI000037 [v]	yüz on milyona almıştım kısaca.	((short laugh))˙	
Trans.	bought (it) for three hundred million, in short.		

OZG000035 [v]		ben	de çalışmaya başlayınca	alacağım.	
Trans.	I'll buy (one) too when I start working.				
BAD000036 [v]	de üç yüze al	dım.			
Trans.	bought it for three hundred as well.				
DER000038 [v]					Çok
Trans.	(so much)				

ASI000037 [v]		((1.5)) sizi çekelim biz de
Trans.	let's take (a picture) of you	
DER000038 [v]	hava atmana gerek yok.	
Trans.	(you) don't have to show off so much.	

OZG000035 [v]							niye sen
Trans.	why, you						
BAD000036 [v]					((0.1))	bişey	
Trans.	Something						
ASI000037 [v]	arkadaşlar.		çeke	biliriz.			
Trans.	friends. (we) can take						
DER000038 [v]		yo beni çek	meyin.				
Trans.	no, don't include me.						

OZG000035 [v]		çekme. sen bi yeme. sen bi içme.		ne	Oluyor
Trans.	don't take (one). just don't eat. just don't drink. what's happening				
BAD000036 [v]	diyeceğim.		sa	na bi	
Trans.	I'll say (something). (you) now				

OZG000035 [v]		ya Allah Allah.	((0.3)) marjinal.	
Trans.	Oh, God. marjınal.			
BAD000036 [v]	Geçireceğim	zaten ((XXX)).		((0.8)) flaşını
Trans.	I will hit/slap you right now. (the flash)			

BAD000036 [v]	açalım mı?		
Trans.	Shall we switch on the flash?		
DER000038 [v]			((0.5)) tamam çekin ya
Trans.	oh well, ok, take (a picture)		

The interactants are taking photographs and at the same time talking about the topic 'camera'; when they bought their first, how much it cost and when they are planning to get one if they do not have one already. One of the speakers ASI encounters conventionalized impoliteness which is triggered due to her repeated violations of maxims of conversation.

ASI first flouts the maxim of quantity by giving too many details about when she bought the camera and how much she paid for it. First, she says 'I bought it when I was in my final year at university' then encouraged by BAD's comment, 'she spent a lot of money at the time really. right? I remember you (doing) that' she gives the exact year and the amount of money she had spent on the camera, taking her time to speak, as the repetition of the phrase the year indicates, in the conversation: 'the year two thousand' trying to remember exactly, 'year two thousand six' 'yes. I bought it for three hundred million, in short.' followed by a short laugh. The fact that she completes her turn by saying 'in short,' she is signalling that she is aware that her turn on the details of when she bought the camera and how much she paid for it had taken up too much time in the conversation. She then gives a short laugh as she might be thinking of what she had just said 'in short' and might have found it contradictory since she is aware she has flouted the maxim of quantity in two ways both with the exact year and the exact price. The exact year and the price are not asked for or are not noteworthy pieces of information for the conversation at that point. Therefore, the information ASI gives is both irrelevant and superfluous.

What follows ASI's violation of the maxim of quantity is an example of impoliteness. The impoliteness unfolds gradually in stages. It begins with DER's comment: 'you don't have to show off so much' (*çok hava atmana gerek yok*), which is in fact a pointed criticism and personalized negative assertion, followed by OZG's comment 'I am going to buy one myself when I start working.' Right after DER's comment 'you don't have to show off so much,' there is a long pause, 1.5 seconds, the longest compared to 0.8, 0.1 and 0.3 seconds in the conversation. Although ASI does not respond to DER's assertion, explicitly, the fact that she takes this pause of 1.5 seconds implicates that the message had an effect on her. ASI's next turn is, 'let's take a photograph of you, friends' (*sizi çekelim bizde arkadaşlar*). 'Friend' (*arkadaş*) is a term of endearment in Turkish which could have been replaced with 'girls' (*kızlar*) in this context. However, it is 'friends' ASI prefers to use and it signals her attempt to repair the assertion that she is showing off. Still, DER replies 'no, don't include me.' ASI is insisting '(we) can take' and with her insistence, she is imposing what she wants to do upon the others. This point in the conversation is critical: ASI has violated the maxim of quantity; her violation of it is interpreted as showing off by her friend and her friend has verbalized this as a criticism and negative assertion directed at ASI. However, the other participants OZG and BAD do not align with DER; on the contrary, they align with ASI. OZG's disapproval of DER comes with the utterance 'why, you. don't take (one). just don't eat. just don't drink. what is happening, God? ((0.3)) marginal' (*niye, sen. çekme. sen bi yeme. sen bi içme, ne oluyor ya Allah Allah, marjinal*). There is a strong dismissal by repeated silencers in the form of negative imperative 'why, you. don't take (one). just don't eat. just don't drink' (*niye, sen. çekme. sen bi yeme. sen bi içme*), and a message enforcer in the form of question ending with an interjection 'what is happening, God!' (*ne oluyor ya Allah Allah*). The pragmatic effect of the interjection 'ya' and the phrase 'Allah Allah' have been given by an exclamation mark instead of a question mark in the translation. Especially, with *(ne oluyor ya Allah Allah)* OZG stresses her confusion and disapproval of DER's comment 'you don't have to show off so much' (*çok hava atmana gerek yok*), and behaviour that she does not want to appear in the photograph. OZG dismisses DER one more time with a personalized negative assertion 'marginal' (*marjinal*) meaning ASI does not fit in. Moreover, the pause of 0.3 second indicates the possibility that whatever impact the comment (*marginal)* is to achieve: the speaker, OZG, takes a pause, which signals a face-sensitive issue.

Overlapping with OZG's utterance 'why, you. don't take (one)' (*niye, sen. çekme*), BAD has also taken a turn by the utterance, '((0.1)) I'll say something' (*bişey diyeceğim*), which has the function of preparing the stage for something negative that will follow. '*Bişey*' (something) is both a euphemism of what she is going to say and a hedge for the impact her utterance is going to make. The pause 0.1 is noteworthy; it is not long. Nevertheless, its presence signals that again a face-sensitive issue is about to arise. BAD then says, 'I'll hit/slap you right now' (*sana bi geçireceğim zaten*), which is a form of a threat. In this utterance, the word 'zaten', which includes the meanings of 'anyway' and 'in fact', is translated as 'right now', as opposed to 'now' due to the impact of 'bi', which signals anger, as discussed below, and increases the intensity of the threat.

While Ruhi (2010) discusses how important it is to go beyond the discussion of interaction with other documents to examine the indexicality of face, following the ethnomethodological approach proposed by Garfinkel (1967) and Hak (1995), she studies photographs taken at a wedding ceremony as parallel documents showing how closely membership categorization is related to the face issue. Quoting from Sudnow (1972:264), Ruhi emphasizes the symbolic action of taking photographs: 'Persons regard the photograph to be produced … as a document of their appearances, actions, movements, relationships, aspects, moods, etc.' (Ruhi, 2010:2135). Coincidentally, this extract is a case of a photograph-taking. When DER announces that she does not want to appear in the photograph, after the comment she made to ASI, 'you don't have to show off so much,' (*çok hava atmana gerek yok*), she is jeopardizing the friendly atmosphere by indexing herself out of the membership of the group and acting against social expectations. Implying that being part of the group through verbal and behavioural channels is not a desirable act, she is attacking the positive face of the group. This is met with a strong reaction from OZG and BAD, with impoliteness. The scale of impoliteness is surprisingly high, a strong dismissal utterance 'why, you. don't take (one). just don't eat. just don't drink. what is happening, God? ((0.3)) marginal' (*niye, sen. çekme. sen bi yeme. sen bi içme, ne oluyor ya Allah Allah, marjinal*), and a threat of physical harm 'I'll hit/slap you right now' (*sana bi geçireceğim zaten*) for a friendly gathering in the extract. One possible reason for the high scale of impoliteness is that DER is not attacking the positive face of one individual but the sum of positive faces of all the participants who are willing to appear in the picture.

In her attempt to arrive at universal properties of face2, Terkourafi (2007) also refers to the notion of the multiplicity of face:

> [...] the intentionality (or directedness) of Face toward an Other means that Self will have several faces concurrently, as many as there are Others involved in a situation. Putting this somewhat schematically, if I am interacting with an interlocutor in front of an audience, I make (and am aware of making) a bid for face not only in the eyes of my interlocutor, but also in the eyes of each of the members of that audience taken separately and as a group. And the same applies to each of them.

Following Terkourafi (2007), Bousfield (2008) points out:

> With two interactants (a dyad) there are two salient types of face being constituted and shaped as the interaction proceeds. With three interactants there are six salient types of face constituted and shaped as the interaction proceeds (3 interactants multiplied by 2 types of face constituted for each individual. (p. 41)

In other words, there is the group face which is constructed by the sum of faces constituted in the interaction, which is inevitably dependent on factors such as previous interactions (p. 42). This confirms that the number of participants in an interaction, especially if they align and present a joint stance, can aggravate face more – as the face here is the group face – and in turn generate a high degree of impoliteness regardless of the context, which is a friendly gathering in this example. The joint action and alignment pushes DER to repair her behaviour and she agrees to be in the picture: 'oh well, ok, take (a picture)' (*tamam çekin ya*). The interjection 'ya' is translated as 'oh well' to create the implicature that the speaker is conceding to being included in the photograph and adds an emotive element to the utterance.

As mentioned earlier, Culpeper (2011b) classifies implicational impoliteness in three categories: form-driven and convention-driven: internal and external; and context-driven: unmarked behaviour and the absence of behaviour. By form-driven, Culpeper (2011b) is referring to the 'implicit messages which are triggered by formal surface or semantic aspects of a behaviour and which have negative consequences for certain individuals' (p. 157). He explains that form-driven implicational impoliteness may look similar to the off-record politeness super strategy; however, there are two major differences. One, this notion is not linked to politeness and two, with the incidences of impoliteness, an alternative interpretation of politeness is impossible to make (p. 157). With the form-driven category, Culpeper (2011b) proposes the Gricean cooperative principles and the echoic mention view (e.g. Sperber and Wilson 1981, 1995 [1986]). The reason why Culpeper (2011b) brings Grice's cooperative principle, which is usually associated with politeness, into the discussion of impoliteness is that when Grice's maxims are flouted, the utterance can be interpreted differently from what it literally means since it acts like indirect speech (see Section 2.2) and is implicational. What this implies then for the extract is that taking too much time to speak or too many turns in conversation leads to violation of Gricean maxims and generates implicational impoliteness. In the extract, ASI flouts the maxim of quantity by giving too many details about when she bought the camera and how much she paid for it by taking too many turns. In Turkish culture, a possession, which is the topic of the conversation, requires a show of modesty. This explains why she encounters the negative assertions 'you don't need to show off so much' (*çok hava atmana gerek yok*) and 'why, you. don't take (one). just don't eat. just don't drink. what is happening, God? ((0.3)) marginal' (*niye sen çekme sen bi yeme. sen bi içme ne oluyor ya Allah Allah, marjinal*) and a threat 'I'll hit you right now' (*sana bi geçireceğim zaten*).

Figure 4.3 below displays the speech analysis for the utterances of OZG, 'why, you. don't take (one). just don't eat. just don't drink. what is happening, God? ((0.3)) marginal' (*niye, sen. çekme. sen bi yeme. sen bi içme, ne oluyor ya Allah Allah, marjinal*) and of BAD 'I'll hit/slap you right now' (*sana bi geçireceğim zaten*). The analysis was effectuated with PRAAT, the speech analyser developed by Paul Boersma and David Weenink, University of Amsterdam (cf. http://www.fon. hum.uva.nl/praat/) and its application Spectrograme, which the waveform or the spectral energy of a sound over time. Although Praat offers applications that lend themselves for indepth analysis of speech such as pitch F0 / Pitch or pitch range, a simpler analysis through Spectrograme was chosen to provide a visual display of the intensity and the high-accent pitch of the speakers OZG and BAD while they are being impolite to DER.

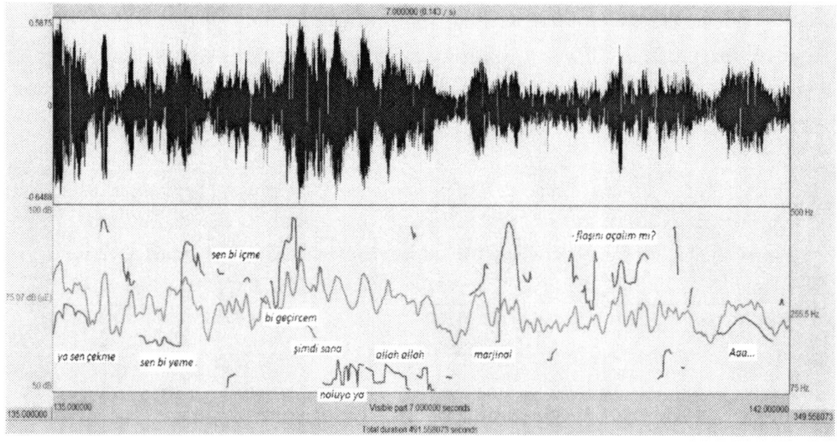

Figure 4.3. Praat display for the STC Extract 1

Intensity is the amount of energy a sound has over an area. If a sound is more intense you hear it in a smaller area and sounds with higher intensity are louder. Pitch shows the length of a sound, whether the soundwave is long or short. Pitch depends on the frequency of a soundwave and the number of wavelengths that fit into one unit of time. In Figure 4.3, the blue line (the lower line of the two lines in the figure) represents the speakers' pitch and the green line (the lower line of two lines in the figure) represent the speakers' sound intensity. The increased pitch and intensity coincides with the utterances for threat (*geçircem*) and dismissal (*çekme, yeme, marjinal*). The transcription in the STC follows a standard orthography so the utterances (*ne oluyor*) and (*geçireceğim*) are displayed in the figure as they are pronounced in the audio, (*noluyo*) and (*geçircem*). The utterances fit into vocal characteristics of emotions anger and frustration, which come in slightly faster tempo and tense articulation (Culpeper, 2011b:170; Murray and Arnott, 1993:1103–4).

In this extract, the utterance from BAD (*sana bi geçireceğim zaten* ((XXX))) is translated as 'I am going to hit/slap you right now' because the semantic prosody (Sinclair, 1998) of the utterance (*sana bi geçireceğim*) required it. Sinclair

(2004) reviews the basic distinctions in semantics and points out the denotative/ connotative and literal/figurative (or metaphorical or idiomatic) distinctions. He argues that although literal/denotative meaning is considered to be the central and obligatory meaning of a word as opposed to the others which are 'unpredictable variants,' 'a lexical item is characteristically phrasal, although it can be realized in a single word' (p. 122). The terminology he proposes for this status of meaning is semantic prosody (Sinclair, 1998), which is the only obligatory element aside from the core word or words:

> It is called a prosody because, like prosodies in phonology, there are often uncertainties about its exact realization, and it ranges over the whole lexical item, in that all the other elements are interpreted within the framework it provides, including classifying aspects of meaning. The important matter is the effect, i.e. what communicative job the lexical item performs, and that is expressed or pointed up by the semantic prosody. (p. 122)

Morley and Partington (2009) summarize the importance of Sinclair's work as the following:

> Sinclair's work has helped demolish the old 'mail order' concept of discourse production, which saw discourse as built up one word at a time, each word delivering its separate parcel of meaning. Semantic prosody instead is the mechanism which shows how one elemental type of meaning-evaluative meaning – is frequently shared across units in discourse and by ensuring consistency of evaluation or evaluative harmony, plays a vital role in keeping the discourse in its cohesion. (p. 139)

Other scholars (Partington, 2004b; Bednarek, 2008) discussed whether there is a distinction between collocational meaning and evaluative meaning, respectively between semantic preference and semantic prosody. For instance, Partington (2004b) suggested that semantic preferences are more or less automatically 'build-up' or 'form' (pp. 150–1), which is in line with the following argument in corpus linguistics: 'lexical item x occurs with negative items (i.e. it has negative semantic preference); ergo, it has evaluative meaning (i.e. a negative semantic prosody)' (Bednarek, 2008:131). However, for Bednarek (2008), for example, such an argument does not always hold because the analysis of semantic prosody is much more subjective and problematic than the analysis of semantic preference (p. 131). The example 'I am going to hit/slap you right now' (*sana bi geçireceğim zaten* ((XXX))', which will be discussed briefly here also shows how complex it is to look into the role of semantic prosody for lexical items, which are inevitably interpreted in the framework and discourse they appear in (Sinclair 1998, 2004; Morley and Partington, 2009; Bednarek, 2008).

The verb *geçir-* has a number of denotative meanings in Turkish. However, in this context it has acquired an idiomatic, metaphorical meaning which matches with 'hit' or 'slap'. In order to answer the question of what might have triggered the negative evaluation of the utterance (*sana bi geçireceğim zaten*) which is a threat and a conventionalized impoliteness formula (Culpeper, 2010), the relationship between the nodes in the collocate have been investigated. The nodes '*geçireceğim*' and '*bi*' are looked into with the consideration that '*sana*' ([to] you) and '*bi*' (right now) are already increasing the intensity of the threat by making the threat personalized and adding immediacy to the motion of hitting. Because Turkish is an object-drop language, the personalization effect is a result of the use of the object pronoun '*sana*' ([to] you). With the nodes, both semantic and corpus analyses are carried out. The corpus analysis was run on a written corpus of Turkish, METU Turkish Corpus (Say, B., Zeyrek, D., Oflazer, K., and Özge, U., 2002) from a collection of 2 million words of written text comprising the years from 1990 to 2000, taken from ten different genres.

In order to find out what triggered the semantic prosody to come into play and created a negative meaning in the utterance (*sana bi geçireceğim zaten*), first of all, a dictionary analysis was carried out for the verb *geçir-* to see if the verb has that denotative meaning. The following entries, extracted from Türk Dil Kurumu (Turkish Language Institute), TDK hereafter, Büyük Türkçe Sözlük (The Dictionary of Turkish, retrieved from http://www.tdk.gov.tr/index. php?option=com_bts) in reference to Güncel Türkçe Sözlük (The Dictionary of Contemporary Turkish), are translated in the same order of the entries above as:

geçirmek

(-i) 1. Geçme işini yaptırmak, geçmesini sağlamak. 2. *(-e)* Bir şeyi bir yandan öbür yana götürmek. 3. *(-i, -e)* Bir şeyi bir yerden başka yere taşımak, nakletmek. 4. *(-i, -e)* Tespit etmek, yazmak, kaydetmek. 5. *(-i, -e)* Bir şeyi kendisine ayrılmış olan yere yerleştirmek, takmak. 6. *(-i, -e)* Yola çıkan birini uğurlamaya gitmek, selametlemek, teşyi etmek. 7. *(-i, -de)* Bir süre yaşamak, oturmak, kalmak. . *(-e, nsz)* Giymek, giyinmek. '9. *(-den)* Bir işi birden çok kişi üzerinde uygulamak. 10. *(-i, -den)* Herhangi bir durumu yaşamış olmak. 11. Etmek, yapmak. 12. *(-i, -e)* Hastalık bulaştırmak.13. Zaman harcamak. 14. Bir gereksinimi eldeki imkânla karşılamak. 15. *(-e)* Vurmak. 16. *mec.* Alışverişte aldatmak, kötü mal satmak, kazıklamak. 17. *(-e) argo* Birine kötü söz söylemek.

The entries are translated in the same order of the entries above as:

1. to get through, 2. to pass, 3. to transfer, 4. to notch, 5. to insert, 6. to see someone off, 7. to pass through, 8. to put sth. over, 9. to run sth. over more than one person, 10. to undergo, 11. to engage, 12. to get over (a disease), 13. to pass time doing sth., 14. to permeate, 15. to hit, 16. (idiomatic) to rip off, 17. (slang) to insult.

The entry number 15 shows that *geçir-* is also listed as 'to hit;' however, the additional information the entries give point to an interesting aspect of the entry number 15. The entries give information about the usage of the verb in regard to whether it is used with the direct object indicated as *(-(y)I)* above or with the indirect object *(-(y)A)* in Turkish. The entries number 15, 'to hit' and 17, 'to insult' are the two entries specified as only to be used with the indirect object case marker *(-(y)E)*. If the reason for the semantic prosody coming into play here is that the verb *geçir-* acquires a negative meaning when it is used with indirect object, then why is it that it does not acquire a negative meaning in other entries that are also used with indirect object such as entry number 2, 'to pass?' Since this question cannot be answered at this stage, further analysis needs to be carried out. However, since the main purpose of the further analysis is to find out the subtlety of the semantic prosody, it is necessary to look at real language data to see how the verb collocates and in what context it is used with negative meaning. In order to look at real language data, a corpus analysis was run.

A query of the verb *geçir-* and the possible derivatives in the verb form (e.g. *geçirdim, geçirdi*, etc.) was run in the METU Turkish Corpus (Say, B., Zeyrek, D., Oflazer, K., and Özge, U., 2002). All the years from 1990 to 2000, including all types of genres and the writers the corpus provides were scanned and 58 hits were obtained. The list below gives all the hits. Many of the hits of the verb were repeated without any difference in the form or meaning in the results, which is why the list is comprised of only 18 items (Table 4.2).

The analysis was significant in that *geçir-* has never been used in the meaning TDK gives with its entry number 15. Although it could also be coincidental and that the verb has a negative denotative meaning just to see if the semantic prosody comes into play within the collocation the verb is used in the utterance 'I'll hit/slap you right now' (*sana bi geçireceğim*), a further analysis is followed with *bi*. The steps were the same as what was followed for the verb *geçir-*: first a semantic analysis, and then a corpus analysis were carried out to see whether the results matched, and whether they confirmed each other or brought out conflicting findings requiring further theorization.

Table 4.2. METU Turkish Corpus Hits for *–geçir*

hayata geçirmek	to implement
ele geçirmek	to conquer
denemeden geçirmek	to try out
vakit geçirmek	to pass time
gözden geçirmek	to look through
gereklerini yerine getirerek geçirmek	to reckon over
geceyi birlikte geçirmek	to pass the night
gözlerinin önünden geçirmek	to pass one's life in review
vakit geçirmek	to pass time doing sth.
değerleri yaşama geçirmek	to act on a thought
aklımdan geçirmek	to cross one's mind
Kızının Fethi 'yi geçirmek üzere	to show the way to somebody
onaydan geçirmek	to hang out with someone
sözünü geçirmek	to assert one's authority
harekete geçirmek	to put in action
belleğine geçirmek	to put in one's memory
balayını geçirmek	to honeymoon

Bi is considered to be the phonologically attenuated form of *bir*, which is the indefinite article/number one in Turkish. Therefore, a semantic analysis was first carried out to see if this is confirmed in dictionary entries with the consideration that there might be a semantic difference indicated, which in turn could give a clue as to why *bi* adds a negative meaning to the verb *geçir-* if it does. The entries in TDK (http://www.tdk.gov.tr/index.php?option=com_bts), and references in *Türkiye Türkçesi Ağızları Sözlüğü (The Dictionary of Turkish Dialects of Turkey)* confirm that *bi* is the spoken variety of *bir*. Considering that *bi* in the utterance (*sana bi geçireceğim*) might have been used as in the meaning of *bir*, a semantic analysis for *bir* was run and the following results were found. Table 4.3 illustrates the dictionary entries of *bir* with examples given in English and Turkish.

Table 4.3. TDK dictionary entries for *bir*

Dictionary Entry	Examples English/Turkish Translation
1. First of numbers	She is number **one** on the list. Listede **bir** numara.
2. The word to express the number 1	There was just **one** car parked on the street. Caddede sadece park etmiş **bir** araba vardı.
3. The same, similar, identical	Sorrow or happiness, they feel **the same**. Elem de **bir** sevinç de.
4. Together, united	Together, we are one. Hep beraber **bir**iz.
5. A, an	I bought a pencil. **Bir** kalem aldım.
6. Some	I spoke to a teacher at the school. **Bir** öğretmenle konuştum okulda.
7. Unique, single, sole	There is one God. Allah **bir**dir.
8. Shared, owned in common	We have one aim as a team, which is to win. Takımımızın **bir** hedefi var; kazanmak.
9. Equal in importance, indifferent	Public or private, they are the same. Devlet de **bir** özel de.
10. Any	I am going to buy a T-shirt. Bir T-shirt alacağım.
11. Once	She looked at me once. Bana **bir** kez baktı.
12. But, except	All is taken care of **but** this! Herşey bitti, **bir** bu kaldı!
13. only	Only you can do this! Bunu **bir** sen yapabilirsin!

Table 4.3 indicates that the entries for *bir* do not give any clues as to why in the utterance (*sana bi geçireceğim*) *geçir-* is interpreted as 'to slap/hit.' This brings us back to investigating *bi* instead of *bir*. As a complementary second step, a corpus analysis in the METU Turkish Corpus (Say, B., Zeyrek, D., Oflazer, K., and Özge, U., 2002) was carried out to see the context in which *bi* is used and reach an insight

on whether it is associated with negativity in usage. One hundred and sixty-four hits were retrieved from a corpus from between 1990 and 2000, from all genres and all writers. Almost all samples were from spoken Turkish; speakers seemed to take turns to speak or sounded like they were having a conversation with themselves or talking to themselves. Below are five examples of *bi* from the corpus hits. The hits are translated with their best equivalents in Turkish and since *bi* is the phonologically attenuated form of *bir*, in the English translations immediately before the phrase *bi* appears in original sentences in Turkish, the word 'one' is added, bolded and underlined for the readers:

1. Ona, bu sopayla bi vururum!
    I would so one hit him with this stick.
2. Bak bi de elin itini koruyo ... Benim kitabımda arada yüzük olmadan kızkardeşime zırt pırt telefon edilmesi yazmıyo kızım.
    Look how she one protects that bastard. His calling my sister all the time without a ring on her finger... that doesn't fly in my book.
3. Bakma sen, baban beni döverken ses etmiyorum ... Beyimdir, döver de sever de ... Ama elin adamı fazla oldu artık ... Ben gidip şu herifi bi parçalıyım. ..
    Look, I don't say anything when your father beats me. He is my husband, he can beat me and he can love me. But this guy has finally crossed the line. I am gonna go and one rip him to shreds.
4. Bak hâlâ konuşuyo ... İskicem belanı, kapa lan şu telefonu, bi daha da Sıdıka'ya takıldığını duyarsam, yersin bıçağı ... Duydun mu Lale?
    Look he is still talking. ...., I am gonna fuck your life up, hang up the damn phone, and if I one get wind of you hanging around Sıdıka, I am gonna stab you. Did you hear me Lale?
5. Galdırdım mı elimin tersiyle şap diye vuruverürün cadaloz ... . İki dakka diziyi seyredicez şurda car car etme, bi sus bakayın bi kere ...
    I would lift my hand and slap you silly. I am gonna watch this show for two minutes so stop yakking, just one shut up for once.

Out of 164 hits 46 hits were used in a negative context, which equals 28.04%. Most of these hits were threats such as the examples above. Despite the relatively common use of *bi* in negative contexts such as threats, there were also cases where *bi* was used for polite requests with imperatives:

1. Nazan Şoray'ın kasedi vardı torpidoda bi onu bul bakiim, teybe şeedelim ... Bu, morfin dediğin şey sıvı mı? Nası bişey şimdi ...

> Nazan Şoray's cassette was in the glove compartment, just one have a look for it, let's (put) it into the cassette player ... Is this thing you call morphine a liquid? Just what kind of a thing is it?

2.   Alo, Sıdıka, Elifsu ben ... Bana bak, senden bi ricam olucak.
     Hello, Sıdıka, its Elifsu ... Look, I am gonna one ask you a favour.

This observation indicates that *bi* functions as a diminutive in Turkish. Diminutive is an affix added to a word to convey the meaning of *small*. In discussing the role of the diminutive suffix – cVk (the V stands for a high vowel motivated by vowel harmony), Zeyrek (2001: 52) maintains that it expresses familiarity, informality, and endearment similar to languages such as Polish (Wierzbicka, 1985) and Greek (Sifianou, 1992). She refers back to Brown and Levinson (1987:109, 251) who mention that the particle meaning 'a little' is observed frequently in polite conversation, especially among women, in Tzeltal. In her example, for instance, the hostess who is offering more food to guests uses the diminutive suffix in 'Why don't you take another piece-DIM', (*Bir parçacık daha alsana*) and will be 'successfully alleviating the possibility of imposition that may be induced by her insistence' (p.52). Zeyrek (2001) refers to Wierzbicka (1985:167) who explains that the effect of the diminutive in the utterance for Polish would be as in 'Don't resist! It's a small thing I'm asking you to do – and a good thing!' She points out that the use of the diminutive is an example of how Turkish people practice cordiality; the insistence is not an imposition but rather an act of generosity (Zeyrek, 2001:53). Bayyurt and Bayraktaroğlu (2001:227) also refer to diminutives as a solidarity consolidating address term, which is 'attached to all address terms, and always together with the possessive pronoun for the first person singular (i.e. Ahmetciğim Ahmet + DIM+ first Person possessive suffix, similar to "my little Ahmet")'. In the two examples above where *bi* is used in polite requests, the meaning it conveys seems to be in line with the discussion that it is used to reduce the possibility of imposition. Although the use of the diminutive is associated with smallness and refers to physical phenomena, considering the five examples where it is used in threats, its varying pragmatic functions makes it quite interesting to study. Bulak (2011) in his discussion of the function and effect of the subjunctive (-(s)A), gives an example (*Erkeksen bana bir yumruk vursana!*), literally translated as 'If you are a man, hit me with a punch!' He explains that the example among others indicate challenge and conflict. Although his main discussion is about the subjunctive mood and the example he gives is to show how the subjunctive mood reflects challenge and conflict, the presence of '*bir*' in the example is interesting. Jurafsky (1996) points out that diminutives may signal both a positive emotional attitude and a pejorative meaning, with both intensifying and attenuating force effects. Badarneh (1996) drew attention to the contradictory use of diminutives showing that they can be used for contempt as well as glorification. He also studied its effect in negative politeness contexts:

> The diminutive in CJA [colloquial Jordanian Arabic] is thus used both as a positive politeness strategy, oriented toward expressing affection and endearment and establishing a friendly context for the interaction, and as a negative politeness strategy aimed at minimizing imposition and softening negative statements. (Badarneh, 2010:153)

The recognition that *bi* can have both positively and negatively associated meanings requires a conscious look at the context to see what verb it is used with and how it changes the interpretation for politeness. The samples collated from the METU Turkish Corpus and the sample in the extract discussed show that *bi* is used to modify verbs (e.g. 'hit him with this stick', 'rip him to shreds', 'get wind of you hanging around Sıdıka' and 'shut up') and when used to modify verbs, it acquires a quantifying function. By quantifying the verb, it quantifies the event. In this case, *bi* seems to create a quantity maxim implicature by which the activity or the action is intensified. In the utterance 'I'll (one) hit/slap you right now' (*sana bi geçireceğim*), *bi* (one) gives the meaning 'I will hit you once only so forcefully that it will be enough.' It is also important to note that the data indicate that this effect of *bi* seems to appear with verbs that have negative connotations. Another item that seems to intensify the message in the threat in 'I'll (one) hit/slap you right now' (*sana bi geçireceğim*) is the overt use of the pronoun 'sana' ([to] you), which is optional in Turkish because it is a pro-drop language. Due to the personalization effect it creates, the threat aimed at the recipient of the action sounds more forceful. These observations confirm how context-sensitive semantic prosody is and how important it is to be aware of the concept while extracting or analysing impoliteness. The lengthy undertaking above of semantic analysis combined with corpus analysis illustrates the subtlety that semantic prosody adds to utterances. The fact that it triggers a negative evaluation of the utterance confirms once more that impoliteness studies require a wider understanding of methodological concerns for extraction and for theorization at the analysis level.

Overall, in this extract, the impoliteness with the utterance 'I will hit/slap you right now' (*sana bi geçireceğim zaten*) is triggered first by DER's comment 'you don't need to show off so much' (*çok hava atmana gerek yok*) and then her act of excluding herself from the rest of the group by not wanting to appear in the photo when she says 'no, don't include me' (*yo beni çekmeyin*). The impoliteness strategy is a threat, which is responded to by DER through a change in her behaviour as she says 'oh well, ok, take (a picture)' (*tamam çekin ya*). This change in behaviour might be considered as an attempt to repair the impoliteness DER has generated in the beginning by acting according to membership organization assumptions in the group. Moreover, conceding by saying 'oh well, ok, take (a picture)' (*tamam çekin ya*) she is both protecting her face and complying with the membership assumptions imposed by the group. This is closely related to the concept of coercive power (see the BNC Extract 7). What OZG and BAD utter generates a coercive action on DER's part.

Extract 2:

In this extract, which is taken from the same conversation 113_090404_00004 as Extract 1, the participants ASI000037, BAD000036, OZG000035, and DER000038 (ASI, BAD, OZG and DER henceforth) are talking about going online and chatting on the MSN. BAD is the focus of impoliteness because when she is online on MSN, she does not chat with the girls. The reason she has given for that, apparently, is that when she is online, she watches TV series on the computer and so by implication she cannot chat. This behaviour and the excuse given for that trigger impoliteness in the form of sarcasm and irony.

Extract 2. 113_090404_00004

OZG000035 [v]		msn olan bu • di mi?			
Trans.	this is msn				
BAD000036 [v]	(onay)...			hı-hı sende var zaten.	
Trans.	(approval) yeah, you have (it) anyway.				
ASI000037 [v]					((0.4))

ASI000037 [v]	var var.	((0.6)) blockladım	ama	olsun.	
ASI000037 [c]				((laughing))	
Trans.	yeah, yeah (I have it).but (I) blocked (it) anyway				
DER000038 [v]					((0.8)) ya bende de
Trans.	yes, on my (msn)(she)				

DER000038 [v]	giriyor.	‿hatun meşgul. selam bile vermiyor.	((0.3))
DER000038 [c]	((lengthening))	((humorous tone))	
Trans.	goes online. the lady is busy. (she) doesn't even say hello.		

OZG000035 [v]		c o artık	bi iş kadını.			Bak
Trans.	well, she is a business woman now. aha,					
ASI000037 [v]				dizi izliyormuş	ve dizi	
Trans.	she watches TV series and because of watching					
DER000038 [v]	büyümüş.	⌐dizi izliyor.				
DER000038 [c]	((change intone of voice))					
Trans.	(she) has grown up. (she) watches series.					

OZG000035 [v]	bak!		
Trans.	look at that!		
ASI000037 [v]		izlemekten...	((0.9)) ama dizi izlemek ((0.3)) önemli
Trans.	TV series.... but watching TV series is an important		

OZG000035 [v]	hangi dizi?					
Trans.	which one?					
BAD000036 [v]			evet ö	nemli bi sanat.		evet.
Trans.	(that is) right, (it is) an important art. yes.					
ASI000037 [v]	bi sanat.	((1.7))	e	e˙	Desperate	Housewives.
Trans.	art. err Desperate Housewives					

BAD goes online. She watches TV series on the computer but presumably does not communicate with the girls participating in the conversation. She does not even give a simple greeting and this behaviour is not acceptable for the girls. Both ASI and DER have BAD added to their MSN but ASI has blocked her, which is already a form of dismissal to BAD. Just after ASI says 'yeah yeah, (I have it). but (I) blocked (it), anyway' overlapping with DER's alignment 'yes, on my (msn) (she) goes online the lady is busy. (she) does not even say hello.' ASI shows her reaction to BAD, who does not 'even' say 'hello' by blocking her. DER also reacts to it because she thinks saying 'hello' on MSN is simple and easy, which is indicated by her use of 'even', and mocks BAD's excuse that she is busy by saying 'the lady is busy.' She continues her sarcastic comment by saying 'she has grown up. (she) watches TV series' while OZG comments 'of course, she is a business woman now.'

DER shows her disapproval of BAD quite sarcastically in different ways. First, she depersonalizes BAD by referring to her in third person in her presence 'the lady' (*hatun*). Second, she calls BAD *hatun*. 'The lady' (*hatun²*) is used in a negative way

2. 'The lady' (*hatun*) is used to depersonalize the person it refers to and creates a negative meaning opposite to 'woman' in the BNC Extract 4.

to distance the speaker from the person to whom she is talking. The word produces a contextual mismatch in terms of address since it is slightly pejorative for the age group in this context even though it is used as an honorific historically in Turkish. By implication BAD's face is also threatened with this usage. Third, having put a distance between her and BAD, DER emphasizes, with the use of 'even' that what they expect from BAD is such a small thing to do – 'she does not even say hello.' She then pauses for 0.3 seconds, takes a hypocoristic tone and says 'she has grown up' as if she is talking to a child. This again adds to the distance DER is putting between BAD and herself by implying BAD does not belong to the group. OZG agrees by saying 'well, she is a business woman now.' 'Now' in this utterance is important as it reinforces the impact of DER's comment 'she has grown up.'

The extract is significant for the metapragmatics of impoliteness because it shows that BAD has apparently violated netiquette norms and politeness rules for this group of participants in the MSN environment by not following ways of maintaining relational contract. Graham (2008) states that when notions of politeness in an electronic setting are examined, it is important to acknowledge 'the parameters of the medium' (p.281). He quotes Smith and Kollock (1999):

> [There are] a number of features of this [electronic] world that make conflict more likely and more difficult to manage than in real communities: wide cultural diversity; disparate interests, needs and expectations; the nature of electronic participation (anonymity, multiple avenues of entry, poor reliability of connections and so forth); text-based communication; and power asymmetry among them. (p.160)

One parameter of MSN is that if a participant is added on the contact list, the participant is visible to the other participants in the list. Going online onto MSN can be compared to sitting at a table with people you have agreed to sit with. Just as saying hello is a norm in such a gathering and violating that expectation would be evaluated as inappropriate, so is going on MSN and not saying hello to the others currently online. This emphasizes the point that underlying norms with which people interact should be analysed further in relation to impoliteness phenomena.

Another issue that comes up in the extract with the use of 'the lady' (*hatun*) and 'well, she is a business woman now' (*ee o artık bi iş kadını*) is related to the metapragmatics of impoliteness and the concept of indexicality of face and membership categorization (Ruhi, 2010, discussed in the STC Extract 1). Both DER with the utterance 'the lady' and OZG with the utterance 'well, she is a business woman now' are distancing BAD and in doing so they are indexing BAD out of their group. The membership of the group seems to have formed during the interaction through DER and OZG's alignment but is based on their common understanding of netiquette norms. They both think going online and not saying hello is inappropriate. In this sense, with their utterances and their move towards kicking BAD out of the group, they form a new indexicality of membership as far as the topic of the interaction is concerned. An interesting point that needs further attention here is that the speakers DER and OZG are using 'indexing' as a strategy similar to what Culpeper (2010) defines as dismissal, which is a conventionalized impoliteness formula. However, here the dismissal is metalinguistic but is reflected through use linguistic terms such as 'the lady' and 'well, she is a business woman now.' This observation highlights that further studies are required to investigate the concept of indexicality of face described in Ruhi (2010) in line with the argument mentioned in the BNC Extract 1 that impoliteness studies should go beyond the discussion of interaction with other documents (Ruhi, 2010; Garfinkel, 1967; Hak, 1995).

It is also noteworthy that the expression 'the lady' (*hatun*) in Figure 4.4 indicates that it is uttered by a high-pitch accent with the blue line making a high peak. It is possible that the irony created by the expression shows itself in the prosody in this way. Contradiction in the tone of voice between DER's utterance '(she) goes online. the lady is busy. (she) does not even say hello' (*ya ben de giriyor hatun, meşgul selam bile vermiyor*) and OZG's utterance 'she is a business woman now' (*ee o artık bi iş kadını*) is also noticeable in the sound file. '([S]he) goes online. the lady is busy. (she) does not even say hello' (*ya ben de giriyor hatun, meşgul selam bile vermiyor*) is uttered in a hypocoristic, humorous tone but 'she is a business woman now' (*ee o artık bi iş kadını*) is uttered in a serious tone. Although it is only impressionistic, the Praat sound analysis demonstrates the change in the tone of voice with the blue line (*ya ben de giriyor hatun, meşgul selam bile vermiyor*) following a higher pitch than the utterance (*ee o artık bi iş kadını*). With the mismatch of the prosodic nuances – humorous versus serious – the two speakers DER and OZG adopt, the intensity of the irony is increased.

ASI also joins in to mock with an echo 'she has been watching TV series and because she watches TV series ...' and violates the maxim of quantity in two ways: she is repeating the information with the first half of her utterance 'she has been watching TV series' and links her utterance with 'and' as if she is going to give some more information but does not complete her utterance 'and because she is watching TV series ...,' which leads to the interpretation that she implying something. The co-text gives the clue that what could follow her utterance is that 'she is busy watching TV shows and so she cannot say hello to us' which again emphasizes their disapproval of BAD's behaviour. OZG takes this as an opportunity to ironically mock BAD by saying 'aha look at that!' (*bak bak*!). It is at this critical point ASI is impolite '((0.9)) but watching TV series ... ((0.3)) is an important art' (((0.9)) *ama dizi izlemek* ((0.3)) *önemli bi sanat*).

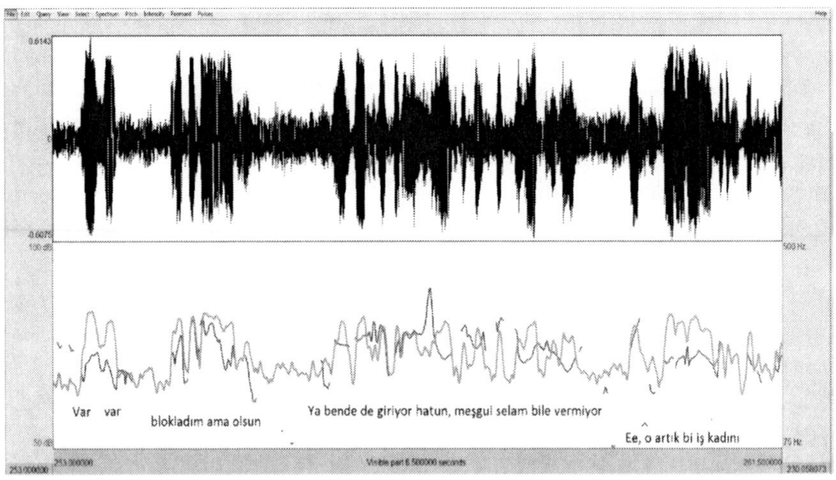

- Var var, blokladım ama olsun
- Ya bende de giriyor hatun, meşgul selam bile vermiyor
- Ee, o artık bi iş kadını

Figure 4.4. Praat display for the change of voice in the STC Extract 2

Culpeper (2011b:165–6) discusses convention-driven implicational impoliteness as follows: '[T]hey very often involve mixed messages in some way. More specifically, they mix features that point towards a polite interpretation and features that point towards an impolite interpretation.' In explaining verbal formula mismatches, under the title of convention-driven implicational impoliteness, Culpeper (2011b:174), points out that he looks into the 'mismatches created out of conventionalized politeness formula in the context of either conventionalized impoliteness formula or a behaviour that otherwise expresses impoliteness.' One example he gives is 'Could you just fuck off?' with the mismatch *could* and *fuck off* present. The other examples below come from British talent shows, *X Factor* and *Britain's Got Talent*, from Simon Cowell, the judge of these talent shows, quoted by Cowell in his book *I hate to be rude, but ... Simon Cowell's book of nasty comments* (2006):

> She was amazing and, but she is completely and utterly barking mad. (p. 41)
> I admire Paula for admiring me. (p. 60)
> You are gorgeous, but your voice isn't. (p. 67)
> I think you are amazing: amazingly dreadful. (p. 73)
> That was extraordinary. Unfortunately, extraordinarily bad. (p. 73)

Culpeper further discusses the strategy by focusing on how mismatch of a conventionalized politeness utterance can create impoliteness through the contrast or the mismatch with the context predictable from the co-text. Repetition and pauses are central to this interpretation:

> Again, they mix conventionalized politeness with conventionalized impoliteness: the contrast is with contexts projected by the co-texts and not the situation. In some cases, the contrast is formalized by *but*, a word that gives rise to the conventional implicature that there is a contrast between its conjuncts. In other cases, the two parts are held together by repetition. The fact that there are two halves is something that Cowell exploits. By beginning with conventionalized politeness these utterances construct a 'garden path' pragmatic strategy: the listener is led towards an understanding that Cowell thinks positively of them, and Cowell invariably pauses to allow understanding to linger. He completes the rhetorical strategy by violently derailing the polite interpretation. (p. 174)

Similarly, with ASI's utterance '((0.9)) but watching TV series ... ((0.3)) is an important art' (((0.9)) *ama dizi izlemek* ((0.3)) *önemli bi sanat)*, can be taken as a complement and conventionalized politeness formula as at the point it occurs in the conversation: all the three speakers ASI, OZG and DER, have informed BAD of their disapproval of not saying hello with the excuse of watching TV series, and politely, they want to end the tension and establish a friendlier interaction. In the rest of the conversation, which is not given here since it is not the focal point of the discussion, the participants start talking about various series they watch and the seasons they have covered watching so far. However, other clues in the immediate context lead to a contradictory interpretation, so '((0.9)) but watching TV series ... ((0.3)) is an important art' (((0.9)) *ama dizi izlemek* ((0.3)) *önemli bi sanat)* is a sarcastic comment and a criticism pointed at BAD.

First, there is a mismatch between the object, watching TV series, and the reference to the object being an art and in fact, an important art, intensified with the adjective *important*. It is contrary to common knowledge that watching TV series is an art and hence further interpretation as to whether the comment is sarcastic is required. Second, the pauses are quite striking not only in this utterance but in all proceeding utterances. As quoted above, Culpeper (2011b:174) points out that pausing is a part of the strategy that Simon Cowell, the judge of British talent shows, *X Factor* and *Britain's Got Talent*, uses: 'By beginning with conventionalized politeness these utterances construct a "garden path" pragmatic strategy: the listener is led towards an understanding that Cowell thinks positively of them, and Cowell invariably *pauses to allow understanding to linger* (emphasis mine).'

Third, given the co-textual clues discussed above indicated by utterances 'but I blocked it,' 'hatun,' and 'she has grown up' by the message enforcers such as 'even' and 'now' by the violations of maxim of quantity and the pauses and the contextual clues that the girls are disapproving of BAD's behaviour of not saying hello because she is watching TV series, the utterance '((0.9)) but watching TV series ... ((0.3)) is an important art' (((0.9)) *ama dizi izlemek* ((0.3)) *önemli bi sanat*) creates a mismatch or contrast to the co-text and the context. Therefore, it is sarcastic and functions as a pointed criticism, which is a conventionalized impoliteness formula (Culpeper, 2010, 2011b).

BAD responds to the irony by '(that is) right. (it is) an important art.' (*evet önemli bi sanat.*). Her tone of voice to counteract ASI's (*ama dizi izlemek (0.3) önemli bi sanat*) high-pitch accent is a considerably lower-pitch accent as Figure 4.5 illustrates.

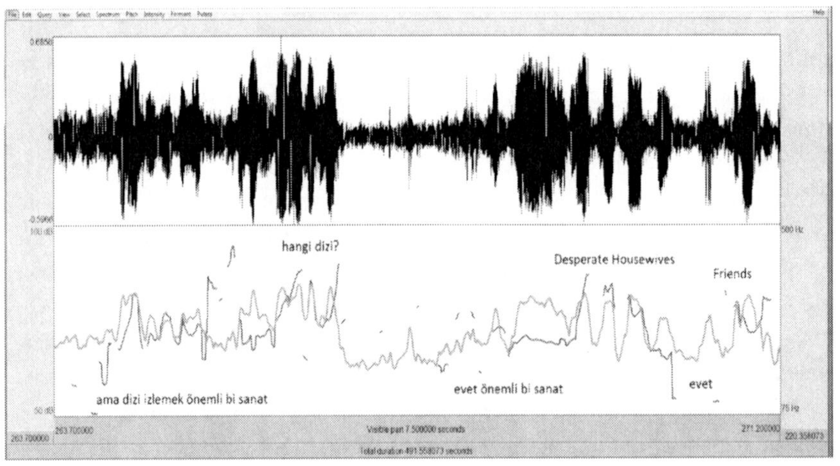

Figure 4.5. Praat display for irony in the STC Extract 2

This observation that BAD's response is uttered in a very different tone of voice can be interpreted as BAD's acknowledging the irony and in return, taking a serious tone to agree. With this serious tone and agreement, she is in fact twisting the irony to the direct propositional meaning of ASI's comment, that is, watching a TV series actually is an important art, and counters the impoliteness.

This extract is also an example of how dynamically in interaction participants index themselves and create different membership categorizations. As soon as ASI says 'I have it. but I blocked it, anyway,' DER aligns with her and joins in with a melodic, humorous tone illustrated in Figure 4.4 and says, '(she) goes online. the lady is busy. (she) does not even say hello' (*ya ben de giriyor hatun, meşgul selam bile vermiyor*). The irony then is carried on between the two speakers even after a third participant, OZG, brings a related but different theme to the topic with her question 'which one (What TV series)?' (*hangi dizi?*) since ASI takes a long pause for 1.7 seconds and acts like she is taking her time to say something significant with a filled pause, 'err' (*ee).* Then she gives an example of a TV series, *Desperate Housewives*, in almost the same high pitch she says '((0.9)) but watching TV series ... ((0.3)) is an important art' (((0.9)) *ama dizi izlemek ((0.3)) önemli bi sanat).* This indicates that she is still being ironic and BAD replies 'yes' (*evet*) with almost the same serious low-pitch accent and says '(that is) right. (it is) an important art' (*evet önemli bi sanat.*). Almost the same serious accent, although in low-pitch, BAD adopts in her utterance '(that is) right. (it is) an important art' (*evet önemli bi sanat.*) in response to ASI's ironic comment '((0.9)) but watching TV series ... ((0.3)) is an important art.' (((0.9)) *ama dizi izlemek ((0.3)) önemli bi sanat*) implies that BAD is being ironic too.

Overall, in this extract, showing dislike to one's taste in an ironical tone, 'but watching TV series ... ((0.3)) is an important art' (*ama dizi izlemek ((0.3)) önemli bi sanat*) preceded by irony '(she) goes online. the lady is busy. (she) does not even say hello' (*ya ben de giriyor hatun, meşgul selam bile vermiyor*) triggers impoliteness. By implication it is a criticism and an insult. This incidence of impoliteness is countered by irony again by BAD with the response '(that is) right. (it is) an important art,' (*evet önemli bi sanat*) which seems like an acknowledgment of the comment, but the irony implies otherwise. The impoliteness is resolved as a result of topic change motivated by a third party OZG's question 'which one?' (*hangi dizi*).

Extract 3:

In this extract, four participants, PER000040, RAM00080, SER000081 and GUL000082, (PER, RAM, SER and GUL hereafter) are involved in a conversation where they are comparing giving birth naturally to having a caesarean. In the transcript in the utterance (*YUS!*), YUS refers to the first three letters of the name RAM calls. The full name the original transcript has been shortened to respect the privacy of the speakers.

Extract 3. 072_090820_00022

PER000040 [v]	⌣çocuğuna bakıyorsun.			nor	Mal
Trans.	(you) look after your baby. with natural birth				
SER000081 [v]		((0.2)) hm-hm˙			
SER000081 [c]		((fast))			
Trans.	mhm mhm.				
GUL000082 [v]			on	dan...	
Trans.	from this...				

PER000040 [v]	doğumda hemen ayaklanıyorsun.	((1.1)) Allah kurtarsın
Trans.	you start walking soon. may God deliver you.[3]	

PER000040 [v]	inşa	llah.				
Trans.	hopefully.					
RAM000080 [v]				olur.	⌣(iyi oluruz).	sen e e kendin
Trans.	fine. ((we) will be fine). well, you err yourself					
SER000081 [v]					gidebilecek misin?	
Trans.	will (you) be able to go?					
GUL000082 [v]		amin.	hadi gide	lim.		
Trans.	amen. let's go.					

RAM000080 [v]	geniş	sin	ya.	
Trans.	are big.			
GUL000082 [v]		ha˙		((inhales)) hah! ((inhales)) ((short laugh))˙
Trans	what? you are joking!			

3. 'May God be with you,' *allah kurtarsın*, is a formulaic expression similar in meaning to 'May God deliver you'. It is used in hard times and difficult situations.

RAM000080 [v]	var mı?				
Trans.	is there/he?				
RAM000080 [c]					((calling
GUL000082 [v]		teessüf ederim. ‿bana şişman mı		demek işte	din?
Trans.	excuse me. are you saying I am fat?				
GUL000082 [c]				((laughing))	

PER000040 [v]			yok. ‿o şekilde demedi herhalde. ‿e	
Trans.	no. she did not mean it like that probably. well,			
RAM000080 [v]	(YUS)!			
RAM000080 [c]	another person in the context))			
SER000081 [v]			((laughs))˙	
GUL000082 [v]		‿((short laugh))˙	((laughs))˙	

PER000040 [v]	e • ne denir böyle?	‿((XXX)) de		ğil anlamı	nda. o anl	Amda
Trans.	err how is it expressed? not in the meaning of (X). in the meaning of					
RAM000080 [v]		vüc	ut.			
Trans.	body.					
GUL000082 [v]			haa˙		yok.	‿şaka
GUL000082 [c]			((lengthening))			
Trans.	oh, I see. no. I was joking.					

PER000040 [v]	(dedi)((XXX))			
Trans.	((she) said) ((XXX))			
RAM000080 [v]			• vücut yapısı.	
Trans.	body shape			
SER000081 [v]				amanın!
SER000081 [c]				((softly))
Trans.	oh no!			
GUL000082 [v]	dedim ben. ‿şaka dedim.			
Trans.	(I) was joking.			

PER, from firsthand experience, explains that having a natural birth is not easy either but at least one is able to look after the baby after a normal birth, which is not the case with a caesarean. The reason for making such a comparison is that

GUL is pregnant and other speakers are offering their thoughts on the issue. When GUL is about to leave, they wish her an easy time with the birth. As GUL suggests going, 'let's go,' SER asks, 'will you be able to go?' which is immediately followed by RAM's comment 'well, you yourself are big' (*sen e e kendin genişsin ya*). As can be seen from the transcription, this comment 'well, you yourself are big' comes immediately after RAM's comment and could be offered as an explanation why SER is asking if GUL is able to go by herself. In the meantime, RAM continues her turn by, apparently looking for another person, and asking 'is (there/he)?') (*var mı?*). Then, she calls out to a person with his name *Yusuf*. The fact that RAM calls for this person just after the question if GUL is able to go by herself even though she is so 'big' (*geniş*) brings out the interpretation that RAM wants Yusuf to accompany her. However, GUL reacts to 'big' with a non-lexical backchannel 'ha,' which precedes RAM's attempt to call the person in the context. The non-lexical backchannel 'ha' is translated as 'what?' to indicate GUL's disbelief to what she has heard. Inhaling, and uttering an interjection, (*hah!*) loudly, which is translated as 'you're joking!' as in 'you cannot really mean what you have just said,' and inhaling again with a short laugh, GUL expresses her surprise at the comment. She reflects her disapproval of the comment with the reply 'excuse me' (*teessüf ederim*), and a confrontation with a direct question to RAM, 'are you saying I am fat?' (*bana şişman mı demek istedin?*) in a jocular manner. The translation 'excuse me' for (*teessüf ederim*) here gives a sense of disagreement with the previous utterance. However, with a direct question, one interjection and the utterance (*teessüf ederim*) in which the lexeme *teessüf* is semantically related to *esef*, meaning contempt, sorrow, regret, sadness, feeling sadness about something and being hurt, the text itself gives away that the jocular manner GUL seems to take does not match with the present tension of the moment. The tension is observed through the uptake of the speaker GUL, which consists of interjections 'what?' (*ha*), and 'you are joking' (*hah!*) with inhales in between and a confrontational question; through the uptake of the speaker PER, who tries to offer an explanation to what RAM did not mean but must have meant by 'no‿ she did not mean like that probably. well, err how is it expressed? not in the meaning of ((XXX)). in the meaning of ((XXX)) ((she) said)' (*yok. ‿o şekilde demedi herhalde‿ ee ne •denir ne denir böyle? ((XXX)) değil anlamında. o anlamda (dedi) ((XXX))*); and through the uptake of SER, which is an interjection uttered softly 'oh no!' (*amanın!*) used to express a warning as in 'eyvah' that the lines in the conversation have been crossed. All these clues cancel the possibility that what is observed here is a case of mock impoliteness: even if GUL is actually misinterpreting RAM's remarks as impolite to generate mock impoliteness and introduce humour into the discourse, despite several instances of laughter, the other participants' perceptions of impoliteness do not match with the context of mock impoliteness. In fact, GUL's reaction and response 'excuse me. are you saying I am fat?' (*teessüf ederim. bana şişman mı demek istedin?*) indicates that GUL took the comment 'well, you yourself are big' (*sen e e kendin genişsin ya*) as an insult, which fits Culpeper's (2010, 2011b) conventionalized impoliteness formulae under insult as personalized negative vocatives with the exception that *geniş* (big) does not necessarily have to be related to *şişman* (fat).

Geniş is semantically related to spatial aspect as *big, spacious* or *large* as opposed to *fat,* which is related to weight and has a negative value judgment as in *overweight*. It is obvious that GUL attaches a connotative meaning to *geniş* and semantic prosody comes into play with her interpretation of *geniş* as fat. She expresses that she feels insulted with the rejoinder *teessüf ederim.* An important question arises here: why is it at this point the semantic prosody comes into play and GUL interprets *big* as *fat*? In other words, in the context, what triggers her interpretation that RAM was implying that she was fat and hence was being impolite?

There are two important cues in the context that bring out GUL's perception of implicational impoliteness (Culpeper, 2011b). The first one is an overlap: when SER asks 'will you be able to go?' RAM was saying '(we) will be fine' (*iyi oluruz),* which could have hindered GUL from hearing SER's question. The significance of the overlap is that if GUL has not heard the question due to the overlap, it is not possible for her to understand that 'well, you yourself are big' (*sen e e kendin genişsin ya*) was an explanation offered to the question 'will you be able to go?' If that is the case, the utterance (*sen e e kendin genişsin ya)* violates the maxim of quantity because it is physically obvious from her stomach that she is pregnant. As a result, GUL attributes impoliteness to RAM's comment. Culpeper (2011b) defines this implicational impoliteness as non-conventionalized implicational form-driven impoliteness. As this excerpt indicates, conversational conventions, an overlap and the turn-taking pattern play a crucial role in GUL's attribution of impoliteness to RAM's comment since they trigger a perception of implied impoliteness by violating maxims of quantity.

The rest of the conversation is also interesting to analyse in terms of how the other participants attempt to restore the perceived impoliteness. PER recognizes what has happened and so tries to offer an explanation 'no⌣ she did not mean like that probably. well, err how is it expressed? not in the meaning of ((XXX)). in the meaning of ((XXX)) ((she) said)' (*yok. ⌣o şekilde demedi herhalde⌣ ee ne •denir ne denir böyle? ((XXX)) değil anlamında. o anlamda (dedi) ((XXX))).* She speaks carefully both by hedging with 'probably' and distancing herself by using a passive structure with 'well, how is it expressed?' After softening and distancing herself, she clarifies the misunderstanding by saying 'not in the meaning of ((XXX))' (*((XXX)) değil anlamında.).* While PER is struggling to come up with a good expression, RAM explains herself by saying 'body' (*vücut*) followed by more explanation 'body structure' (*vücut yapısı*) relating it to anatomy. GUL realizes what has been meant as she utters, (*haa*), a lengthened non-lexical backchannel used to express realization as in 'oh, I see.' She then withdraws her expression of contempt '*teessüf ederim*' by saying 'no. I was joking. (I) was joking' (*yok. şaka dedim ben. ⌣şaka dedim*).

Overall, in this extract, GUL's perception that RAM is being critical of how she looks with her comment 'well, err you yourself are big' (*sen e e kendin genişsin ya*) makes her take it as an insult and her counter-strategy to it is an ironic acknowledgment of the insult. GUL verbalizes her acknowledgment of RAM's insult with 'excuse me. are you saying I am fat?' (*teessüf ederim. bana şişman mı demek istedin?*). A third party, PER, attempts to repair GUL's impoliteness and protect RAM's face and possibly GUL's and her own face as well. GUL, in the end, after sensing the inappropriacy of her behaviour indicated by the interjection *(haa)* meaning 'Oh, I see' denies the face attack and says 'no. I was joking. (I) was joking' (*yok. şaka dedim ben. ⌣şaka dedim*).

Extract 4:

In this conversation, speakers MUS000518, NIL000520, HUM000467 (MUS, NIL and HUM hereafter) are talking about a past event in which one of the participants, YAL, apologized for his behaviour. In the original transcript, when the speakers talk about the event, they refer to each other and YAL with their full names. However, the full names in the transcript below have been replaced with three first capital letters as in MUS. A similar convention is used in the discussions. The type of impoliteness discussed in this extract is different from the others both in the sense that the instance of impoliteness in conversation that took place in the past is narrated by people who participated in the conversation rather than taking place at the time of speaking; and that it could only be extracted since MUS reported YAL's apology in direct speech which included the apology formula 'I am sorry' (*özür dilerim*). The conversation takes place at work and the participants MUS, NIL and HUM are colleagues. The address term 'hoca' that comes up in the transcription is translated as 'teacher' and 'hocam' as 'my teacher.' However, the terms 'hoca' and 'hocam' have a wide coverage; for instance, they can refer to a teacher of any academic title or to a stranger as a deferential address term. The word 'şey' is a multifunctional filler in Turkish (see section 3.4.2), which actually means 'thing.' It can be used to gain time or as a hesitation marker in addition to displaying caution and discretion to mark politeness when assessing something about the self or the other (Yılmaz, 2004). In the translation row in the extract, the point where the filler 'şey' is used, in parentheses 'thing' is written to indicate the filler.

Extract 4. 023_100304_00181

MUS000518 [v]		YAL Hoca şimdi kapıdan girdi
Trans.	look, YAL teacher came through the door.	
HUM000467 [v]	hoca çok komik ya.	
Trans.	the teacher is so funny.	
HUM000467 [c]		

MUS000518 [v]	biz de böyle NIL'le ((0.1)) şey konuşuyoruz.	((0.2)) şöyle
Trans.	we were like talking (thing) with NIL (he) looked	

MUS000518 [v]	bi baktı. ((0.3)) sonra ne yaptım ben?	bişey demedi	sonra.
Trans.	awhile. what did I do then? (he) didn't say anything then.		
HUM000467 [v]			Se
Trans.	(you)		

MUS000518 [v]	ha! • e ne yapıyorsun...				ha-ha˙	
Trans.	right! so how is it going... yeah, right					
HUM000467 [v]	n	şey de demişsin/ hocam		bu NIL değil		demiş	in.
Trans.	you said (thing) too /my teacher this is not NIL (you) said.						
NIL000520 [v]	o	dedi ki bize		ne	yapıyorsunuz	dedi.	
Trans.	he said what are you doing (he)said						

HUM000467 [v]	• ama o i/ o sen şaka yapıyorsun sanmış. ⌐sonra geldi.
Trans.	but he i/ (he) thought you were joking. then (he) came back.

HUM000467 [v]	((inhales)) ama suratı	direkt	kızardı.	((0.7)) falandı beni de
Trans.	but (he) blushed immediately. was like when (he).			

HUM000467 [v]	görünce. ⌐hocam dedim ordaki kardeşim diyorum.	
Trans.	saw me too. my teacher (I)said that is my sister, (I)am saying.	
NIL000520 [v]		Ben
Trans.	I	

MUS000518 [v]		bilmiyor mu	senin ikizin olduğunu on	un?	
Trans.	doesn't (he) know she is your twin?				
HUM000467 [v]				o	Hiç
Trans.	he never				
NIL000520 [v]	böyle çaba	lıyorum.			
Trans.	I am like struggling				
NIL000520 [c]	((laughing))				

MUS000518 [v]		ha˙		dedi ki ne yapıyorsunuz b	Akayım
Trans.	oh! he said so what are you doing.				
HUM000467 [v]	görmemiş yemek	hane	de.		
Trans.	saw (us) in the cafeteria.				
NIL000520 [v]				belki duymadı (bile).	
Trans.	maybe (he) never heard (even).				

MUS000518 [v]	dedi böyle bi.	((0.2)) ((inhales)) ben de şey dedim.	((0.3)) e
Trans.	(he) said like. I said (thing) er		

MUS000518 [v]	ne dedim?		şey de...		çalışma yapıyoruz
Trans.	what did (I) say? in (thing)... (we) are studying				
NIL000520 [v]		((0.5)) e	e	çalışma	yapıyoruz dedi... sonar
Trans.	emm (he) said we are studying... then				

MUS000518 [v]	dedim.		ben ded	i... sonra o da	böyle (şey) bi
Trans.	(I) said. I (he) said. then he like (thing)				
NIL000520 [v]		sen de dedin k	i		HUM'nın
Trans.	And then you said HUM's				

MUS000518 [v]	(bakın yaa)	filan dedi böyle. hep seni/ seni ee	Sandığını
Trans.	look at this or something like that, he said. he thought it was you/ you er all along		
MUS000518 [c]		((change in tone of voice))	
NIL000520 [v]	karde...		sonra ne
Trans.	sis.. then		

MUS000518 [v]	ben anladım.		• hahı!		HUM
Trans.	I realized. yeah! HUM				
NIL000520 [v]	dedi? fa/ • fabri	kasyon...		hı˙ evet.	((laughs))˙
Trans.	what did (he) say? fa/ fabrication....yeah, right.				
NIL000520 [c]				((laughing))	

MUS000518 [v]	olduğunu	düşündüğünü düşündüm. hocam HUM değil
Trans.	(he) thought (I) thought my teacher she is not HUM	

MUS000518 [v]	yalnız o dedim.		sonra		çıktı. Hıı
Trans.	though (I) said then (he) left. I see.				
HUM000467 [v]		((0.1)) iş	te o	es	pri yapıyorsun (sandı).
Trans.	(you) see (he thought) you were joking.				

MUS000518 [v]	fabrikasyon değil mi dedi.		öyle bişey
Trans.	fabrication isn't she (he) said? something like that		
DID000521 [v]		((knocks on the door))	

MUS000518 [v]	dedi.			gel.		
Trans.	(he) said. come in					
HUM000467 [v]	((laughs))˙					
NIL000520 [v]	öyle bişey dedi. ((laughs))˙	((short	laugh))˙		Ge
Trans.	(he) said something like that. Com					
DID000521 [v]				gelebil	ir mi	yim?
Trans.	can I come in?					

MUS000518 [v]		sonra	da gitti. arkasından geldi.	((0.2)) ay çok
Trans.	then he left. then he came back . oh I am			
MUS000518 [c]			((laughing))	((laughing, reporting
NIL000520 [v]	I DID.	gel.		
Trans.	eDID, come in.			

MUS000518 [v]	özür dilerim.
Trans.	so sorry.
MUS000518 [c]	YAL's words))
ALL000001 [v]	((laughter))˙
[nn]	((silence))

In this conversation 'oh, I am so sorry' (*ay çok özür dilerim*) is a metapragmatic comment signalling an impoliteness event that has apparently been perceived to have occurred. The summary of the event is as follows. NIL and HUM are twins. YAL, who could be actually be a teacher, an older colleague or a socially distant colleague who does not know HUM has a twin. MUS seems to be a friend of both HUM and NIL. When MUS and NIL are working on something together YAL comes across them and greets them, 'so what are you doing?' (*e ne yapıyorsunuz bakayım?*). MUS realizes that YAL thinks MUS is talking with HUM and so he points that out to YAL 'she is not HUM though' (*HUM değil yalnız o*). YAL, not having a clue what MUS has meant, thinks MUS is just joking and he replies 'fabrication, isn't she?' (*fabrikasyon değil mi?*). Then as HUM explains, he walks away; sees HUM and comes back: 'but (he) blushed immediately. was like when he saw me too. my teacher (I) said that is my sister (I) am saying' (*ama suratı direk kızardı. beni de görünce. Hocam dedim ordaki kardeşim diyorum*). Realizing what MUS has meant, YAL comes back and apologizes to MUS.

MUS is providing genuine and true information with his utterance 'my teacher she is not HUM though' (*hocam Hümeyra değil yalnız o*). With other words, MUS is adhering to the maxim of quality which requires two premises: (1) do not say what you believe to be false; (2) do not say that for which you lack adequate evidence (Grice, 1975). However, YAL thinks that MUS is joking because the information he provides does not conform to the reality YAL knows of and creates an inconsistency. Realizing later that he failed to follow the real content of the utterance and the misunderstanding, he comes back and apologizes. What needs to be discussed here is this: what brings YAL to apologize? What makes him perceive that his behaviour was impolite?

YAL failed to see the truthfulness of MUS's utterance 'she is not HUM though' (*HUM değil yalnız o*) and misunderstands MUS. Therefore, he responds. If he had assumed that MUS was abiding by the quality maxim, he would have responded differently: perhaps, with a question inquiring why MUS says that the person he sees is not HUM. Instead of the conversational sequence in the form of a (perceived) joke 'she is not HUM though' (*HUM değil yalnız o*) replied by a joke 'fabrication, isn't she?' (*fabrikasyon değil mi?*), a different conversational sequence would have taken place including a question-answer adjacency pair. In the extract, YAL's utterance 'fabrication, isn't she?' (*fabrikasyon değil mi?*) functions as a silencer although it is meant to be a joke. Moreover, YAL leaves the room, which again functions as a silencer as it ends the conversation. Since MUS's utterance, which adheres to the maxim of quality, is confronted with a joke that overlooks the truthfulness of it, YAL's joke creates an awkward moment in the discourse. YAL comes back to apologize because he realizes that his failure in understanding the conversational subtleties silenced MUS. This brings us to an important but a neglected aspect of impoliteness: impoliteness can be perceived to have occurred by formulaic use of linguistic expressions or by failure to attend to the propositional content or the truthfulness of utterances, which is related to the maxim of quality.

Overall, in this extract, impoliteness is triggered by a misunderstanding. There is no impoliteness strategy since misunderstanding occurs as a result of the professor's lack of information and his disbelief in MUS's words. The response coming from MUS is silence and the impoliteness, which is not intentional since it is YAL's perception of having committed it by not knowing that HUM has a twin and for not having taken MUS's word for real, is repaired through an apology when YAL realizes the misunderstanding and apologizes.

Extract 5:

In this extract, ZEY000073, ISA000058, MEH000126 (ZEY, ISA, MEH hereafter) are talking about earthquakes. In the extract there are two Arabic interjections (*ulek!*) and (*hallak*) and the abbreviation 'ara' next to the interjections means Arabic. The word 'şey' comes up twice in ISA's utterances 'well, mostly ...' (*çoğu şey ...*) and 'well, why in ...' (*e niye şeyde*). In the translation row in the extract, the point where the filler 'şey' is (see section 3.4.2 and STC Extract 4), in parentheses 'thing' is written to indicate the place of the filler. However, the effect of its meaning, which is 'well' in both cases, is translated as part of the utterance in English. In ZEY's utterance 'they are your children too!' (*ya o senin çocuğun da o ...*), the emotive emphasis of the interjection 'ya' in the Turkish utterance is given by the exclamation mark at the end of the utterance in the English translation. Other fillers and interjections (e.g. 'yani', 'yav') are translated by using lexical items in English to the closest meaning they connote in the interactional exchange. In the conversation, ZEY is enquiring about whether the city they live in is in the most dangerous earthquake zone in the world or in Turkey, the country the city is in. ISA responds to ZEY's questions and says the city is not in the most dangerous zone in the world but it is the most dangerous one in Turkey. MEH joins in when ZEY comments 'why don't they pass a law here so that ...' (*niye burda bir yasa getirilmiyor da ...*). At this point MEH joins in.

Extract 5. 061_0900712_0045

ZEY000073 [v]	madem burası... dünyanın birinci deprem bölgesi mi burası
Trans.	if it is.... is it the most dangerous earthquake zone in the world

ISA000058 [v]		((0.4)) dünyanın değil. yok.	((0.3)) yani...
Trans.	not in the world. no. I mean...		
ISA000058 [c]		((softly))	
ZEY000073 [v]	Türkiye'nin mi?		((0.3)) Türk
Trans.	or in Turkey? in Turkey.		

ISA000058 [v]		tamam.	((0.1)) hı-	hı˙	
Trans.	Ok. Yeah				
ISA000058 [c]		((change in tone of voice))	((fast))		
ZEY000073 [v]	iye'nin.			ha	h!	((0.1)) Türkiye'
Trans.	right! in Turkey.				

ZEY000073 [v]	nin.	((inhales)) niye burda bir yasa getirilmiyor da...	
Trans.	why don't they pass a law here so that...		
MEH000126 [v]			((0.2))
MEH000126 [c]			ara: ulek!

MEH000126 [v]	(ulek!)	orospu çocuğu kendilerine çimentodan çalıp
Trans.	son of a bitch (they) steal cement and make (constructions)	
MEH000126 [c]	interjection	

ISA000058 [v]				çoğu şey...			
Trans.	well, mostly (thing)...						
ISA000058 [c]				((softly))			
ZEY000073 [v]						o	lur mu yan
Trans.	well, is it fair?						
MEH000126 [v]	yapıyorlar.	hallak	ne yasak	ne de bir bo	k ya	rar.	
Trans.	for themselves. (interjection). no prohibition no shit would work.						
MEH000126 [c]		ara: now				is	

ZEY000073 [v]	i? senin	halkın ölüyor.	ya o senin		çocuğun da o...		

Trans.	your people die. he is your own child too!...					
MEH000126 [v]	yav!		yav s...	çok		sikin	de onun
MEH000126 [c]			((lengthening))	((emphatically))		((fast))
Trans.	right! like (he gives) a f... (he) really (gives) a fuck					

ISA000058 [v]			((1.7)) e niye	şeyde/
Trans.	well, why in (thing)			
ISA000058 [c]				
MEH000126 [v]	senin halkın ölmüşse. çok affedersin.			
Trans.	if your people die. forgive me please.			

MEH's response to ZEY's question, starting with an interjection *ulek!*, in Arabic includes swear words: 'son of a bitch they steal from cement and make (constructions) for themselves' (*orospu çocuğu kendilerine çimentodan çalıp yapıyorlar*). ISA has a limited part in the conversation; he has a soft tone and as MEH is speaking, he says 'well, mostly...' (*çoğu şey ...*). He does not continue since ZEY directs another question after MEH's comment, 'well, is it fair?' (*olur mu yani?*). MEH, who has not completed his turn yet, completes it with another interjection, *hallak*, and comments 'no prohibition no shit would work' (*ne yasak ne de bir bok yarar*). ZEY is emotional with her next comment 'your people die' (*senin halkın ölüyor*) 'he is your own child too!' (*ya o senin çocuğun da o*). The interjection 'ya' adds to the emotive effect. In her utterances, the possessive determiner 'your' and the subject pronoun 'you' is used to refer to third person determiner 'their' and third person pronoun 'they.' Moreover, she personalizes those who die by referring to them in the singular third person pronoun 'he' (o) instead of plural third person pronoun 'they.' It is noteworthy to point out that the singular third person 'o' in Turkish may refer to both males and females. For the sake of simplicity, the 'child' in the utterance 'he is your own child too!' (*ya o senin çocuğun da o*) will be referred to as 'he' although the word 'çocuk' denotes he/she distinction in most cases. Through personalization and use of the interjection 'ya,' ZEY reflects that she is taking an emotional stance and expresses her difficulty in understanding why those people cannot empathize with the people dying. MEH's response to ZEY's emotional reaction with 'your people die' (*senin halkın ölüyor*) 'he is your own child too!' (*ya o senin çocuğun da o*) starts with an interjection 'yav,' which is translated as 'right!' with an exclamation mark to indicate MEH is surprised and being ironic to ZEY. MEH is surprised at ZEY's irrational expectation that the people who can steal from cement to better serve themselves could care for people who die. Therefore, he comments, 'like he gives a f(uck) (*yav s(ikinde)*) he really gives a fuck if your people die' (*çok sikinde onun senin halkın ölmüşse*). In the comment tier, notice how he plays with his tone of voice to emphasize his point. The interjection is lengthened; the word 'really' (*çok*) is accompanied by an ironically emphatic tone, and the swear word 'fuck' (*sikinde*) by a fast tone. Immediately after that comment, MEH apologizes 'forgive me please' (*çok affedersin*). The literal gloss of the original utterance (*çok affedersin*) is 'a lot forgive me' and the word 'a lot' functions as a quantifier to the act of forgiving. The 'forgive' apology formula as in 'forgive me' is used in the translation utterance instead of 'I'm so sorry' because of the implicational difference between the two utterances. In this extract, MEH obviously thinks that he has been impolite. However, he himself does not explain or give clues as to why he thinks he has been impolite and what in the conversation he evaluates to be impolite.

One explanation is that MEH apologizes because he has used swear or taboo words, with a gradually increased level of offensiveness (i.e., 'son of a bitch' [*orospu çocuğu*], 'no shit' [*ne bok*], 'gives a f[uck]' [*yav s{ikinde}*], and 'he really gives a fuck' [*çok sikinde onun*]), one after the other. The taboo words in the expressions he uses are associated with offensiveness and have negative connotations. Having gone against the 'norms' and conventions of the conversation by using bad language, MEH apologizes. In her study examining the metapragmatics of impoliteness in Turkish, Işık-Güler (2008:249) maintains that '[c]ursing and swearing as a style of speech all the time ("küfürlü konuşma"), using slang, vernacular language ("argo") and cursing (e.g. "allah belanı versin," "gebersin") in the company of others – moreso in the company of a female – are seen as impolite ways.' She mentions Hirschon (2001), who states that for Turkish people, certain insults, especially those that associate sexually with individuals' family members are found as more impolite and can be met with physical retaliation. The phrase 'son of a bitch' (*orospu çocuğu*) and the taboo word 'fuck' (*sik*) MEH uses are impolite – more so because they are sexual swear words and he uses them in a female's (ZEY's) company. 'Orospu' means 'whore' in Turkish and 'sik' means male sex organ in a vulgar way. The reasons why swear words and phrases which have sexual connotations 'are usually not taken lightly and they are not let pass as verbal altercations in Turkish' (Işık-Güler, 2008:250). Why they are considered more impolite in the company of a female needs to be analysed with further studies.

Nevertheless, different theoretical models would propose different explanations as to why MEH apologizes in this extract. While discussing examples that did not quite fit the bulk of his data, Culpeper (2011b:42) explains that taboo words create cases where it is difficult to decide what causes these cases to be perceived as impolite: whether the negative connotations of the taboo words themselves threaten the positive face of the participants or their sociality rights, which are not directly about face issues. The example he gives is as follows:

> On the beach in the South of England with my family. My dad has bought me
> a snorkel set but the sea is freezing and I don't use it.
>   'Come on son, be brave.' < said quite jokingly >
>   'I am.'
>   'You're not gonna do much snorkelling there.' < said quite jokingly >
>   (after attempting to get in the sea).
>   'Dad it's freezing ... I don't want to!' < being stubborn >
>   'Oh don't be a wimp.'
>   'No dad I'm not going in.' < being stubborn > (said as I walked up the beach).
>   'Well we might as well throw it in the f**king sea then!' < stress on f**king >

Quoting Brown and Levinson (1987:67), Culpeper (2011b:42) explains that they treat 'irreverence' and 'mention of taboos' as a positive face issue on the basis that 'S indicates that he doesn't value H's values and doesn't fear H's fears.' He, on the other hand, maintains that because 'taboos are less a matter of mediating an individual's self and more a matter of social conventions,' they are primarily related to sociality rights not to face issues. He adds that '[a]lthough not explicitly accommodated within equity rights, one can construct an argument that the producer of something shows lack of consideration for the perceiver by introducing something with strong negative emotions (i.e. it causes them emotional cost)' (p. 42).

If we consider Brown and Levinson's (1987) treatment of mention of taboo words as a positive face issue (with the explanation that 'S indicates that he doesn't value H's values and doesn't fear H's fears'), maintaining that MEH apologizes because he does not value what ZEY values would not be a valid comment. In fact, with his comments, MEH shows his agreement with ZEY about the inconsiderateness of the people who do not care about people's lives, and shares her feelings strongly.

If we consider MEH's apology on the basis that 'the producer shows lack of consideration for the perceiver by introducing something with strong negative emotions' (Culpeper, 2011b:42), and causes emotional cost, maintaining that MEH has caused an emotional cost to ZEY would not be valid either. By implication, through the utterances 'hah! like he gives a f... he gives load of fuck your people die' (*yav! yav s..., çok sikinde onun senin halkın ölmüşse*), MEH means ZEY's expectations that those people should empathize and behave more humanely are irrational and unreasonable. However, arguing that his implication causes an emotional cost to ZEY would not be well-grounded because the context or the co-text does not give any cues in that respect.

Overall, in this extract, MEH seems to be attributing impoliteness to his own use of language on the basis of common understanding that people avoid using bad language because it brings out strong negative connotations. It is important to note that MEH, the speaker and generator of impoliteness (at least from his own point of view), is the only participant in the conversation making judgments about his behaviour. Therefore, although he insults a third party and does not get reactions from the overhearing participants, we do not see a counter-strategy.

In Section 1.3, it was discussed how politeness theory was initially shaped by Lakoff (1973, 1989) and later by Brown and Levinson (1987 [1978]), and it was explained how the hearer was perceived in their framework. For instance, what is proposed for the positive politeness superstrategy (Brown and Levinson, 1987) is that the speaker performs the FTA towards redressing the positive face threat to the hearer (i.e., by claiming common ground, attending to the hearer's needs, etc.). For this framework, the speaker had a more central role in the analysis of face in politeness theories. However, in time, with increasing emphasis on the discursive approach, the focus was given to participants' or hearers' perception, which has also been criticized later for its focus (Haugh, 2007). In the extract being discussed, the speaker MEH is the performer of impoliteness and is the only participant who draws attention to it by an apology 'forgive me please' (*çok affedersin*). Therefore, this extract highlights the importance of including speakers' evaluations of their own utterances in the discussion of politeness and impoliteness theories. Perhaps an emphasis on how speakers form judgments on their impolite behaviour and how they evaluate the impact of their behaviour on their own faces in interaction would bring about new dimensions to impoliteness studies.

4.4 An Overview

This chapter has demonstrated the application of the methodological framework proposed in Chapter 3 together with the analyses of the BNC and the SCT extracts. In this chapter, within the corpus driven approach, impoliteness phenomena in conversation have been explored inductively rather than deductively (Francis, 1993). The analysis has covered the interplay of the context and the co-text through tapping into varying forms of linguistic and paralinguistic clues for impoliteness, from the use of formulaic expressions to the mechanics of conversation such as turn-taking and the impact of voice quality. In Chapter 3, it has been maintained that the cyclic process, i.e., going backwards from collated data to develop the theory or framework is essential both among different studies and within single studies. Within a single study, it is argued that the cyclic process requires *tentativeness* – 'an open mind' (Rühlemann, 2007:1) in terms of the research questions the analyst starts the study with. Perceiving the research questions as tentative means that the researcher is willing to revise or reformulate the questions later as the study unfolds because if the findings from natural data do not fit any existing theories, they will in fact be bringing new dimensions to be explored and revealing answers to questions which the analyst did not have in mind at the beginning. This explains why both the extraction and analysis levels are equally significant and complementary to each other within single studies carried out with a corpus driven approach. In light of the findings and the issues that have arisen during the advancement of the two layers, certain concepts formed around impoliteness have been revisited and new theoretical dimensions are theorized in relation to corpus linguistic studies of impoliteness. The following chapter, which is the end result of the cyclic process, discusses these emerging issues.

CHAPTER 5

Revisiting the Methodological Perspective: Emerging Issues

5.1 Impoliteness and the study

Pragmatic and sociolinguistic studies have mainly focused on politeness and its strategies for many years (Lakoff, 1973; Leech, 1983; Brown and Levinson, 1987; Holmes, 1990; Lane, 1990). Recently, a growing interest has been observed in impoliteness phenomenon (see, e.g. Watts, 2003; Mills, 2003; Culpeper, Bousfield and Wichmann 2003; Culpeper, 2005; Mills 2005; Bousfield, 2008; Bousfield and Locher, 2008; Culpeper, 2011b; Culpeper and Kádár, 2010) The reason why impoliteness has not received much attention until of late is closely related to the assumption that impoliteness is 'rather marginal to human linguistic behaviour in normal circumstances' (Leech, 1983). However, such an approach to impoliteness has been criticized, as it could be said to reflect a 'conceptual bias' (Eelen, 2001). It has been argued that suitable discussion of the dynamics of interpersonal communication should include hostile as well as harmonious communication (Xie, He and Lin, 2005; Bousfield and Locher, 2008). This book tackles with the limitations in this issue with its focus and postulates that impoliteness is very much a part of our daily interactions.

The main purpose of the book is to devise a methodological framework to analyse impoliteness in corpora. In doing so, the book tackles the issue of the methodology of extracting and analysing impoliteness in general corpora in both British English and Turkish. The data have been retrieved from two different corpora, the British National Corpus (BNC) XML edition and the Spoken Turkish Corpus (STC) (Ruhi et al., 2010b). The focus of the extraction and analysis is on informal conversation as a genre in spoken interaction. The discussion has been developed around the issues related to investigating impoliteness in a corpus driven linguistic (CDL) (Tognini-Bonelli, 2001; Römer, 2005) approach. Within the CDL framework, linguistic approaches to investigating the topic of research have been largely developed out of the findings offered by the data itself. In line with the corpus driven approach to investigating language use, the book illustrates that a corpus approach to impoliteness is exploratory and data driven. Therefore, the steps in research are not linear but cyclic. It is argued that the cyclic process, i.e., going backwards from collated data to develop the theory or framework the analysis level will be informed by, is of fundamental importance for impoliteness research. Since the natural data a corpus offers are expected to offer new findings that may not fit the pre-formulated questions, the cyclic process requires tentativeness in terms of the research questions. This book has aimed to illustrate such a methodology.

At the extraction level of the study, among the spoken texts in both the BNC and the databases of the STC, dialogues that include a conflict or an offending event have been selected. In order to identify such dialogues, various methods have been applied. First, spoken texts have been scanned through initial word query, collocation query, question sentences and tags query, query for imperatives, and possible queries that allow for searching of prosodic nuances, as well as inter-ruptions and overlaps. The next stage entailed taking metapragmatic comments, conventionalized impoliteness formulae (Culpeper, 2010, 2011b), cues for non-conventionalized implicational impoliteness (Culpeper, 2011b), conver-sational patterns, and other cues such as semantic prosody into consideration (Sinclair 1998, 2004; Stubbs, 2002; Morley and Partington, 2009; Bednarek, 2008). This means that, bearing in mind that 'neither the expression nor the context guarantee an interpretation of (im)politeness' (Culpeper 2010:3237), the conversations which have been selected as containing impoliteness have been examined discursively, for metapragmatic comments existing in the co-text, as well as having been looked at through the cues existing both in the co-text and context to detect conventionalized impoliteness formulae and non-conventionalized implicational impoliteness.

This method of looking at conversations to extract impoliteness events has two steps:

(a) Studying the co-text for what linguistic expressions come before and after utterances and for metapragmatic comments (e.g. 'you're rude,' 'what she did was rude')

(b) Studying the co-text *for* conventionalized impoliteness formulae, (e.g. 'you are such a hypocrite,' 'Shut up!') and context, and for what is beyond the linguistic expressions for non-conventionalized implicational impoliteness (e.g. the relationship of speakers such as parent-child, prosodic aspects such as pauses, and rises in intonation and pitch)

Step 1 characterizes the discursive approach and Step 2, the cue-based approach. The discursive approach is characterized by its emphasis on how participants in interaction perceive (im)politeness. With this emphasis, this school of researchers (Eelen 2001; Mills 2003; Watts, 2003, Watts, Ide, and Ehlich 2005; Locher, 2004; Locher and Watts, 2005) contests the essentialist view that the notion of politeness is the same across cultures, which has been reinforced by Brown and Levinson's (1987) politeness theory. Since metapragmatic comments and reactive responses open a window to how interactants perceive impoliteness phenomena, they are listed as the two points taken into consideration under the discursive approach for the present study.

The discursive approach has been criticized for its emphasis on participants' perception and it has been argued that it has created questions concerning the validity of researchers' analyses (Haugh, 2007). An approach that complements the discursive approach in light of such criticisms is necessary; therefore, the cue-based approach is proposed in this study as a complement.

The cue-based approach has not been used in previous literature as a term to refer to an approach. Conventionalized impoliteness formulae, non-conventionalized implicational impoliteness, verbal and non-verbal forms signalling interpersonal conflict and semantic prosody all fall under the heading of the cue-based approach. It has been assumed that conventionalized impoliteness formulae, non-conventionalized implicational impoliteness, conversation analysis tools (e.g. turn-taking, pauses) verbal and non-verbal forms signalling interpersonal conflict (e.g. change in structural patterns such as turn-taking, topic change, repetition, seeking disagreement) and semantic prosody create an inclusive model to compensate for what might be neglected by the discursive approach.

Once the extraction level is completed, impoliteness in both languages is examined and compared in regards to how impoliteness is triggered, how the progression of impolite exchanges takes place, and how those instances of impoliteness are resolved, if they are indeed resolved. Other considerations such as context-determined impoliteness, the intentionality of the speaker, and the perception of the hearer are discussed. Finally, as part of the cyclic research pattern required by the CDL approach, the research questions are revisited and the concepts that emerged along with their implications are discussed in relation to existing impoliteness theories and models.

In this chapter, the research questions will be revisited and the findings will be discussed and summarized. Implications of the methodological framework the study is designed with, namely the CDL approach and cyclic research pattern, will be linked to the discussion and suggestions for further studies will be offered.

5.2 Extraction and the methodology: revisiting research questions

There are two questions at this level. The first question is: How can impoliteness be extracted in conversation across languages? In this study, British English and Turkish are the focus. The second question is: do findings at this level of the study provide the researcher with clues about what impoliteness is?

The first research question has a number of aspects to be discussed. The first aspect is the methodological approaches adopted at the extraction level. The method of extraction consists of a combination of two approaches: the discursive and the cue-based. The discursive approach applied in (im)politeness studies has been borrowed from discursive psychology. It has three main strands:

> (i) re-specification and critique of psychological topics and explanations; (ii) investigations of how everyday psychological categories are used in discourse; (iii) studies of how psychological business (motives and intentions, prejudices, reliability of memory and perception, etc.) is handled and managed in talk and text, without having to be overtly labelled as such. (Edwards, 2005:259)

These points explain the close relationship between discursive psychology and conversation, that is, talk that reflects our everyday business without necessarily being discussed.

Examples of impoliteness extracted from the corpora show that the combination of the two approaches with the tools they provide are as effective as they were assumed to be. For instance, some examples would not have been extracted from the BNC and the STC if the cue-based approach had not been included in the extraction. The BNC Extract 5 exemplifies how a conventionalized impoliteness formula 'fuck off' creates tension. Extract 2 shows how non-conventionalized implicational impoliteness is generated through an echo of offensive word 'shit' in 'SHIT TV.' Extract 3 is an example of how conversation analysis tools can be applied to reach conclusions about verbal and non-verbal conflicts which aggravate impoliteness. With immediate topic changes, after question-answer adjacency pairs, participants in interaction silence each other and create interpersonal conflict. The STC Extract 1 is a good example of how semantic prosody comes into play in generating impoliteness (through the use of *bi*, functioning in the text as a diminutive, and the verb *geçir-*) and how context-sensitive both semantic prosody and non-conventionalized implicational impoliteness are.

Overall, the effectiveness of these tools combined with the discursive and cue-based approaches proved to provide a wide enough window to look at impoliteness. In fact, if they were not combined, the subtle ways in which impoliteness is generated would have gone unnoticed in the analysis stage. It is important that further studies be carried out within a similar methodological approach to find out what other tools can be added under the two approaches.

Another aspect of the question is whether the query methods used with the corpora were effective. In order to arrive at conventionalized impoliteness formulae in the corpora to collect conversations that involve impoliteness, a variety of query methods were used. For instance, in the BNC, word and collocation queries were initially run for a list of taboo words such as *sodding, fucking, shit* and conventionalized phrases such as *bugger off, shut up* in the spoken subcorpus with the text type selected as spoken conversation. Most words for queries came from a study from Millwood-Hargrave (2000) cited by Culpeper (2011b). For extracting incidences of impoliteness in the STC, a similar method was used. A list of swear words and expressions was formed. Most words and expressions came from Aydın's (2006) and Güneş's (2009) studies. It was assumed that a list of these words would function well for carrying out the word query for extraction in Turkish, as Millwood-Hargrave's (2000) list used for word query in British English was so effective. Examples of impoliteness arrived at as a result of such word and collocation queries retrieved from the two corpora (e.g. The BNC Extracts 1, 2, 3, 7, the STC Extract 5) indicate that looking for conventionalized impoliteness formulae lends itself well for extraction.

For the word query in the STC, Işık-Güler's (2008) dissertation findings about concepts strongly associated with KABA in Turkish were also used. The lexical items that she found to be strongly associated with KABA in metapragmatic talk on impoliteness – *düşüncesiz, saygısız, nezaketsiz, küstahlık, patavatsızlık, kırıcı, bencil, çirkin, cahil,* and *empati kuramayan,* were not encountered in the extracted conversations. There are three possible reasons for this. First, despite being fairly representative in terms of demographic sampling, the STC is still limited in size. When the STC is expanded, further studies could bring about different findings. Second, people may prefer to not respond to impoliteness (Culpeper, Bousfield and Wichmann, 2003) and even if they do, they may not report it to other people later. For instance, in the STC Extract 4, which is reported impoliteness, we do not have access to the actual interaction that took place between the student and the professor. If the professor had not come back to apologize, and if the student had not reported it fully with the fact that the professor did apologize, this example of impoliteness would have not been available to the researcher. The third, and indeed a more plausible reason could be that there is a mismatch between how people conceptualize impoliteness and verbalize that conceptualization, and how they use the language to generate and react to impoliteness. While they evaluate a behaviour as impolite, people could verbalize their judgment with the lexeme *nezaketsiz,* but they could just as well use other expressions such as the metapragmatic comment (e.g. *teessüf ederim* [excuse me] in the STC Extract 3).

Eelen (2001) suggests that first-order politeness should be distinguished in three categories: expressive politeness, classificatory politeness, and metapragmatic politeness. He describes them as follows:

> Expressive politeness1 [i.e. first-order politeness] refers to politeness encoded in speech, to instances where the speaker aims at 'polite' behaviour: the use of honorifics or terms of address in general, conventional formulaic expressions ('thank you,' 'excuse me' ...), different request formats, apologies, etc. ..., i.e., the usual objects of investigation in most politeness research. Classificatory politeness1 refers to politeness used as a categorizational tool: it covers hearers' judgments (in actual interaction) of other people's interactional behaviour as 'polite' or 'impolite.' Finally, metapragmatic politeness1 covers instances of talk about politeness as a concept, about what people perceive politeness to be all about. (Eelen, 2001:35)

As mentioned above in the example of the STC Extract 3, comments such as *teessüf ederim* (excuse me), are regarded in this study as metapragmatic comments indicating classificatory politeness1. The reason for this is that the study examines impoliteness in interaction and such comments are metapragmatic and classificatory since they show interactants' evaluations of other participants' interactional behaviour as polite or impolite.

Another point that needs to be remembered here about the STC Extract 3 and the metapragmatic comment *teessüf ederim* (excuse me) is that *teessüf ederim* is uttered to express disapproval of what the speaker has heard from another speaker in an interaction. In other words, it expresses that the person who says *teessüf ederim* has taken offence at the violation of her rights and she is asking that the other speaker acknowledge what she has done. Going back to the argument about whether impoliteness is inherent in linguistic expressions or speech acts (see Section 2.2 for discussion), it seems that Culpeper's (2010) dual view that (im)politeness and pragmatic (im)politeness are inter-dependent, is plausible: '([I]m)politeness can be more inherent in a linguistic expression or can be more determined by context, but neither the expression nor the context guarantee an interpretation of (im)politeness' (p. 3237). In discussing mimicry and echoic mention as implicational impoliteness (see Section 2.2), Culpeper (2011b) refers to Sperber and Wilson's (1981) Relevance Theory and echoic irony. Culpeper summarizes Sperber and Wilson (1981:240), where the relevant implicatures are formed on the following conditions:

> [f]irst, on a recognition of the utterance as an echo; second, on an identifi-
> cation of the source of the opinion echoed; and third, on a recognition that
> the speaker's attitude to the opinion echoed is one of rejection or disapproval.

In the case of the STC Extract 3, 'excuse me' in the meaning of *teessüf ederim* fulfils these three conditions of echoic use. This again confirms that word query by itself is not an adequate method for extraction of impoliteness unless contextual clues are taken into consideration. However, they can signal contexts where impoliteness might take place.

Related to what has been discussed regarding 'excuse me,' another complexity that was taken into consideration in the extraction was the role of semantic prosody. As mentioned before in Section 4.3, semantic prosody is closely related to the notion of collocations. The primary function of semantic prosody is to express speaker/writer attitude or evaluation (Louw, 2000:58). Semantic prosodies are typically negative; however, it is also possible that a speaker violates a semantic prosody condition to create an impact such as irony, insincerity, or humour on the hearer (Louw 1993:173). Findings confirm that the nuances semantic prosody brings to the interpretation of impoliteness play a fundamental role in extraction. The examples discussed in relation to semantic prosody with the extracts in this study strongly indicate that a consideration of semantic prosody is a must for research studies focusing on impoliteness.

One other fundamental notion applied in the extraction was Culpeper's (2011b) non-conventionalized implicational impoliteness. As discussed in Section 2.2, Culpeper (2011b) classifies implicational impoliteness in 3 categories: form-driven, convention-driven, internal and external, and context-driven, unmarked behaviour and absence of behaviour. Below is an example Culpeper (2011b:158) gives to demonstrate form-driven impoliteness:

> 'Uh, I'm always tidying this fucking room'-person X
>   Implied I never tidy the living room (which isn't true!)
>   Said in the living room, semi-angry, emphasizing 'always.'
>   Said by a housemate. No one else was there.
>   My response – silent annoyance

This example illustrates how flouting a Gricean maxim creates implicational impoliteness. From the perspective of the hearer, the offender violates the maxim of quality because it is false to say that the speaker is always tidying the room. This example falls into the classificatory politeness1 verbalized later in this way, since the behaviour and evaluation of the behaviour take place in actual interaction.

Through another example, Culpeper (2011b:168) illustrates convention-driven impoliteness.

> A friend that I used to work with came to visit me with his partner (who used to work for me last year). She is pregnant and before she even said hello to me she walked into my house and said 'Yeah Mate – I'm 5 months now and I'm nowhere near as big as you were – you were a monster (laughs) wasn't she Daz' So I replied with 'Oh, hello, come in – very nice to see you again too!'
>
> After saying this in a sarcastic tone, I looked at my friend Darren (the pregnant girl's partner) who cringed + mouthed silently 'sorry' to me and then said 'who's for a nice cup of tea' in a smiley voice.

This is an example of external, convention-driven impoliteness because 'Oh, hello, come in – very nice to see you again too!' is a conventionalized politeness greeting. However, it does not match the context especially since what it is preceded with (i.e., 'you were a monster') is more likely to be associated with impoliteness. This is a case for external mismatch. Again, taking Eelen's (2001) categories into consideration, one might suggest that 'Oh, hello, come in – very nice to see you again too!' indirectly falls into the metapragmatic politeness1 category, although it is a reaction to impoliteness taking place in an actual interaction as in classificatory politeness1 category. Similar to the case in the STC Extract 3, the three categories – expressive, classificatory and metapragmatics that Eelen (2001) suggests – become intertwined in interaction. The insight that has been gleaned from this observation is that extracting implicational impoliteness from corpora required more indepth awareness in terms of what forms and what cues impoliteness might present itself with.

With this in mind, in extraction, as well as in conventionalized impoliteness formulae, cues for different categories of implicational impoliteness were tracked down for both British English and Turkish to compensate for the incidences of impoliteness which could have been otherwise missed because they did not fall into what might be named as conventionalized impoliteness formulae. Although looking for non-conventionalized implicational impoliteness sets out a solid framework for other aspects of impoliteness that are closely linked to the form, conventions and context, the concept of non-conventionalized impoliteness is not broad enough to include the category for implicational impoliteness that is generated by metaphorical, metonymic and idiomatic expressions. The idiomatic expressions in the BNC Extract 1, 'getting too big for their boots,' and Extract 7, with the metaphor of 'crawling into a hole' signal the potential for implicational impoliteness in the sense that they are used to express affective meaning and the emotional effect of what is being experienced. As argued before in Section 4.1, with the BNC Extract 7, in which the emotional effect of having encountered impoliteness is expressed with 'Oh God, I would've crawled into a hole for the rest of my life,' we see that in studying naturally-occurring conversations, metapragmatic comments on emotions may not appear in the form of emotion labels, but rather in the form of idioms, multi-word expressions, and conventional or creative metaphors and metonymies.

The second question is: What do findings at this level of the study provide the researcher about what impoliteness is? In order to answer this question within the CDL framework, scholars evaluate the insights they have gathered from the extracted instances of impoliteness for the reformulation of the research questions or the theory that will be applied to analyse the data. Recent studies also indicate a tendency towards that practice. For instance, Bousfield (2008) allocates a chapter, 'The Dynamics of Impoliteness' (Chapter 7), and discusses 'just what exactly is "context," and more importantly for us here, how does it relate to, and shape, the creation and perceptions of impoliteness?' (p. 169). In this chapter, he introduces the theory of activity type. Thomas (1995:189–190) gives six features of activity type as the following: 1) the goals of the participants, 2) allowable contributions, 3) the degree to which Gricean maxims are adhered to or are suspended, 4) the degree to which the interpersonal maxims are adhered to or are suspended, 5) turn-taking and topic control, and 6) the manipulation of pragmatic parameters. In terms of turn-taking and topic control, for example, Bousfield (2008) explains that 'the degree to which an individual can exploit turn-taking norms in order to control the interaction, to establish his, or her, own agenda, to successfully manage the activity type and achieve their goals is an important and significant area for impoliteness' (p. 173). Through applying the 'activity type' to the analysis of impoliteness, especially with the discussions of allowable contributions, Gricean maxims, turn-taking and topic control, Bousfield (2008), by implication, addresses what is explicitly proposed with this study: the theory of impoliteness in spoken interaction should be explained through both the concept of face and conversational conventions in spoken interaction.

So far, the findings from the extraction level support an integration of theoretical discussion of conversational conventions to the model of impoliteness, and require that the face model be enriched. It is with this awareness that the data will be examined. The research questions and existing theories will be revisited and reformulated before the analysis level starts.

5.3 Analysis: insights from the data

At the analysis level, seven extracts are discussed from the BNC. Extract 4 is given as an example of a conversation in which, despite the use of 'don't be a so stupid woman,' the participant who is being addressed does not evaluate it as impolite. Extract 7 is reported impoliteness (i.e., metapragmatic impoliteness). One of the participants tells about the impoliteness she has encountered for chewing gum at school, when a teacher seeing her comments that she looks like a slut. All the other extracts are incidences of impoliteness taking place during interaction. From the STC, five extracts are analysed, all of which are examples of impoliteness happening during an interaction, except Extract 4, which is reported impoliteness. Table 5.1 below gives a summary of the findings reached at the end of the detailed analysis in Chapter IV. In the table the box for the second question regarding STC Extract 4 is empty since the question is not applicable to the extract. Although the chart abridges the details of the analysis, it provides a visual tool to arrive at conclusions, within the limits of the number of conversations analysed, about impoliteness in British English and Turkish.

It seems that both in British English and Turkish, showing dislike of a feature of someone, which is a form of face attack, commonly triggers impoliteness. As Extracts 1 in both the BNC and STC exemplify, acting against pre-formed membership organizations, as well as assumptions and expectations related to membership categorization bring out the potential for impoliteness. In the BNC Extract 1, two of the card players are assumed to have formed new alliances (Figure 4.1), which in turn prompts reaction from the other two members. Similarly, in the STC Extract 1, one of the participants excludes herself from the group of people who are taking a photograph together in reaction to one of the members who has been irritating. However, her behaviour of excluding herself from the group and the implication that she is indexing herself differently is responded to with impoliteness by two members of the group. The use of offensive language and a misunderstanding are the two other issues that have triggered impoliteness. In Extract 5 in the BNC, 'fuck off' is uttered in reaction to what the other speaker was saying: the teacher has asked them to write about 6,000 words for a paper due soon. However, 'fuck off' is not neutralized, and in return triggers counter-impoliteness from the other participant, 'you do.' In the STC in Extract 5, offensive language is used again to react, but it is verbalized in a way that it is obviously targeted at an outsider or a third party. After saying 'son of a bitch' (*orospu çocuğu*), and 'he gives a fuck' (*çok sikinde onun*), the speaker apologizes to the present participants for being impolite. In the STC Extract 4, a misunderstanding occurs between a professor and students on the propositional content of what the student is saying. Based

Table 5.1. Research Questions and the BNC and STC

The BNC					
Research Questions	Extract 1	Extract 2	Extract 3	Extract 5	Extract 6
What triggers impoliteness in interaction among the speakers of British English?	Forming alliance against background assumptions	Showing dislike to one's taste	Showing dislike to one's use of language	Offensive language	Showing dislike to one's behaviour
What impoliteness strategies are employed in interaction by speakers of British English?	Insult	Insult	Insult	Insult	Insult
How is impoliteness countered in interaction by speakers of British English?	Attempt to prove adequacy	Excluding oneself from the group and indexing oneself with a different group	Ironical acknowl-edgment of the insult	Direct response with the same phrase	Warning
What is the role of countering strategies in relation to face in interaction employed by speakers of British English?	Attempt to repair impoliteness	Topic Change	Closure by topic change	Closure	Denial Closure by topic change

The STC					
Research Questions	Extract 1	Extract 2	Extract 3	Extract 5	Extract 6
What triggers impoliteness in interaction among the speakers of Turkish?	Excluding oneself from the group and indexing oneself with a different group	Showing dislike to one's taste	Showing dislike to one's appearance	Misunderstanding	Offensive language directed to a third party
What impoliteness strategies are employed in interaction by speakers of Turkish?	Threat	Insult	Insult		Insult
How is impoliteness countered in interaction by speakers of Turkish?	Change in behaviour	Ironical acknowledgment of the patronizing behaviour	Ironical acknowledgment of the insult	No reply	No reply
What is the role of countering strategies in relation to face in interaction employed by speakers of Turkish?	Attempt to repair impoliteness	Topic change	Denial	Apology	Apology

on his own understanding, the professor makes a joke, but later, when he realizes there was a misunderstanding, he comes and apologizes for the joke. Looking at what triggers impoliteness in interaction, especially the BNC Extract 5 and the STC Extracts 4 and 5, the debate on whether intention is a determining factor in generating impoliteness and whether an intentional face attack is attributed to the impoliteness seem extraneous. Culpeper's (2011b:23) current definition of what impoliteness is seems to be in line with the data:

> Impoliteness is a negative attitude towards specific behaviours occurring in specific contexts. It is sustained by expectations, desires and/or beliefs about social organization, including, in particular, how one person's or a group's identities are mediated by others in interaction. Situated behaviours are viewed negatively – considered 'impolite' – when they conflict with how one expects them to be, how one wants them to be and/or how one thinks they ought to be. Such behaviours always have or are presumed to have emotional consequences for at least one participant, that is, they cause or are presumed to cause offence. Various factors can exacerbate how offensive an impolite behaviour is taken to be, including, for example, whether one understands a behaviour to be strongly intentional or not.

Thus, regardless of whether the impoliteness events encountered in the extracts are performed intentionally or not, looking at the chart, insult seems to be applied or perceived to be applied the most as a strategy with one exception in the STC Extract 1, which is a threat. The close relationship between insults and notions of punishment and harm has been discussed earlier in Chapter IV. There are different types of harm: physical harm, such as punching or stabbing; and deprivation of resources such as in robbery and social harm (Tedeschi, 1970). Social harm is an important type for impoliteness, since it damages the social identity of a person by lowering their status. It can be executed through insults, reproaches, sarcasm, and impolite behaviour, and linguistic impoliteness. Negative evaluations, mild reproaches, and disagreements may be perceived as identity attacks, even when they are not intended to be (Tedeschi and Felson, 1994:171). In Extract 7 in the BNC, while reporting the impoliteness she experienced, the participant talks about how she felt. The emotion she describes is embarrassment because her social identity face is being attacked, and as a result social harm is being inflicted. This extract also illustrates a case for the need to study the role of emotions in impoliteness. Although Spencer-Oatey (2011) pointed out that the role of emotions has always been an implicit thread of discussion in relation to politeness theory (Brown and Levinson, 1987; Lakoff, 1989; Ide, 1989; Leech, 1983; Goffman, 1967), there has been little research on it in politeness studies (Spencer-Oatey, 2011; Culpeper, 2011b, and Ruhi, 2009a).

The STC Extract 1, 'I'll hit/slap you right now' (*sana bi geçircem zaten*) was identified as the impoliteness category of a threat with its semantic prosody that came into play through *bi*, which is functioning in the text as a diminutive with its pragmatic function as an emphasizer/intensifier quantifying the verb *geçir-*. Semantic prosody is context-sensitive in the sense that the same combination of the diminutive and verb, as in the utterance (*sana bi geçircem [bu bereyi] right* now) which is translated as 'I'll put [this beret on] you now', would not be interpreted as impolite under normal circumstances. When the contextual sensitivity of semantic prosody is taken into consideration, one could argue that what is considered as a conventionalized impoliteness formula could as well turn out to be a neutral expression, as it is the case in the *beret* example. This acknowledgment demands an approach to extraction and analysis for studies similar to the present study. Otherwise, it is possible to miss incidences of impoliteness triggered or verbalized through non-conventionalized expressions that are impolite due to the effect of semantic prosody.

In terms of how impoliteness is countered in interaction, the extracts show that a variety of strategies are employed in British English and Turkish. An attempt to prove adequacy when inadequacy is implied through insults (e.g. 'psychological'), excluding oneself from the group and indexing oneself with a different group (e.g. 'the best people are'), responding directly with the same phrase perceived to be impolite to the performer of impoliteness (e.g. 'you do! (fuck off)'), warning (e.g. 'don't talk to me like that. I don't appreciate the way you're talking to me'), ironical acknowledgment of the insult (e.g. 'I stand corrected'; 'yes an important art' (*evet önemli bi sanat*)), change of behaviour (e.g. 'oh well, take (a picture)', (*tamam çekin ya*)), and not replying are used as strategies to counter impoliteness. For the last question about the role of countering strategies, it would not be wrong to say that in both languages, when a participant responds to impoliteness in some way, there is somewhat of a change in the behaviour. The performer of the impolite behaviour may try to repair the act, either the performer of the act or another participant may change the topic, or either the performer or another participant denies that an impolite act has been performed and closes the incident. These findings point to a significant direction about how the notion of face is perceived in interaction. As Arundale (2010) argues face seems to be conceptualized differently from a person-centred construct considered as self image or social identity (Goffman, 1955) or social wants (Brown and Levinson, 1987). Within his model of interaction, namely, Conjoint Co-Constituting Model of Communication, Arundale (2010) proposes that in interaction, face is conceptualized as relational connectedness and separateness conjointly co-constituted during the course of interaction, which places face and facework on social constructivist ground. Haugh (2009; Haugh and Bargiela-Chiappini 2010) expands on the notion of face on a similar ground focusing on jocular mockery. He (2010: 21116) concludes that face is arguably co-constitutive of interaction and attention to local details practiced by Conversation Analysis as well as to a broader historicity should be given in analysis. In the analyses of the extracts, there have been several cases the notion of face has been referred to, which confirms that face is a construct pertaining to the individuals and collectives (Spencer-Oatey, 2007) and as an interaction construct (Arundale, 2006a; Haugh,2007) and is always at play in impoliteness phenomena. However, other issues related to an approach grounded in ethnomethodology (e.g. membership organization) or conversation analysis (e.g. turn-taking) have accompanied the discussions. In fact, it is through recognition and discussion of clues arising from such issues it has been possible that we see how discussions about participants' understandings are incorporated into the analysis. This is in line with what Haugh and Bargiela-Chiappini (2010:2074) are critical of conversation analysts and suggest:

> Another issue for conversation analysts or ethnomethodologists is that the analyst's perspective is elevated above that of the participants themselves, since both Brown and Levinson and Goffman are committed to an ontology where the analyst alone decides what kind of face(work) has arisen in the interaction. In neither approach, then, do we see how the participants' understandings might be incorporated into the analysis. Thus, if we are really committed to an analysis of face in interaction, the conceptualisation of face needs to be shifted to an epistemology grounded in social constructionism (Berger and Luckmann, 1966; Garfinkel, 1967), where "meaning comes into existence and out of our engagement with the realities in our world" (Crotty, 1998:8), and an ontology grounded in interpretivism (Sacks, 1992), "where social reality is regarded as the product of processes by which social actors negotiate the meanings for actions and situations" (Crotty,1998:11).

Overall, reaching conclusive remarks about the speakers of British English or Turkish would be unwarranted given that the number of impoliteness extracts analysed in the study is not big enough to make generalizations. However, this is not necessarily a drawback. The aim of contrastive studies should not be to make generalizations about speakers of languages at the cultural level. Culpeper and Kádár (2010:14) describe the importance of contrastive studies as follows: '[c]omparative analysis is an important task, because comparing politeness practices and their contexts should enable [one] to gain insights into the general mechanism of the interactional function of linguistic (im) politeness." Ruhi and Kádár (2011), for instance, carried out a contrastive analysis of how face was conceptualized during the late nineteenth- and early twentieth-century in Turkish and Chinese through the use of word 'face.' Although their study is an example of one in historical impoliteness, their aim, which is to take a step towards generating cross-cultural research, is closely linked to the aim of this study.

5.4 Contrastive Level: British English and Turkish

The question at this level is: What are the implications of the study for impoliteness and face theory? The suggestion that CA tools should be integrated into the discussion of what impoliteness is has been confirmed to be useful for discussions of debated issues, such as the role of disagreement sequences. In Chapter IV, in the BNC Extract 3, the notion of disagreement has emerged as a topic that needs to be discussed further. As mentioned, early in the field there was a conceptual tendency (Locher, 2004; Waldron and Applegate, 199; Kakavá, 1993) to regard disagreement as a form of conflict. When disagreement was linked to CA studies, the same line of thought that disagreement indicated conflict (Hutchby, 1996Q1) ruled the discussions. It was within this dominant perspective that disagreement was linked to the issue of face, and it was maintained that disagreement posed a threat to face (Brown and Levinson 1987; Leech, 1983). However, over time that tendency took a different direction, and scholars argued that as an adjacency pair, disagreements produced longer turn-taking sequences (Kotthoff, 1993; Sifianou, 2012) and therefore had face-maintaining or face-enhancing effects as well (Angouri and Locher, 2012). In the BNC Extract 3, disagreement is analysed in relation to CA and is treated as an adjacency pair. It was observed that the disagreement in the extract did not produce longer sequences, although its effect seemed to open a new sequence of opinion-disagreement. It was then observed that the immediate topic change after the disagreement created a silencing effect. Therefore, it was theorized that the pattern of disagreement followed by immediate topic change functions as an impoliteness strategy. It was through CA analysis tools that this conclusion was arrived at. This claim has implications about what impoliteness is and whether face theory should be central for impoliteness theory, and, if yes, what other ways face can be analysed.

With the three strands of the discursive approach, one of which is studying how psychological business (motives and intentions, prejudices, reliability of memory and perception, etc.) is handled and managed in talk and text (Edwards, 2005), the discussion on face predominantly looks into interaction. However, as Haugh and Bargiela-Chiappini (2010:2074) pointed out, what we mean by interaction may differ:

> In its most fundamental sense, interaction refers to situations in which two or more people communicate. Face is uncontroversially interactional in this sense in that face necessarily involves evaluation by others, which in turn presupposes that interaction has indeed taken place (Arundale, 1999; Haugh and Hinze, 2003; Ho, 1976). The move in pragmatics – albeit not always accepted – towards examining samples of real-life interaction is thus largely consistent with a conceptualisation of face as interactional in this ordinary sense. However, interaction can also be understood in a more technical sense, namely, as the reciprocal influence two or more persons have on each other in communicating, through which fundamentally non-summative outcomes emerge (that is, meanings which are not necessarily synonymous with what the speaker might have intended nor with what the recipient might have understood). (Arundale, 2006a:196)

Different orientations towards looking into face in interaction have been taken up by scholars. For instance, Ruhi (2010) proposes that face should be analysed not only through an examination of interaction in the ordinary sense, but also through parallel documents, as suggested by Garfinkel (1967) and Hak (1995), to reach an understanding of how background assumptions and categorizations affect face in interaction in the 'technical' sense. Ruhi and Kádár's (2011) comparative study of folk concepts of face in Chinese and Turkish is another example for grounding analysis of face in 'the first-order emic concepts' (Haugh and Schneider, 2012:128–9). Arundale (2005:212) also grounds face in the ethnography of interaction in a general sense:

> The alternative, more culture-general conceptualization of face developed here is grounded in an observation considerably more general than Goffman's: all humans engage in communication within a matrix of relationships with other human beings. From the perspective of theory in human communication, interaction in relationships is basic to explaining human sociality. But given this particular observational and theoretical framing, one needs to ask if the alternative view of face as relational and interactional is a culturally bounded conceptualization. Of course it is. No human construction can be otherwise.

Spencer-Oatey (2007) is another scholar who aims to bring a broader analysis of face in interaction. As mentioned in Chapter 2, while discussing the question what kind of data is needed for research into face, she argues that post-event comments offer valuable information on people's evaluative reactions or attributions, which may vary from person-to-person and culture-to-culture. Chang and Haugh (2011) use a different term for post-interviews: ethnographic interviews. Although they applied this method in their study together with recordings of naturally occurring interactional data, they acknowledge that doing an ethnographic interview could also be face threatening by itself (p. 2952) since it creates a new interaction. Mills (2009:1049) argues that a distinction between impoliteness at an individual level and at a societal level should be made and analytical frameworks should be developed to analyse impoliteness at a societal level. This can be achieved through an analysis of 'Communities of Practice' norms. In conclusion, the analysis of face in interaction in the ordinary sense (Haugh and Bargiela-Chiappini, 2010) falls short for impoliteness studies, and different analytical approaches should be developed to go beyond this type of analysis. This is implied as well with this study, which examined the interaction in the ordinary sense, but went relatively further by integrating the CA approach and tapping on issues such as membership organization assumptions in the context the interaction took place. In this sense, for this study, interaction is conceptualized more in line with the "the reciprocal influence" which has implications as to how face is conceptualized along with it as Haugh and Bargiela-Chiappini (2010: 2074) explain:

> In its most fundamental sense, interaction refers to situations in which two or more people communicate. Face is uncontroversially interactional in this sense in that face necessarily involves evaluation by others, which in turn presupposes that interaction has indeed taken place (Arundale, 1999; Haugh and Hinze, 2003; Ho, 1976). The move in pragmatics – albeit not always accepted – towards examining samples of real-life interaction is thus largely consistent with a conceptualisation of face as interactional in this ordinary sense. However, interaction can also be understood in a more technical sense, namely, as the reciprocal influence two or more persons have on each other in communicating, through which fundamentally non-summative outcomes emerge (that is, meanings which are not necessarily synonymous with what the speaker might have intended nor with what the recipient might have understood (Arundale, 2006:196).

5.5 Emerging concepts: face and impoliteness

The BNC Extract 1 and the STC Extracts 1, 3, and 4 are examples of impoliteness in which violation of Gricean conversational maxims directly or indirectly triggers impoliteness. This indicates that the Gricean maxims need to be taken into consideration in interaction. With repeated violation of the maxims in spoken conversation, speakers are perceived to be impolite and they encounter impoliteness (e.g. the STC Extract 1). This brings the notion of 'speaker rights theory' (Wilson 1987, 1989) and related notions such as Spencer-Oatey and Jiang's (2003) sociopragmatic interactional principles (SIPs) into play in addition to the notion of face, which has been at the centre of impoliteness theory so far. As Haugh and Bargiela-Chiappini (2010: 2073) point out there is a need to 'move towards a theory of face that is (albeit temporarily) divorced from a focus on (im)politeness.' Since 'conflation of politeness with face' create endless controversies, they maintain, in the special issue *Journal of Pragmatics* 42, that '[w]hile acknowledging the important role face plays in politeness and impoliteness research, it is suggested that the time has come for face to be theorized on its own terms.'(Haugh and Bargiela-Chiappini, 2010: 20073).

Wilson (1987, 1989) argues that a conversation can only be defined through an 'equal distribution of speaker rights' (1987:96). This argument is different than participants taking equal turns: 'It is rather recognition of the fact that in conversation, speakers have equal rights in terms of initiating talk, interrupting, responding, or deciding not to do any of these (Warren, 2006:8).' Wilson (1989) claims that the 'speaker rights theory' (SRT) is what distinguishes conversation from other types of discourse.

Warren (2006:8) explains that:

> When it is claimed that the participants in conversation are of equal status, this does not mean that one can never converse with one's employer, for example. What is meant is that for the duration of a conversation, the external status set aside, and for the purposes of conducting the conversation, the participants are deemed to be of equal status. In this way the participants perceive themselves to be of equal status or the purposes of holding a conversation. This distinguishes conversation from specialized discourse types in which the status of participants is unequal, which in turn has consequences for the resulting discourse. ... [e]ven if in reality a particular conversation is dominated verbally by one or more of the participants, the responsibility for the discourse remains shared. Moreover, the participants in a conversation can only share responsibility for it if they perceive themselves to be of equal status. This is not the case in specialized discourse types in which it is the speaker(s) who is designated as dominant and who has the ultimate responsibility for the discourse.

STR can also be related to Spencer-Oatey's (2000) Rapport Management Model. It consists of three interconnected aspects: the management of face, the management of sociality rights and obligations, and the management of interactional goals. For

Spencer-Oatey face is similar to how Goffman (1967:5) defines it: 'the positive social value a person effectively claims for himself [*sic*] by the line others assume he has taken during a particular contact' (quoted in Spencer-Oatey, 2000:13). The management of sociality rights and obligations are about social expectancies, meaning that they reflect people's concerns about fairness and appropriateness of behaviour. Interactional goals are the tasks people have when they interact with each other (Spencer-Oatey, 2000:14). What is important about perceived sociality rights and obligations is that people develop a sense of behavioural expectations and in cases where these expectations are met differently or not met at all, the interpersonal relationship is influenced. She summarizes the bases of perceived sociality rights and obligations under three headings: 1) contractual/legal agreements and requirements, 2) explicit and implicit conceptualizations of roles and positions, and 3) behavioural conventions, styles and protocols. She expands the last heading by giving an example: work groups, for instance, usually develop conventions for managing team meetings on issues such as who sits where, and whether where they sit should depend on their status or role or not. Although the first base, contractual/legal agreements and requirements are more rigid, it is possible that they were generated as a result of some normative behaviour. Not surprisingly, the normative behaviour is what frequently or typically takes place in a context, but these norms may not be arbitrary:

> They may reflect efficient strategies for handling practical demands, and they may also be manifestations of more deeply-held values. For example, conventions in relation to *turn-taking and rights to talk* (emphasis mine) at business meetings are partly a reflection of the need to deal effectively with the matters at hand, but they are also likely to reflect more deeply-held beliefs about hierarchy and what is socially appropriate behaviour for a given role-relationship. In other words, people typically hold value-laden beliefs about the principles that should underpin interaction. (Spencer-Oatey, 2000:16)

Spencer-Oatey and Jiang (2003) call these beliefs sociopragmatic interactional principles (SIPs), two of which are equity and association. It is essential to expand on these two principles since they are the principles that link both Culpeper's (2011b) and Bousfield's (2008) models to Spencer-Oatey's Rapport Management model. The dimension Spencer-Oatey brings to the model of impoliteness with the theory of Rapport Management is of fundamental importance, as it pinpoints the relationship between impoliteness and conversation, which is the main focus of this study. In fact, with the example of turn-taking and rights to talk, in relation to the SIPs, especially with equity and interactional involvement, the model Rapport Management brings us back to the basics of conversational analysis, which should be supported with references to broader societal context (Chang and Haugh, 2011; Haugh, 2009; Haugh and Watanabe, 2009; Ruhi, 2010). This is very important to acknowledge, as what has been at the heart of the impoliteness model so far is the concept of face. This study confirms that impoliteness theory should link the two, namely face and interaction analysis, together at least as far as spoken interaction is concerned. What has arisen from the findings of both layers, namely extraction and analysis, in the study confirms what Chang and Haugh (2011:412–13) postulate:

> We suggest evaluations of im/politeness are closely tied to converging and diverging interpretations of actions and meanings that are interactionally achieved in situated discourse (Arundale 2006, 2010; Haugh 2007, 2010b), as well as the empirical and moral norms relative to which such evaluations arise. Empirical norms, in this analysis, are defined as encompassing (linguistic) behaviour interactants think is *likely* to be occasioned in particular, localised contexts based on the sum of their individual experiences, while moral norms are defined as involving (linguistic) behaviour interactants think *should* be occasioned, with the latter constituting part of the moral structures of socio-cultural networks (Culpeper 2008: 29; Haugh 2003: 399–400; cf. Eelen 2001: 127–158). In invoking norms in our interactional analysis, then, we are presuming that such evaluations of im/politeness are not only being made by the participants, but *could* be made by others who share similar sociocul-turally-situated frames of reference. It then becomes an empirical question as to what extent similar evaluations would be distributed across sociocultural groups.

5.6 The cyclic research pattern

As explained in Section 3.2 with Figure 3.1, this study follows a cyclic research pattern. The cyclic process demands going backwards. After taking the insights from collated data into consideration, the theory or the framework with which the analysis level will be discussed is formed. It is assumed that since the main focus of the study is on natural data in interaction, data will require a theorization that does not necessarily fit the pre-formulated assumptions and existing theories. The cyclic process of going backwards from collated data to develop a theory requires tentativeness in terms of the research questions the analyst starts the study with. Perceiving the research questions tentatively means that the researcher is willing to revise the questions or discuss emerging issues later as the study unfolds.

During the course of the study, certain issues emerged and insights gathered about these issues are summarized in this section. The issues will be expressed as two further research questions, followed up by the findings and perspectives. These questions are different from the research questions the researcher started the study with in the beginning and treated as tentative to be revised later in the light of new findings. Although these new questions have not necessarily replaced the earlier ones, they have come out as the study proceeded. Therefore, they are considered as part of the cyclic approach.

Related to corpus linguistics and contrastive studies with corpora the first question, is: to what extent is the extraction of impoliteness possible when the corpora used for a study, the BNC and the STC in the case of this study, are not fully comparable? To what extent can such semi-comparable corpora be used for contrastive studies, which in this case is the present study?

Although scholars have not reached an agreement on the terminology they are using for different types of corpora, generally three types of corpora involving more than one language are referred to. If the original texts in one language are translated into another, this type of corpora is referred to as translation corpus (Aijmer, 1996). If two monolingual corpora are designed using the same sampling frame, they are referred to as comparable corpora (McEnery and Wilson, 1996:57Q9; Hunston, 2002:15). If the corpora are a combination of the types mentioned, the combination is referred to as parallel corpora (Johansson and Hofland 1994; Johansson, 1998).

The BNC and STC can be considered as comparable corpora despite their differences in size because the principles governing the issue of representativeness are similar. However, due to certain differences, it would not be right to claim these two corpora as fully comparable. The BNC spoken sub-corpus is general, since it contains as many text types (e.g. public speeches, sport commentaries, etc.) as possible, whereas STC in its current state is specialized, since it contains only conversations, despite its focus on the variety of topic distribution in speech contexts. However, taking a look at leisure speech which consists of speeches, sports commentaries, talks to clubs, broadcast shows, phone-ins, and club meetings in the BNC (see section 3.4.1) and the subcategories of 'conversation' in the STC under family, friends, family and friends, workplace and education (see section 3.4.2), the STC appears to be designed to represent a wider range of natural conversation compared to the BNC spoken corpora. Another difference which has directly affected both the extraction and the analysis levels of the present study is that the BNC and STC encoding systems are different. The BNC provides opportunities for a detailed analysis of both linguistic and paralinguistic data. Carrying out frequency analysis both at the word and phrase level and including demographic data about the population by whom these words and phrases are used are among the analyses which can be carried out quite easily on the corpus. Paralinguistic data are provided in the XML format, which enables the researchers to do an analysis, although not in a visually accessible way due to the reasons explained in Section 1.4. The STC provides both linguistic and paralinguistic data in a visually more accessible format through various output formats (e.g. the RTF) and allows for a frequency or demographic analysis similar to the BNC. Both the BNC and STC supply whole transcriptions of conversations recorded; however, reaching a whole conversation in the BNC requires a complex series of steps as explained in Chapter 2, where extraction methods are described. Moreover, despite a recent publication of some sound files, the BNC is monomodal and the STC is multimodal in that the latter has the transcriptions and sound files of conversations and video recordings of some conversations.

Despite all the differences, the present study proved that it is possible to do a contrastive analysis with even semi-comparable corpora. The BNC provided a larger pool of data to extract from, and the STC provided features that enabled the researcher to do a more indepth analysis with the RTF files and sound files, which then were analysed using Praat software. Culpeper, Bousfield and Wichmann (2003:1577) note some areas related to impoliteness in need of further studies. Two of them are that they have focused on parking disputes but '[d]ifferent phenomena and patterns remain to be found in other discourse types' and '[t]here is much more to be said about turn-taking and about non-verbal aspects.' The genre approach to the study with the focus on conversation using the larger pool of the BNC and the corpus features of the STC in terms of the subcategories of conversation, the study addresses the need for further research in other discourse types. Moreover, by making use of the musical score notation which displays turn-taking phenomena, annotations especially describing voice quality and sound files to examine components of prosody such as pitch and loudness with the data provided by the STC, the study attends to turn-taking and non-verbal aspects Culpeper, Bousfield and Wichmann (2003) refer to.

The second question to emerge from the cyclic process is related to prosody and impoliteness: to what extent can prosody be used as a cue to impoliteness despite its being gradient and relative? Culpeper (2011a) argues that prosody plays a key role in triggering evaluations about an utterance, in terms of whether it is impolite, and he shows the ways in which prosody functions in this respect. In discussing the difference between paralanguage and prosody, he defines prosody as 'local dynamic vocal effects, variations in loudness, pitch, tempo, and so on' and paralanguage as more general vocal characteristics such as 'voice setting, voice quality, characteristics such as whining, laughing, whispering, etc., as well as vocalizations such as "uh-huh" or "mhm"' (p. 60). He treats paralanguage as a superordinate term, and focuses on more specific aspects that fall into prosody. In this study, prosody is treated with the same focus. Three parts from the STC extracts were analysed by Praat to show how prosody is illustrative of impoliteness. In Extract 1, a threat '*sana bi geçireceğim zaten* ((XXX))' (I am going to hit/slap you right now [[XXX]])' comes with a higher-pitch accent in the local context (see Figure 4.3). In Extract 2, the irony in non-conventionalized implicational impoliteness generated by the utterances '(she) goes online. the lady is busy. (she) does not even say hello' (*ya ben de giriyor hatun, meşgul selam bile vermiyor*) and 'she is a business woman now' (*ee o artık bi iş kadını*) is demonstrated with the mismatch between a humorous tone and a serious tone (see Figure 4.4). How this irony in implicational impoliteness is being acknowledged, ironically as a counter strategy, is illustrated in Figure 4.5, again through the discussion of change of voice and mismatches between vocal effects.

One of the issues Culpeper (2011a) demonstrates is that the layperson's views on prosody show the important role it has in evaluations of impolite behaviour. He gives examples of comments people put on weblogs, and convincingly maintains that 'it [impoliteness] is not what you said, it's how you said it.' He emphasizes that prosody in impoliteness studies has been neglected, and although prosody is gradient and relative to some degree, it can provide insights as long as context is taken into consideration and linked to the discussion (p. 79). This study is also a small step towards taking the suggestion to broaden the research on prosody and impoliteness and how that can be linked to the local context.

5.7 Areas for future research

The present study proposes a methodological approach to extracting and analysing impoliteness in spoken interaction. The methodological perspective it proposes takes long-debated issues into consideration, and addresses them with applicable and analytical suggestions. The progression of the study itself confirms that the proposed framework has been effective. There are a number of questions that have arisen during the extraction and analysis levels on which further future studies might focus. The questions are as follows:

1. What other categorical methods, other than conventionalized impoliteness formulae and non-conventionalized implicational impoliteness, can we apply while extracting impoliteness from spoken corpora?
2. What are the roles of alignment (Goffman, 1974, 1981) and membership categorization (Sacks, 1989) in relation to face issues in aggravating

impoliteness? What motivates the participants to form or disrupt alliances with the other participants during interaction?

3. What is the role of metaphorical and metonymic words and expressions verbalizing impoliteness?

4. What is the role of semantic prosody in impoliteness? How can it be used as an extraction method for impoliteness?

    •   These questions will bring valuable insights for impoliteness theories and supply further implications for future studies.

CHAPTER 6

Conclusion

6.1 Final Word

In this book, a methodological perspective on how two corpora, despite their different features, can be used and read to extract and analyse impoliteness across two languages has been demonstrated. Tognini-Bonelli (2001, 2010) maintains that a text and a corpus require a qualitatively different reading. The text is to be read horizontally with special attention given to the boundaries between units while a corpus is examined in KWIC format to be read vertically to scan for the patterns and nodes. The function of a text is 'communicative' since it is situational and refers to a wider cultural context. A corpus, on the other hand, is designed for the purpose of linguistic analysis. The information drawn from a text is interpreted within the context it occurs in relation to both verbal and non-verbal actions and the consequences of those actions. However, the information gathered from a corpus is meaningful only as far as it can be generalized to the language as a whole. In Saussurian terminology, a text is 'an instance of *parole* while the patterns shown up by corpus evidence yield insights into *langue*' (Tognini-Bonelli, 2010: 19–20)

Nevertheless, as illustrated in the book through the steps for the extraction and discussion in the analysis layers, a corpus can be read similarly to how a text is read; in fact, the extracts themselves qualify as texts. However, through query methods used to extract instances of impoliteness in the corpora especially with the 'KWIC' format used in the BNC (see section 3.6), corpus reading methods are applied, and the additional steps (e.g. creating Word files small enough to read through as explained in section 3.6) enabled doing a text reading with the corpora. This explains best why a quantitative analysis in its traditional sense (e.g. a frequency analysis of taboo words) has been replaced by a qualitative analysis, which at times has been supported by data gathered quantitatively (e.g. the use of METU Turkish corpus for the STC Extract 1 discussed in section 4.3).

Tognini-Bonelli (2010:17) also elaborates on the revolution corpus linguistics has made in three stages. In the first stage, the computer was seen simply as a tool, in the second stage 'not only was it providing an abundance of new evidence, it was by its nature affecting the methodological frame of enquiry by speeding it up, systematizing it, and making it applicable in real time to ever larger amounts of data.' The third stage took place in 1990s and necessitated going beyond method-ological concerns:

> Not only could language researchers speed up the process of analysis, they could carry out procedures which were just not feasible before computers became available. The difference of scale led to a qualitative difference in the observations. It is strange to imagine that just more data and better counting could trigger philosophical repositionings, but that indeed is what has happened. (p. 18)

The proposed cyclic method in the book addresses the philosophical stance that has come out of the third stage Tognini-Bonelli (2010) describes through the process of going backwards from collated data to develop a theory and considering the research questions *tentative* so that the researcher is willing to revise the research questions later as the study unfolds and reconceptualize existing theories. The discussions on the emerging issues in Chapter 5 are the end result of the cyclic process applied within this single study.

As far as the proposed methodological perspective in the book is concerned, in addition to how to read corpora and how to proceed through the (cyclic) steps of the research, a methodology for extracting impoliteness has been put forward through the combination of 'tools' characterized by the discursive and cue-based approaches. Metapragmatic comments and reactive responses counted for the features of the discursive approach while conventionalized impoliteness formulae (Culpeper, 2010, 2011b), cues for non-conventionalized implicational impoliteness (Culpeper, 2011b), conversation management tools (e.g. turn-taking, pauses, etc.), verbal and non-verbal forms signalling interpersonal conflict (e.g. change in structural patterns such as turn-taking, topic change, repetition, seeking disagreement) and other cues such as semantic prosody (Sinclair 1998, 2004; Stubbs, 2002; Morley and Partington, 2009; Bednarek, 2008) counted for the cue-based approach. Along with the line of genre approach to studying impoliteness (Garcés-Conejos Blitvich, 2010; Garcés-Conejos Blitvich *et al.*, 2010), conversation, which has been selected as the discourse type for the study, has been approached through the lens of conversation analysis (CA).

For the conversation analysts, conversation is regarded as 'the basic environment for language use' and the aim of CA is 'to capture the temporal production of utterances in turns-at-talk and thus make available for analysis how participants understand and respond to one another' (Clift, Drew and Hutchby, 2009: 40). How participants understand and respond to one another in temporal production of utterances, supported by the evaluation of other the clues (e.g. acoustic prosody and semantic prosody) salient both in the immediate and the wider context and co-text, along with clues offered by conventionalized impoliteness formulae (Culpeper, 2010, 2011b) and non-conventionalized implicational impoliteness (Culpeper, 2011b) has also been explored in this study. The undertaking of separating extraction from the analysis layer, looking for as many clues as possible for extraction and analysing the extracts with an open mind (Rühlemann, 2007) aims to address 'empirical normativity' and 'interpretive relevance' in impoliteness studies. Haugh (2007) states:

> However, while the analyst should avoid reifying his or her own personal assessments of (im)politeness as norms, a theory of politeness necessarily involves an understanding of both what people think *should* happen (moral norms) and what people think *is likely to* happen (empirical norms) (Eelen 2001: 140; Haugh 2003: 400). One possible window into "moral normativity" is a careful analysis of "talk" about politeness (metapragmatic politeness1), including etiquette guides, media discourse on (im)politeness, and conversations explicitly focusing on what is considered (im)polite behaviour. To better understand empirical normativity, on the other hand, requires corpus-based work where expectations about (im)politeness are grounded in an analysis of participant uptake (Terkourafi 2001, 2005a, 2005b; cf. Usami 2002, 2006). Thus, while a theory of politeness2 should be non-evaluative and non-normative in relation to the analyst's own personal interpreting, it will always be evaluative and normative in the sense that it seeks to better understand the process by which evaluations of (im)politeness are made, and how common understandings (although not necessarily practices) of norms are shared or constructed across social networks, including so-called "cultures." (p.308)

In discussing the discursive challenge as to how the notions of politeness1 and politeness2 are dealt with, Haugh (2007) maintains that it is possible to overcome some of the epistemological and ontological issues formed around a discursive approach to impoliteness by the Conjoint Co-Constituting Model of Communication (Arundale 1999, 2004, 2006a) as a theoretical foundation. Haugh (2007) suggests this framework since 'it is consistent with a conceptualization of (im)politeness as being interactionally achieved in a collaborative, non-summative manner through interaction by participants, whilst carefully avoiding the ontological trap of conflating the analysts' and participants' perspectives' (p.309). Not conflating the two perspectives will establish the 'interpretive relevance' (Arundale, 2006b). Moreover, during the analysis, new concepts such as alignment of participants and membership organization in relation to impoliteness have arisen. The emergence of new concepts such as these that the analyst did not start with in the beginning of the study indicates that the extraction and analysis levels should not be considered as one. It has been observed that the overlap between the extraction layer and the analysis layer in cases where the clue used for the extraction is used as a tool to analyse impoliteness in an extract is inevitable to a certain extent. However, this does not take away from the non-normative aspect in the methodology proposed here.

Considering the findings and methodological issues that have arisen during the course of this study, one area similar studies could further delve into in future research is how the extraction layer can be enriched in terms of the tools used and how non-formulaic implicational impoliteness (Culpeper, 2011b) can be expanded so that both the extraction and the analysis layers are better addressed. The conversation management tools borrowed from CA, the concept of semantic prosody and nuances provided by acoustic prosody have broadened the study. Further studies will shed light onto why and how instances of impoliteness may have gone unnoticed in this study.

References

Aarts, J. 2002. 'Review of *Corpus Linguistics at Work*.' *International Journal of Corpus Linguistics* 7 (1): 118–23. http://dx.doi.org/10.1075/ijcl.7.1.09aar.

Aijmer, K. 1996. *Conversational Routines in English*. London: Longman.

Angouri, J., and M.A. Locher. 2012. 'Theorising disagreement.' *Journal of Pragmatics* 44 (12): 1549–53. http://dx.doi.org/10.1016/j.pragma.2012.06.011.

Arndt, H., and R.W. Janne. 1987. *Intergrammar: Toward an Integrative Model of Verbal, Prosodic and Kinesic Choices in Speech*. Berlin: De Gruyter. http://dx.doi.org/10.1515/9783110872910.

Arundale, R.B. 1999. 'An alternative model and ideology of communication for an alternative Politeness theory.' *Journal of Pragmatics* 9 (1): 119–53.

Arundale, R.B. 2004. Co-constituting face in conversation: An alternative to Brown and Levinson's politeness theory. Paper presented to the National Communication Association, Chicago, IL.

Arundale, R.B. 2005. Face as relational and interactional: alternative bases for research on face, facework, and politeness. Paper presented at the 9th International Pragmatics Association Conference, Riva Del Garda, Italy.

Arundale, R.B. 2006a. 'Face as relational and interactional: A communication framework for research on face, facework, and politeness.' *Journal of Politeness Research* 2 (2): 193–216.

Arundale, R. 2006b. Arguing participants' achieving of relationship in talk: Notes towards an examination. Unpublished manuscript, University of Alaska, Fairbanks.

Arundale, R. 2010. 'Constituting face in conversation: Face, facework, and interactional achievement.' *Journal of Pragmatics* 42 (8): 2078–105. http://dx.doi.org/10.1016/j.pragma.2009.12.021.

Atkinson, J.M., and P. Drew. 1979. *Order in Court: The Organization of Verbal Interaction in Judicial Settings*. London: Macmillan.

Austin, J.L. 1962. *How To Do Things With Words*. Oxford: Oxford University Press.

Aydın, H. 2006. 'G.O.R.A. Filmindeki argo ve küfür kullanımının mizahi işlevi.' *Millî Folklor* 71: 90–2.

Badarneh, M.A. 1996. Translation of the Arabic diminutive into English. M.A. Thesis. Yarmouk University, Jordan.

Badarneh, M.A. 2010. 'The pragmatics of diminutives in colloquial Jordanic Arabic.' *Journal of Pragmatics* 42 (1): 153–67. http://dx.doi.org/10.1016/j.pragma.2009.05.004.

Bald, W.D. 1995. 'Gegenstands und Zielbestimmungen der anglistischen Sprachwissenschaft im Lichte der fachinternen Entwicklunden.' In *Anglistische Lehre Aktuell: Probleme, Perspektiven, Praxis*, ed. B. Korte and K.P. Müller, 93–107. Trier: Wissenschaftlicher Verlag Trier.

Bargiela-Chiappini, F. 2003. 'Face and politeness: New (insights) for old (concepts).' *Journal of Pragmatics* 35 (10–11): 1453–69. http://dx.doi.org/10.1016/S0378-2166(02)00173-X.

Barsoux, J.L. 1993. *Funny Business. Humour, Management and Business Culture*. London: Cassell.

Bayraktaroğlu, A., and M. Sifianou, eds. 2001. *Linguistic Politeness Across Boundaries: A Case of Greek and Turkish*. Amsterdam/ New York: John Benjamins. http://dx.doi.org/10.1075/pbns.88.

Bayyurt, Y., and A. Bayraktaroğlu. 2001. 'The use of pronouns and terms of address in Turkish service encounters.' In *Linguistic Politeness Across Boundaries: A Case of Greek and Turkish*, ed. A. Bayraktoroğlu and M. Sifianou, 209–40. Amsterdam/New York: John Benjamins. http://dx.doi.org/10.1075/pbns.88.09bay.

Beattie, G. 1983. *Talk: An Analysis of Speech and Nonverbal Behaviour in Conversation*. Milton Kaynes: Open University Press.

Bednarek, M. 2008. 'Semantic preference and semantic prosody re-examined.' *Corpus Linguistics and Linguistic Theory* 4 (2): 119–39. http://dx.doi.org/10.1515/CLLT.2008.006.

Biber, D. 1988. *Variation Across Speech and Writing*. Cambridge: Cambridge University Press. http://dx.doi.org/10.1017/CBO9780511621024.

Biber, D. 1993/2004. 'Representativeness in corpus design.' *Literary and Linguistic Computing* 8 (4): 243–57. Reprinted in G. Sampson and D. McCarthy (eds) (2004) *Corpus Linguistics: Reading in a Widening Perspective*, 174–97. London: Continuum.

Billig, M. 1997. 'Rhetorical and discursive analysis: how families talk about the Royal family.' In *Doing Qualitative Analysis in Psychology*, ed. N. Hayes, 39–54. Hove: Psychology Press.

Billig, M. 1999a. 'Whose terms? Whose ordinariness? Rhetoric and ideology in conversation analysis.' *Discourse and Society* 10 (4): 543–58. http://dx.doi.org/10.1177/0957926599010004005.

Billig, M. 1999b. 'Conversation analysis and claims of naivety.' *Discourse and Society* 10 (4): 572–6. http://dx.doi.org/10.1177/0957926599010004007.

Black, A. 1988. 'The syntax of conversational coherence.' *Discourse Processes* 11 (4): 433–55. http://dx.doi.org/10.1080/01638538809544712.

Blum-Kulka, S. 1992. 'The metapragmatics of politeness in Israeli society.' In *Politeness in Language: Studies in Its History, Theory and Practice*, ed. J.R. Watts, S. Ide, and K. Ehlich, 255–80. Berlin: Mouton de Gruyter.

Boersma, P., and D. Weenink. 2013. Praat: doing phonetics by computer [computer program]. Version 5.3.42. Retrieved 2 March 2013 from http://www.praat.org/.

Bourdieu, P. 1991. *Language and Symbolic Power*. Cambridge, MA: Harvard University Press.

Bousfield, D. 2008. *Impoliteness in Interaction*. Amsterdam: John Benjamins. http://dx.doi.org/10.1075/pbns.167.

Bousfield, D., and M. Locher. 2008. *Impoliteness in Language: Studies On Its Interplay With Power in Theory and Practice*. Berlin: Walter de Gruyter.

Brown, P., and C.S. Levinson. 1987. *Politeness: Some Universals in Language Usage*. Cambridge: Cambridge University Press (Original work published 1978).

Bulak, Ş. 2011. '"-sA" Ekinin İşlevleri.' *A. Ü. Türkiyat Araştırmaları Enstitüsü Dergisi* 46: 25–38.

Bublitz, W. 1996. 'Semantic prosody and cohesive company: somewhat predictable.' *Leuvense Bijdragen: Tijdschrift voor Germaanse Filologie* 85 (1–2): 1–32.

Burnard, L. 2007 [2000]. *Encoding the British National Corpus, BNC Users' Reference Guide*. Edited by Burnard, L. Retrieved from http://www.natcorp.ox.ac.uk/docs/Burnage93a.htm#4.4.

Büyük Türkçe Sözlük. 2013. Retrieved 10 December 2012 from http://www.tdk.gov.tr/index.php?option=com_bts.

Cameron, D. 2001. *Working With Spoken Discourse*. London: Sage Publication.

Carter, R. 2004. *Language and Creativity: The Art of Common Talk*. London, New York: Routledge. http://dx.doi.org/10.4324/9780203468401.

Cashman, H.R. 2006. 'Impoliteness in children's interactions in a Spanish/English bilingual community of practice.' *Journal of Politeness Research* 2 (2): 217–46.

Chang, W.-L.M., and M. Haugh. 2011. 'Strategic embarrassment and face threatening in business interactions.' *Journal of Pragmatics* 43 (12): 2948–63. http://dx.doi.org/10.1016/j.pragma.2011.05.009.

Cheepen, C., and J. Monaghan. 1990. *Spoken English: A Practical Guide*. London: Pinter.

Clift, R., P. Drew, and I. Hutchby. 2009. 'Conversation analysis.' In *The Pragmatics of Interaction*, ed. S. D'hondt, J. Östman, and J. Verschueren, 40–54. Amsterdam: John Benjamins. http://dx.doi.org/10.1075/hoph.4.02cli.

Coleman, J., L. Baghai-Ravary, J. Pybus, and S. Grau. 2012. A British National Corpus spoken audio sampler. Retrieved from http://www.phon.ox.ac.uk/SpokenBNC.

Coulter, J. 1979. *The Social Construction of Mind: Studies in Ethnomethodology and Linguistic Philosophy*. London: Macmillan.

Coulter, J. 1989. *Mind in Action*. Oxford: Polity.

Coupland, N. 2007. *Style: Language Variation and Identity*. Cambridge, New York: Cambridge University Press. http://dx.doi.org/10.1017/CBO9780511755064.

Crystal, D., and D. Davy. 1969. *Investigating English Style*. London: Deutsch.

Culpeper, J. 1996. 'Towards an anatomy of impoliteness.' *Journal of Pragmatics* 25 (3): 349–67. http://dx.doi.org/10.1016/0378-2166(95)00014-3.

Culpeper, J. 2005. 'Impoliteness and *The Weakest Link*.' *Journal of Politeness Research* 1 (1): 35–72.

Culpeper, J. 2010. 'Conventionalized impoliteness formulae.' *Journal of Pragmatics* 42 (12): 3232–45. http://dx.doi.org/10.1016/j.pragma.2010.05.007.

Culpeper, J. (2011a) '"It's not what you said, it's how you said it": prosody and impoliteness.' In *Discursive Approaches to Politeness*, ed. I. Kecskes and Linguistic Politeness Group, 57–84. Berlin, Boston: De Gruyter Mouton. http://dx.doi.org/10.1515/9783110238679.57.

Culpeper, J. 2011b. *Impoliteness: Using Language to Cause Offence*. New York: Cambridge University Press. http://dx.doi.org/10.1017/CBO9780511975752.

Culpeper, J., D. Bousfield, and A. Wichmann. 2003. 'Impoliteness revisited: with special reference to dynamic and prosodic aspect.' *Journal of Pragmatics* 35 (10–11): 1545–79. http://dx.doi.org/10.1016/S0378-2166(02)00118-2.

Culpeper, J., and D.Z. Kádár, eds. 2010. *Historical (Im)politeness*. Bern: Peter Lang.

de Kadt, E. 1998. 'The concept of face and its applicability to the Zulu language.' *Journal of Pragmatics* 29 (2): 173–91. http://dx.doi.org/10.1016/S0378-2166(97)00021-0.

Doğançay-Aktuna, S., and S. Kamışlı. 2001. 'Linguistics of power and politeness in Turkish: Revelations from speech acts.' In *Linguistic Politeness Across Boundaries: A Case of Greek and Turkish*, ed. A. Bayraktoroğlu and M. Sifianou, 75–104. Amsterdam, New York: John Benjamins. http://dx.doi.org/10.1075/pbns.88.05dog.

Donaldson, S.K. 1979. 'One kind of speech act: how do we know when we are conversing?' *Semiotica* 28 (3–4): 259–99.

Durkheim, E. 1924. *The Early Forms of Religious Life*. London: Allen and Unwin. New York: Macmillan.

Edwards, D. 2005. 'Discursive psychology.' In *Handbook of Language and Social Interaction*, ed. K.L. Fitch and R.E. Sanders, 257–273. Mahwah, NJ: Lawrence Erlbaum.

Edwards, J. 1993. 'Principles and contrasting systems of discourse transcription.' In *Talking Data – Transcription and Coding in Discourse Research*, ed. J. Edwards and M. Lampert, 3–31. Hillsdale: Erlbaum.

Eelen, G. 2001. *A Critique of Politeness Theories*. London: St Jerome Publishing.

Ehlich, K., and J. Rehbein. 1976. 'Halbinterpretative Arbeitstranskriptionen (HIAT).' *Linguistische Berichte* 45: 21–41.

Fairclough, N. 2003. *Analyzing Discourse: Textual Analysis for Social Research*. London: Routledge.

Fillmore, C.J. 1981. 'Pragmatics and the description of discourse.' In *Radical Pragmatics*, ed. P. Cole, 143–66. New York: Academic Press.

Finnegan, E. 1999. *Language Its Structure and Use*. New York: Hartcourt Brace and Company.

Foucault, M. 1972. *The Archaeology of Knowledge*. Trans. A.M. Sheridan Smith. New York: Pantheon (Original work published 1969).

Francis, G. 1993. 'A corpus-driven approach to grammar.' In *Text and Technology. In Honour of John Sinclair*, ed. M. Baker, G. Francis, and E. Tognini-Bonelli, 137–56. Amsterdam and Philadelphia, PA: John Benjamins. http://dx.doi.org/10.1075/z.64.10fra.

Fraser, B., and W. Nolen. 1981. 'The association of deference with linguistic form.' *International Journal of the Sociology of Language* 27: 93–109.

Garcés-Conejos Blitvich, P. 2010. 'A genre approach to the study of impoliteness.' *International Review of Pragmatics* 2 (1): 46–94. http://dx.doi.org/10.1163/18773 1010X491747.

Garcés-Conejos Blitvich, P., N. Lorenzo-Dus, and P. Bou-Franch. 2010. 'A genre approach to impoliteness in a Spanish television talk show: evidence from corpus-based analysis, questionnaires and focus groups.' *Intercultural Pragmatics* 7 (4): 689–723. http://dx.doi.org/10.1515/iprg.2010.030.

Garfinkel, H. 1967. *Studies in Ethnomethodology*. Englewood Cliffs, NJ: Prentice-Hall.

Gavioli, L. 2005. *Exploring Corpora for ESP Learning*. Amsterdam: John Benjamins. http://dx.doi.org/10.1075/scl.21.

Goffman, E. 1955. 'On face-work.' In *Social Theory: The Multicultural Readings* (2010), ed. C. Lemert, 338–43. Philadelphia, PA: Westview Press.

Goffman, E. 1967. *Interaction Ritual*. Chicago, IL: Aldine Publishing.

Goffman, E. 1971. *Relations in Public: Micro Studies of the Public Order*. New York: Basic Books.

Goffman, E. 1974. *Frame Analysis*. New York: Harper and Row.

Goffman, E. 1981. *Forms of Talk*. Oxford: Oxford University Press.

Graham, S.L. 2008. 'A manual for (im)politeness? The impact of the FAQ in an electronic community in practice.' In *Impoliteness in Language*, ed. D. Bousfield and M.A. Locher, 281–304. Berlin, New York: Mouton de Gruyter.

Grice, H.P. 1975. 'Logic and conversation.' In *Speech Acts*, ed. P. Cole and J.L. Morgan, 41–58. New York: Academic Press.

Grice, H.P. 1989. *Studies in the Way of Words*. Cambridge, MA: Harvard University Press.

Gu, Y. 1990. 'Politeness phenomena in modern Chinese.' *Journal of Pragmatics* 14 (2): 237–57. http://dx.doi.org/10.1016/0378-2166(90)90082-O.

Gumperz, J. 1992. 'Contextualization revisited.' In *The Contextualization of Language*, ed. P. Auer and A. di Luzio, 39–54. Amsterdam and Philadelphia, PA: John Benjamins. http://dx.doi.org/10.1075/pbns.22.04gum.

Güneş, A. 2009. 'Mizah dergilerinde ve İnternette küfürlü sözlerin yazımları.' *Acta Turcica Çevrimiçi Tematik Türkoloji Dergi* 2 (1): 61–67.

Hak, T. 1995. 'Ethnomethodology and the institutional context.' *Human Studies* 18 (2–3): 109–37. http://dx.doi.org/10.1007/BF01323206.

Hammersley, M. 2003. 'Conversation analysis and discourse analysis: methods or paradigms.' *Discourse and Society* 14 (6): 751–81. http://dx.doi.org/10.1177/09579265030146004.

Hatipoğlu, Ç. 2007. '(Im)politeness, national and professional identities and context: Some evidence from e-mailed "Call for Papers".' *Journal of Pragmatics* 39 (4): 760–73. http://dx.doi.org/10.1016/j.pragma.2006.11.014.

Haugh, M. 2005. 'The importance of "place" in Japanese politeness.' *Intercultural Pragmatics* 2:41–68.

Haugh, M. 2007. 'The discursive challenge to politeness research: an interactional alternative.' *Journal of Politeness Research* 3 (2): 295–317.

Haugh, M. 2009. Face and interaction. In: Francesca Bargiela-Chiappini and Michael Haugh (eds.), *Face, Communication and Social Interaction*, 1–30. London: Equinox.

Haugh, M., and Y. Watanabe 2009. Analysing Japanese 'face-in-interaction': Insights from intercultural business meetings. In: Francesca Bargiela-Chiappini and Michael Haugh (eds.), *Face, Communication and Social Interaction*, 78–95. London: Equinox.

Haugh, M., and F. Bargiela-Chiappini. 2010. 'Face in interaction.' *Journal of Pragmatics* 42 (8): 2073–7. http://dx.doi.org/10.1016/j.pragma.2009.12.013.

Haugh, M., and K.P. Schneider. 2012. 'Im/politeness across Englishes.' *Journal of Pragmatics* 44 (9): 1017–21. http://dx.doi.org/10.1016/j.pragma.2012.05.010.

Hecht, M., J.R. Warren, E. Jung, and J.L. Krieger. 2005. 'A communication theory of identity: development, theoretical perspective, and future directions.' In *Theorizing about Intercultural Communication*, ed. W.B. Gudykunst, 257–78. Thousand Oaks, CA: Sage.

Heritage, J. 1984. *Garfinkel and Ethnomethodology*. Cambridge, UK: Polity Press.

Hirschon, R. 2001. 'Freedom, solidarity and obligation: The socio-cultural context of Greek politeness.' In *Linguistic Politeness Across Boundaries: A Case of Greek and Turkish*, ed. A. Bayraktoroğlu and M. Sifianou, 17–42. Amsterdam/ New York: John Benjamins. http://dx.doi.org/10.1075/pbns.88.03hir.

Hoey, M. 2005. *Lexical Priming: A new Theory of Words and Language*. London, New York: Routledge. http://dx.doi.org/10.4324/9780203327630.

Holmes, J. 1990. 'Politeness Strategies in new Zealand Women's Speech.' In *New Zealand Ways of Speaking English*, ed. A. Bell and J. Holmes, 252–75. Avon: Multilingual Matters Ltd.

Holmes, J., and S. Schnurr. 2005. 'Politeness, humor and gender in the workplace: negotiating norms and identifying contestation.' *Journal of Politeness Research* 1 (1): 121–49.

Hunston, S., and G. Thompson, eds. 1999. *Evaluation in Text: Authorial Stance and the Construction of Discourse*. Oxford: Oxford University Press.

Hunston, S., and G. Francis. 2000. *Pattern Grammar. A Corpus-Driven Approach to the Lexical Grammar of English*. Amsterdam: John Benjamins. http://dx.doi.org/10.1075/scl.4.

Hunston, S. 2002. *Corpora in Applied Linguistics*. Cambridge: Cambridge University Press. http://dx.doi.org/10.1017/CBO9781139524773.

Hunston, S. 2007. 'Semantic prosody revisited.' *International Journal of Corpus Linguistics* 12 (2): 249–68. http://dx.doi.org/10.1075/ijcl.12.2.09hun.

Ide, S. 1989. 'Formal forms and discernment: two neglected aspects of linguistic politeness.' *Multilingua* 8 (2–3): 223–48. http://dx.doi.org/10.1515/mult.1989.8.2-3.223.

Ide, S. 1993. 'Preface: the search for integrated universals of linguistic politeness.' *Multilingua* 12 (1): 7–12. http://dx.doi.org/10.1515/mult.1993.12.1.7.

Işık-Güler, H. 2008. Metapragmatics of (im)politeness in Turkish: an explanatory emic investigation. Unpublished PhD dissertation. Middle East Technical University, Turkey.

Jay, T. 1992. *Cursing in America: A Psycholinguistic Study of Dirty Language in the Courts, in the Movies, in Schoolyards and on the Streets*. Philadelphia, PA: John Benjamins. http://dx.doi.org/10.1075/z.57.

Jefferson, G. 1984. 'Notes on the Systematic deployment of the acknowledgment tokens "yeah" and "hm mm".' *Papers in Linguistics (Edmonton)* 17 (2): 197–216. http://dx.doi.org/ 10.1080/08351818409389201.

Johansson, S. 1998. 'On the role of corpora in cross-linguistic research.' In *Corpora and Cross-linguistic Research*, ed. S. Johansson and S. Oksefjell, 1–24. Amsterdam and Atlanta, GA: Rodolpi.

Johansson, S., and K. Hofland. 1994. 'Towards an English-Norwegian parallel corpus.' In *Creating and Using English Language Corpora*, ed. U. Fries, G. Tottie, and P. Schneider, 25–37. Amsterdam: Rodopi.

Jucker, A. 1988. 'Relevance theory and the communication of politeness.' *Multilingua* 7: 375–84.

Jurafsky, D. 1996. 'Universal tendencies in the semantics of the diminutive.' *Language* 72 (3): 533–78. http://dx.doi.org/10.2307/416278.

Jurafsky, D. 2004. 'Pragmatics and computational linguistics.' In *Handbook of Pragmatics*, ed. R.H. Laurence and W. Gregory, 578–606. Oxford: Blackwell. Pre-print retrieved from http://citeseerx.ist.psu.edu/viewdoc/summary?doi=10.1.1.16.2419

Kahneman, D., and A. Tversky. 1984. 'Choices, values, and frames.' *American Psychologist* 39 (4): 341–50. http://dx.doi.org/10.1037/0003-066X.39.4.341.

Kakavá, C. 1993. Negotiation of disagreement by Greeks in conversations and classroom discourse. Ph.D. dissertation. Georgetown University: Washington, DC.

Kakavá, C. 2002. 'Opposition in Modern Greek discourse: cultural and contextual constraints.' *Journal of Pragmatics* 34 (10–11): 1537–68. http://dx.doi.org/10.1016/S0378-2166(02)00075-9.

Kangasharju, H. 2002. 'Alignment in disagreement: forming oppositional alliances in committee meetings.' *Journal of Pragmatics* 34 (10–11): 1447–71. http://dx.doi.org/10.1016/S0378-2166(02)00073-5.

Kennedy, G. 1998. *An Introduction to Corpus Linguistics*. London: Longman.

Kleinig, J. 1973. *Punishment and Desert*. Berlin: Springer.

Kotthoff, H. 1993. 'Disagreement and concession in disputes: on the context sensitivity of preference structures.' *Language in Society* 22 (2): 193–216. http://dx.doi.org/10.1017/S0047404500017103.

Lakoff, R. 1973. The logic of politeness; or minding your ps and qs. *Papers from the Ninth Regional Meeting of the Chicago Linguistics Society*, 292–305. Chicago, IL: Chicago Linguistics Society.

Lakoff, R. 1989. 'The limits of politeness: therapeutic and courtroom discourse..' *Multilingua* 8 (2–3): 101–29. http://dx.doi.org/10.1515/mult.1989.8.2-3.101.

Lakoff, R., and S. Ide (eds). 2005. *Broadening the Horizons of Linguistic Politeness*. Amsterdam: John Benjamins. http://dx.doi.org/10.1075/pbns.139.

Lane, C. 1990. 'The sociolinguistics of questioning in District Court Trials.' In *New Zealand Ways of Speaking English*, ed. A. Bell and J. Holmes, 221–51. Avon: Multilingual Matters Ltd.

Langlotz, A., and M.A. Locher. 2012. 'Ways of communicating emotional stance in online disagreements.' *Journal of Pragmatics* 44 (12): 1591–606. http://dx.doi.org/10.1016/j.pragma.2012.04.002.

Lauer, P. 1996. Linguistic politeness in letters of complaint. Unpublished MA Dissertation. University of Reading: UK.

Leech, G. 1969. *A Guide to English Poetry*. London: Longman.

Leech, G. 1980. *Explorations in Semantics and Pragmatics*. Amsterdam: John Benjamins. http://dx.doi.org/10.1075/pb.i.5.

Leech, G. 1981. *Semantics: The Study of Meaning* (2nd edn). Harmondsworth: Penguin Books (Original work published 1974).

Leech, G. 1983. *Principles of Pragmatics*. London: Longman.

Leech, G. 1992. 'Corpora and theories of linguistic performance.' In *Directions in Corpus Linguistics: Proceedings of Nobel Symposium 82, Stockholm, 4–8 August 1991*, ed. J. Svartvik, 105–22. Berlin: Mouton de Gruyter. http://dx.doi.org/10.1515/9783110867275.105.

Leech, G. 2005. 'Is there an East-West divide in politeness?' *Journal of Foreign Languages* 6:1–30.

Lee-Wong, Song Mei 1998. 'Face Support – Chinese Particles As Mitigators: a Study of Ba a/Ya and Ne.' In *Pragmatics : quarterly publication of the International Pragmatics Association* 8 (3): 387–404.

Levinson, S.C. 1983. *Pragmatics*. Cambridge, England: Cambridge University.

Levinson, S.C.. 1992 [1979]. 'Activity types and language.' In *Talk at Work: Interaction in Institutional Settings*, ed. P. Drew and J. Heritage, 66–100. Cambridge: Cambridge University Press.

Lim, T., and J.W. Bowers. 1991. 'Facework: solidarity, approbation, and tact.' *Human Communication Research* 17 (3): 415–50. http://dx.doi.org/10.1111/j.1468-2958.1991.tb00239.x.

Locher, M.A. 2004. *Power and Politeness in Action: Disagreements in Oral Communication*. Berlin and New York: Mouton de Gruyter. http://dx.doi.org/10.1515/9783110926552.

Locher, M.A., and R.J. Watts. 2005. 'Politeness theory and relational work.' *Journal of Politeness Research* 1 (1): 9–33.

Locher, M. 2006. 'Polite behaviour within relational work: the discursive approach to politeness.' *Multilingua* 25 (3): 249–67. http://dx.doi.org/10.1515/MULTI.2006.015.

Locher, M.A., and R.J. Watts. 2008. 'Relational work and impoliteness: negotiating norms of linguistic behavior.' In *Impoliteness in Language: Studies on Its Interplay with Power in Theory and Practice*, ed. D. Bousfield and M.A. Locher, 77–99. Berlin and New York: Mouton de Gruyter. http://dx.doi.org/10.1515/9783110208344.

Louw, B. 1993. 'Irony in the text or insincerity in the writer? The diagnostic potential of semantic prosodies.' In *Text and Technology: In Honour of John Sinclair*, ed. M. Baker, G. Francis, and E. Tognini-Bonelli, 157–76. Amsterdam: John Benjamins. http://dx.doi.org/10.1075/z.64.11lou.

Louw, B. 2000. 'Contextual prosodic theory: bringing semantic prosodies to life.' In *Words in Context: A Tribute to John Sinclair on His Retirement*, ed. C. Heffer, H. Sauntson, and G. Fox, 48–94. Birmingham: University of Birmingham.

Martı, L. 2006. 'Indirectness and politeness in Turkish-German bilingual and Turkish monolingual requests.' *Journal of Pragmatics* 38 (11): 1836–69. http://dx.doi.org/10.1016/j.pragma.2005.05.009.

Matsumoto, Y. 1988. 'Reexamination of the universality of face: politeness phenomena in Japanese.' *Journal of Pragmatics* 12 (4): 403–26. http://dx.doi.org/10.1016/0378-2166(88)90003-3.

McCarthy, M., and A. O'Keeffe. 2010. 'Historical perspective: what are corpora and how have they evolved?' In *The Routledge Handbook of Corpus Linguistics*, ed. A. O'Keeffe and M. McCarthy, 3–13. New York: Routledge.

McEnery, T., and A. Wilson. 2001. *Corpus Linguistics*. Edinburgh: Edinburgh University Press.

McEwen, W.J., and B.S. Greenberg. 1970. 'The effects of message intensity on receiver evaluations of source message and topic.' *Journal of Communication* 20 (4): 340–50. http://dx.doi.org/10.1111/j.1460-2466.1970.tb00892.x.

Meyer, C.F. 2004. *English Corpus Linguistics*. Cambridge: Cambridge University Press.

Mills, S. 2003. *Gender and Politeness*. Cambridge: Cambridge University Press. http://dx.doi.org/10.1017/CBO9780511615238.

Mills, S. 2005. 'Gender and impoliteness.' *Journal of Politeness Research* 5 (1): 263–80.

Mills, S. 2009. 'Impoliteness in a cultural context.' *Journal of Pragmatics* 41 (5): 1047–60. http://dx.doi.org/10.1016/j.pragma.2008.10.014.

Millwood-Hargrave, A. 2000. Delete expletives: research undertaken jointly by the Advertising Standards Authority, British Broadcasting Standards Commission and the Independent Television Commission. ASA, BBC, BSC and ITC, London.

Mindt, D. 1985. 'Das Tempus in einer didaktishen Grammatik am Beispiel des futurishen Zeitbesug im Englishen.' *Anglistik & englischunterricht* 27: 171–83.

Mindt, D. 1987. *Sprache-Grammatik-Unterrichtsgrammatik: Futurisher Zeitbezug im Englishen I*. Frankfurt am Main: Diesterweg.

Mindt, D. 1991. 'Syntactic evidence for semantic distinctions in English.' In *English Corpus Linguistics: Studies in Honour of Jan Svartvik*, ed. K. Aijmer and B. Altenberg, 182–96. London: Longman.

Mindt, D. 1992. *Zeitbezug im Englischen. Eine Didaktische Grammatik des Englishen Futurs*. Tübingen: Narr.

Morley, J., and A. Partington. 2009. 'A few Frequently Asked Questions about semantic – or evaluative – prosody.' *International Journal of Corpus Linguistics* 14 (2): 139–58. http://dx.doi.org/10.1075/ijcl.14.2.01mor.

Mukherjee, J. 2004. 'The state of the art in corpus linguistics: three book-length perspectives.' *English Language and Linguistics* 8 (1): 103–19. http://dx.doi.org/10.1017/S1360674304001261.

Murdock, M.C., and R.M. Ganim. 1993. 'Creativity and humor: integration and incongruity.' *Journal of Creative Behavior* 27 (1): 57–70. http://dx.doi.org/10.1002/j.2162-6057.1993.tb01387.x.

Murray, I.R., and J.L. Arnott. 1993. 'Toward the simulation of emotion in synthetic speech: a review of the literature on human vocal emotion.' *Journal of the Acoustical Society of America* 93 (2): 1097–108. http://dx.doi.org/10.1121/1.405558.

O'Driscoll, J. 1996. 'About face: a defence and elaboration of universal dualism.' *Journal of Pragmatics* 25 (1): 1–32. http://dx.doi.org/10.1016/0378-2166(94)00069-X.

O'Driscoll, J. 2007. 'Brown and Levinson's face: how it can and can't help us understand interaction across cultures.' *Intercultural Pragmatics* 4 (4): 463–92.

Partington, A. 1998. *Patterns and Meanings*. Amsterdam: John Benjamins. http://dx.doi.org/10.1075/scl.2.

Partington, A. 2004a. '"Utterly content in each other's company": semantic prosody and semantic preference.' *International Journal of Corpus Linguistics* 9 (1): 131–56. http://dx.doi.org/10.1075/ijcl.9.1.07par.

Partington, A. 2004b. 'Corpora and discourse: a most congruous beast.' In *Corpora and Discourse*, ed. A. Partington, J. Morley, and L. Haarman, 11–20. Bern: Peter Lang.

Pizziconi, B. 2007. 'Facework and multiple selves in apologetic metapragmatics comments in Japanese.' In *Metapragmatics in Use*, ed. W. Bublitz and A. Huebler, 49–72. Amsterdam: John Benjamins. http://dx.doi.org/10.1075/pbns.165.05piz.

Pomerantz, A. 1984. 'Agreeing and disagreeing with assessments: some features of preferred/dispreferred turn shapes.' In *Structures of Social Action: Studies in Conversation Analysis*, ed. J.M. Atkinson and J. Heritage, 75–101. Cambridge: Cambridge University Press.

Pomerantz, A., and B.J. Fehr. 1997. 'Conversation analysis: An approach to the study of social action and sense-making practices.' In *Discourse as a Social Interaction*, ed. T. Van Dijk, 1–37. Thousand Oaks, CA: Sage.

Pratto, F., and O.P. John. 2005. 'Automatic vigilance: the attention-grabbing power of negative social formation.' In *Social Cognition*, ed. D.L. Hamilton, 250–65. London: Taylor and Francis. (Original work published 1991.)

Römer, U. 2005. *Progressives, Patterns, Pedagogy: A Corpus-Driven Approach to English Progressive Forms, Functions, Contexts and Didactics*. Philadelphia, PA: John Benjamins. http://dx.doi.org/10.1075/scl.18.

Ruhi, Ş. 2005. Türkçede inceliğin kavramlaştırılması: *yüz* ve *gönül* ile ilgili sözcük ve deyimler üzerine bir inceleme. Paper presented at the 14th National Linguistics Conference, 20–21 May 2005, Harran Üniversitesi.

Ruhi, Ş. 2006. 'Politeness in compliment responses: a perspective from naturally occurring exchanges in Turkish.' *Pragmatics* 16 (1): 43–101.

Ruhi, Ş. 2008. 'Intentionality, communicative intentions and the implication of politeness.' *Intercultural Pragmatics* 5 (3): 287–314. http://dx.doi.org/10.1515/IPRG.2008.014.

Ruhi, Ş. 2009a. 'Evoking face in self and other-presentation in Turkish.' In *Face, Communication and Social Interaction*, ed. F. Bargiela-Chiappini and M. Haugh, 155–74. London: Equinox Publishing.

Ruhi, Ş. 2009b. Face and the 'negativity bias:' A view from Turkish and British English. Paper presented at Linguistic Impoliteness and Rudeness II (LIAR II), Lancaster University, United Kingdom, 30 June–2 July 2009.

Ruhi, Ş. 2010. 'Face as an indexical category in interaction.' *Journal of Pragmatics* 42 (8): 2131–46. http://dx.doi.org/10.1016/j.pragma.2009.12.020.

Ruhi, Ş., K. Eyrılmaz, and M.G.C. Acar. 2012.. A platform for creating multimodal and multilingual spoken corpora for Turkic languages: Insights from the Spoken Turkish Corpus. Paper presented at the First Workshop on Language Resources and Technologies for Turkic Languages, LREC 2012. İstanbul, 57–63. Retrieved from http://www.lrec-conf.org/proceedings/lrec2012/workshops/02.Turkic%20Languages%20Proceedings.pdf.

Ruhi, Ş., Ç. Hatipoğlu, B. Eröz-Tuğa, H. Işık-Güler, M.G.C. Acar, K. Eryılmaz, H. Can, Ö. Karakaş, and D. Çokal Karadaş. 2010a. Sustaining a corpus for spoken Turkish discourse: Accessibility and corpus management issues. *Language Resources: From Storyboard to Sustainability and LR Lifecycle Management*, LREC 17–24 May 2010, Malta: 44–48. http://lrec-conf.org/proceedings/lrec2010/workshops/W20.pdf#page=52.

Ruhi, Ş., Ç. Hatipoğlu, B. Eröz-Tuğa, and H. Işık-Güler. (2010b) *A Guideline for Transcribing Conversations for the Construction of Spoken Turkish Corpora Using EXMARaLDA and HIAT*. ODTÜ-STD: Setmer Basımevi. (available on request through http://std.metu.edu.tr)

Ruhi, Ş., and H. Işık-Güler. 2007. 'Conceptualizing face and relational work in (im) politeness: revelations from politeness lexemes and idioms in Turkish.' *Journal of Pragmatics* 39 (4): 681–711. http://dx.doi.org/10.1016/j.pragma.2006.11.013.

Ruhi, Ş., H. Işık-Güler, Ç. Hatipoğlu, B. Eröz-Tuğa, and D. Çokal Karadaş. 2010c. 'Achieving representativeness through the parameters of spoken language and discursive features: the case of the Spoken Turkish Corpus.' In *Language Windowing through Corpora. Visualización del Lenguaje a través de Corpus. Part II*, ed. I. Moskowich-Spiegel Fandino, B. Crespo García, and I. Lareo Martín, 789–799. Universidade da Coruna.

Ruhi, Ş., and D.Z. Kádár. 2011. 'Face across historical cultures: A comparative study of Turkish and Chinese.' *Journal of Historical Pragmatics* 12 (1–2): 25–48. http://dx.doi.org/10.1075/jhp.12.1-2.02ruh.

Rühlemann, C. 2007. *Conversation in Context: A Corpus-driven Approach*. London, New York: The Continuum International Publishing Group.

Sacks, H. 1973/1987. 'On the preference for agreement and contiguity in sequences in conversation.' In *Talk and Social Organisation*, ed. G.B. Button and J.R.E. Lee, 54–69. Clevedon: Multilingual Matters.

Sacks, H. 1984. 'Notes on methodology.' In *Structures of Social Action: Studies in Conversation Analysis,* ed. Jefferson, G. from unpublished lectures, ed. J.M. Atkinson and J. Heritage, 21–27. Cambridge: Cambridge University Press.

Sacks, H. 1986. 'On the analyzability of stories by children.' In *Directions in Sociolinguistics. The Ethnography of Communication*, ed. J.J. Gumperz and D. Hymes, 325–45. Oxford: Basil Blackwell.

Sacks, H. 1989. 'Lecture six. The M.I.R.: membership categorization device.' *Human Studies* 12 (3–4): 271–81. http://dx.doi.org/10.1007/BF00142771.

Say, B., D. Zeyrek, K. Oflazer, and U. Özge. 2004. 'Development of a corpus and a Treebank for present-day written Turkish (Proceedings of the Eleventh International Conference of Turkish Linguistics, August, 2002).' In *Current Research in Turkish Lingustics*, ed. K. İmer and G. Doğan, 183–92. Cyprus: Eastern Mediterranean University Press.

Schank, R., and R.P. Abelson. 1977. *Scripts, Plans, Goals and Understanding: An Inquiry into Human Knowledge Structures*. London and New Jersey: Lawrence Earlbaum.

Schegloff, E.A. 1972. 'Sequencing in conversational openings.' In *Directions in Sociolinguistics. The Ethnography of Communication*, ed. J.J. Gumperz and D. Hymes, 346–380. New York: Holt, Rinehart and Winston.

Schegloff, E.A. 1981. 'Discourse as an interactional achievement: Some uses of "uh huh" and other things that come between sentences.' In *Georgetown University Roundtable on Languages and Linguistics*, ed. D. Tannen, 71–93. Washington, DC: Georgetown University Press.

Q6Schegloff, E.A. 1992. 'Introduction.' In *Sacks, H. Lectures on Conversation*, vol. 1. ed. G. Jefferson and E.A. Shegloff, ix–xii. Oxford and Cambridge, MA: Basil Blackwell.

Schegloff, E.A. 1997. 'Whose text? Whose context?' *Discourse and Society* 8 (2): 165–87. http://dx.doi.org/10.1177/0957926597008002002.

Schegloff, E.A. 1999. 'Schegloff's texts as "Billig's data": a critical reply.' *Discourse and Society* 10 (4): 558–72. http://dx.doi.org/10.1177/0957926599010004006.

Schegloff, E.A., and H. Sacks. 1973. 'Opening up closings.' *Semiotica* 7 (3–4): 289–327.

Schlenker, B.R., and B.A. Pontari. 2000. 'The strategic control of information: impression management and self-presentation in daily life.' In *Psychological Perspectives on Self and Identity*, ed. A. Tesser, R.B. Felson, and J.M. Suls, 199–232. Washington, DC: American Psychological Press. http://dx.doi.org/10.1037/10357-008.

Schmidt, T., and K. Wörner. 2009. 'EXMARaLDA – Creating, analysing and sharing spoken language corpora for pragmatic research.' *Pragmatics* 19: 565–82.

Schmidt, T. 2010. 'Another extension of the stylesheet metaphor: Visualising multi-layer annotations as musical scores.' In *Linguistic Modeling of Information and Markup Languages*, ed. A. Witt and D. Metzing, 23–44. Dordrecht: Springer. http://dx.doi.org/10.1007/978-90-481-3331-4_2.

Schriffin, D. 1994. *Approaches to Discourse*. Oxford: Blackwell.

Schwartz, S.H. 1992. *Universals in the Content and Structure of Values: Theoretical Advances and Empirical Tests in 20 Countries*, Vol. 25. Ed. M.P. Zanna, 1–65. Advances in Experimental Social Psychology. San Diego: Academic Press.

Schwartz, S., G. Melech, A. Lehmann, S. Burgess, M. Harris, and V. Owens. 2001. 'Extending the cross-cultural validity of the theory of basic human values with a different method of measurement.' *Journal of Cross-Cultural Psychology* 32 (5): 519–42. http://dx.doi.org/10.1177/0022022101032005001.

Selting, M. 2012. 'Complaint stories and subsequent complaint stories with affect displays.' *Journal of Pragmatics* 44 (4): 387–415. http://dx.doi.org/10.1016/j.pragma.2012.01.005.

Shaver, P., J. Schwartz, D. Kirson, and C. O'Connor. 1987. 'Emotion knowledge: further exploration of a prototype approach.' *Journal of Personality and Social Psychology* 52 (6): 1061–86. http://dx.doi.org/10.1037/0022-3514.52.6.1061.

Sifianou, M. 1992. *Politeness phenomena in England and Greece*. Oxford: Clarendon Press.

Sifianou, M. 2012. 'Disagreements, face and politeness.' *Journal of Pragmatics* 44 (12): 1554–64. http://dx.doi.org/10.1016/j.pragma.2012.03.009.

Sinclair, J. 1987. *Looking Up*. London, Glasgow: Collins.

Sinclair, J. 1991. *Corpus, Concordance, Collocation*. Oxford: Oxford University Press.

Sinclair, J. 1996. 'The search for units of meaning.' *Textus* IX: 75–106.

Sinclair, J.M. 1998. 'The lexical item.' In *Contrastive Lexical Semantics*, ed. E. Weigand, 1–24. Amsterdam: John Benjamins. http://dx.doi.org/10.1075/cilt.171.02sin.

Sinclair, J.M. 2004. *Trust the Text: Language, Corpus, and Discourse*. London, New York: Routledge.

Sinclair, J.M., and M. Coulthard. 1975. *Towards an Analysis of Discourse*. Oxford: Oxford University Press.

Smith, M.A., and Kollock, P. 1999. *Communities in Cyberspace*. London: Routledge.

Spencer-Oatey, H. 2000. *Culturally Speaking: Culture, Communication and Politeness Theory*. London: Continuum International Publishing Group.

Spencer-Oatey, H. 2002. 'Managing rapport in talk: using rapport-sensitive incidents to explore the motivational concerns underlying the management of relations.' *Journal of Pragmatics* 34 (5): 529–45. http://dx.doi.org/10.1016/S0378-2166(01)00039-X.

Spencer-Oatey, H. 2005. '(Im)politeness, face and perceptions of rapport: unpackaging their bases and interrelationships.' *Journal of Politeness Research* 1: 95–119.

Spencer-Oatey, H. 2007. 'Theories of identity and the analysis of face.' *Journal of Pragmatics* 39 (4): 635–656. http://dx.doi.org/10.1016/j.pragma.2006.12.003.

Spencer-Oatey, H. 2011. 'Conceptualizing "the relational" in pragmatics: insights from metapragmatics emotion and impoliteness comments.' *Journal of Pragmatics* 43 (14): 3565–78. http://dx.doi.org/10.1016/j.pragma.2011.08.009.

Spencer-Oatey, H., and W. Jiang. 2003. 'Explaining cross-cultural pragmatic findings: moving from politeness maxims to sociopragmatic interactional principles (SIPs).' *Journal of Pragmatics* 35 (10–11): 1633–50. http://dx.doi.org/10.1016/S0378-2166(03)00025-0.

Spencer-Oatey, H., and J. Xing. 2004. 'Rapport management problems in Chinese-British business interactions: a case study.' In *Multilingual Communication*, ed. J. House and J. Rehbein, 197–221. Amsterdam: Benjamins. http://dx.doi.org/10.1075/hsm.3.13spe.

Sperber, D., and D. Wilson. 1981. 'Irony and the use-mention distinction.' In P. Cole (ed.) *Radical Pragmatics*, 295–318. New York: Academic Press. Reprinted in S. Davis (ed.) 1991. *Pragmatics: A Reader*, 550–63. Oxford: Oxford University Press.

Sperber, D., and D. Wilson. 1995. *Relevance: Communication and Cognition*. 2nd ed. Oxford and Malden, MA: Blackwell (Original work published 1986).

Stewart, D. 2010. *Semantic Prosody a Critical Evaluation*. New York: Routledge.

Stubbs, M. 1995. 'Collocations and semantic profiles: On the cause of the trouble with quantitative studies.' *Functions of Language* 2 (1): 23–55. http://dx.doi.org/10.1075/fol.2.1.03stu.

Stubbs, M. 1996. *Text and Corpus Analysis*. Oxford: Blackwell.

Stubbs, M. 2001. *Words and Phrases: Corpus Studies of Lexical Semantics*. Oxford: Blackwell.

Stubbs, M. 2002. 'Two quantitative methods of studying phraseology in English.' *International Journal of Corpus Linguistics* 7 (2): 215–44. http://dx.doi.org/10.1075/ijcl.7.2.04stu.

Sudnow, D. 1972. 'Temporal parameters of interpersonal observation.' In *Studies in Social Interaction*, ed. D. Sudnow, 259–79. New York: Free Press.

Swales, J. 1990. *Genre Analysis. English in Academic and Research Settings*. Cambridge: Cambridge University Press.

Tannen, D. 1984. *Conversational Style: Analyzing Talk Among Friends*. Norwood, NY: Ablex publishing Company.

Tannen, D. 1993. 'The relativity of linguistic strategies: rethinking power and solidarity in gender and dominance.' In *Gender and Discourse*, ed. D. Tannen, 19–52. Oxford: Oxford University Press.

Taylor, C. 2011. 'Negative politeness features and impoliteness: A corpus-assisted approach.' In *Situated Politeness*, ed. B. Davies, A. Merrison, and M. Haugh, 209–31. London: Continuum.

Tedeschi, J.T. 1970. 'Threats and promises.' In *The Structure of Conflict*, ed. P. Swingle. New York: Academic Press.

Tedeschi, J.T., and R.B. Felson. 1994. *Violence, Aggression, and Coercive Actions*. Washington, DC: American Psychological Association. http://dx.doi.org/10.1037/10160-000.

TEI Consortium, eds. 2013. *Guidelines for Electronic Text Encoding and Interchange*. 17 January 2013. Retrieved from http://www.tei-c.org/Guidelines/P5/.

Terkourafi, M. 2001. Politeness in Cypriot Greek: a frame-based approach. Unpublished PhD. Dissertation. University of Cambridge, UK.

Terkourafi, M. 2005a. 'Beyond the micro-level in politeness research.' *Journal of Politeness Research* 1 (2): 237–62.

Terkourafi, M. 2005b. 'Pragmatic correlates of frequency of use: the case for a notion of "minimal context".' In *Reviewing Linguistic Thought: Converging Trends for the 21st Century*, ed. S. Marmaridou, K. Nikiforidou, and E. Antonopoulou, 209–33. Berlin: Mouton de Gruyter. http://dx.doi.org/10.1515/9783110920826.209.

Terkourafi, M. 2007. 'Toward a universal notion of face for a universal notion of co-operation.' In *Explorations in Pragmatics*, I. Kecskés and L. Horn, 313–44. Berlin: Mouton de Gruyter.

Teubert, W. 2005. 'My version of corpus linguistics.' *International Journal of Corpus Linguistics* 10 (1): 1–13. http://dx.doi.org/10.1075/ijcl.10.1.01teu.

Thomas, J. 1995. *Meaning in Interaction*. London, New York: Longman.

Tognini-Bonelli, E. 1996. *Corpus Theory and Practice*. Birmingham: TWC.

Tognini-Bonelli, E. 2001. *Corpus Linguistics at Work*. Amsterdam: Benjamins. http://dx.doi.org/10.1075/scl.6.

Tognini-Bonelli, E. 2010. 'Theoretical overview of the evolution of corpus linguistics.' In *The Routledge Handbook of Corpus Linguistics*, ed. A. O'Keeffe and M. McCarthy, 14–27. New York: Routledge.

Tsui, A.B.M. 1994. *English Conversation*. Oxford: Oxford University Press.

Waldron, V.R., and J.A. Applegate. 1994. 'Interpersonal construct differentiation and conversational planning: an examination of two cognitive accounts for the production of competent verbal disagreement tactics.' *Human Communication Research* 21 (1): 3–35. http://dx.doi.org/10.1111/j.1468-2958.1994.tb00337.x.

Warren, M. 2006. *Features of Naturalness in Conversation*. Amsterdam: John Benjamins. http://dx.doi.org/10.1075/pbns.152.

Watanabe, Y. 2011. 'Conflict, culture and face.' In *Politeness Across Cultures*, ed. F. Bargiela-Chiappini and D.Z. Kádár, 216–36. Basingstoke: Palgrave Macmillan.

Watts, R.J. 1992. 'Linguistic politeness and politic behaviour.' In *Politeness in Language: Studies in Its History, Theory and Practice*, ed. J.R. Watts, S. Ide, and K. Ehlich, 43–69. Berlin: Mouton de Gruyter.

Watts, R.J. 2003. *Politeness*. Cambridge: Cambridge University Press. http://dx.doi.org/10.1017/CBO9780511615184.

Watts, R.J., S. Ide, and K. Ehlich. 1992. 'Introduction.' In *Politeness in Language: Studies in Its History, Theory and Practice*, ed. J.R. Watts, S. Ide, and K. Ehlich, 1–20. Berlin: Mouton de Gruyter.

Watts, R.J., S. Ide, and K. Ehlich, eds. 2005. *Politeness in Language: Studies in Its History, Theory and Practice*. Berlin: Mouton de Gruyter. http://dx.doi.org/10.1515/9783110199819.

Wilson, J. 1987. 'On the topic of conversation as a speech event.' *Research on Language and Social Interaction* 21 (1–4): 93–114. http://dx.doi.org/10.1080/08351818709389286.

Wilson, J. 1989. *On the Boundaries of Conversation*. Oxford: Pergamon Press.

Wierzbicka, A. 1985. 'Different cultures, different languages, and different speech acts.' *Journal of Pragmatics* 9 (2–3): 145–78. http://dx.doi.org/10.1016/0378-2166(85)90023-2.

Wittgenstein, L. 1953. *Philosophical Investigations*. ed. G. Anscombe. Oxford: Basil Blackwell.

Wooffitt, R. 2005. *Conversation Analysis and Discourse Analysis: A Comparative and Critical Introduction*. London: Sage Publications.

Xie, C., Z. He, and D. Lin. 2005. 'Politeness: Myth and truth.' *Studies in Language* 29 (2): 431–61. http://dx.doi.org/10.1075/sl.29.2.07xie.

Yılmaz, E. 2004. A pragmatic analysis of Turkish discourse particles: Yani, işte and şey. Unpublished doctoral dissertation. METU, Ankara.

Zeyrek, D. 2001. 'Politeness in Turkish and its linguistic manifestations: A socio-cultural perspective.' In *Linguistic Politeness Across Boundaries: A Case of Greek and Turkish*, ed. A. Bayraktoroğlu and M. Sifianou, 43–73. Amsterdam/ New York: John Benjamins. http://dx.doi.org/10.1075/pbns.88.04zey.

Index

CPSIA information can be obtained at www.ICGtesting.com
Printed in the USA
BVOW05*0242220715

408642BV00002B/2/P